Our America

Post-Contemporary Interventions

Series Editors: Stanley Fish and Fredric Jameson

Our America

Nativism, Modernism, and Pluralism

Walter Benn Michaels

DUKE UNIVERSITY PRESS   *Durham and London 1995*

© 1995 Duke University Press
All rights reserved
Printed in the United States of America on acid-free paper ∞
Typeset in Berkeley Medium by Keystone Typesetting, Inc.
Library of Congress Cataloging-in-Publication Data appear
on the last printed page of this book.

To Becky and Sascha

Contents

Acknowledgments

I first studied modernism with Hugh Kenner and Herbert N. Schneidau; although neither is likely to agree with many of the views expressed in this book, I owe a great deal to both of them and am grateful for the opportunity to acknowledge that debt. My own students at Johns Hopkins—especially Shelly Eversley, Maria Farland, Jared Gardner, Todd Jackson, Cathy Jurca, Alex Love, Dan McGee, Mark McGurl, Mark Schoening, Michael Szalay, and Joanne Wood—have made significant contributions to this project, as have many colleagues at Hopkins and elsewhere: Deborah Chay, Jerome Christensen, Arnold Davidson, Neil Hertz, Stanley Fish, Henry Louis Gates Jr., Amy Kaplan, Ruth Leys, W. J. T. Mitchell, Stephen Nichols, Donald Pease, Ross Posnock, Michael Rogin, and the two anonymous readers for Duke University Press. Finally, *Our America* would not have been possible without Sharon Cameron, Frances Ferguson, Michael Fried, and Steven Knapp.

Our America

Land of the Kike Home of the Wop

THE REVEREND SHEGOG'S Easter sermon in the fourth chapter of
William Faulkner's *The Sound and the Fury* (1929) repeats and
interlaces that novel's twinned fantasies about language and the
family—about language, that the word can be made flesh and, about
family, that endogamy can supplant exogamy—by invoking the Eucharistic miracle that turns the sign of Christ's blood into the blood itself and
by reimagining a congregation as a collection of blood relations: "Breddren
en sistuhn," the Reverend Shegog says, "I got de ricklickshun en de blood
of de Lamb."[1] In *The Sound and the Fury*, the desire to make words into
things and the desire to sleep with your sister are inseparable or even, as
is the case with Quentin's "*I have committed incest I said*" (49), indistinguishable. To commit incest by saying that you've committed incest is
to make the words the thing; to say you've committed incest and thus to
commit incest is to keep your sister forever in your family—"if I could tell
you we did it would have been so and then the others wouldnt be so and
then the world would roar away" (107–8). In *The Sound and the Fury*,
these ambitions are doubly linked, first because they both involve a
repudiation of arbitrary or conventional relations (between word and
thing, between husband and wife) and, second, because the repudiation
of those relations is everywhere deployed in defense of a tautology that
will find its definitive formulation in the proposition "blood is blood and
you can't get around it" (146).

The Sound and the Fury repeatedly insists that what people and things
do or mean is a function of what they are; it insists, that is, on identity as
the determining ground of action or significance. In this, as the following

pages will make clear, it is typical of the major American texts of the 1920s and in particular of those texts—ranging from *The Professor's House* (1925) by Willa Cather to the Immigration Act of 1924 and from *The Rising Tide of Color* (1920) by Lothrop Stoddard to Hemingway's *The Sun Also Rises* (1926)—that belong to the discourse of what I will call nativist modernism. Nativism, according to its most distinguished scholar, John Higham, can be defined as "intense opposition to an internal minority on the grounds of its foreign (i.e. 'un-American') connections," opposition that, while it may "vary widely" in target and intensity, ultimately expresses in each case "the connecting, energizing force of modern nationalism."[2] But while the pages that follow will often engage the kinds of hostility that Higham describes—Quentin Compson's joke, "Land of the kike home of the wop" (76) is one example—my main focus will be less on the hostility itself (which will, in any case, prove to be only one of several affective stances made available by nativism) than on the changing conceptions of identity sometimes articulated by that hostility. I will argue that nativism in the period just after World War I involved not only a reassertion of the distinction between American and un-American but a crucial redefinition of the terms in which it might be made. America would mean something different in 1925 from what it had meant at, say, the turn of the century; indeed, the very idea of national identity would be altered. My use of the term "nativist modernism," as opposed to nativism *tout court*, is meant in part to suggest what I will describe as the distinctive nature of nativism in the '20s.

It is also meant to suggest that the nativism discussed here is simultaneously a modern and a *modernist* phenomenon. Although there are many different accounts of literary modernism, probably all of them acknowledge its interest in the ontology of the sign—which is to say, in the materiality of the signifier, in the relation of signifier to signified, in the relation of sign to referent. My point, then, in beginning this book with an exploration of the relation between a certain fantasy about the sign—that it might function, in effect, onomatopoetically, without reliance upon a system of syntactic and semantic conventions—and a certain fantasy about the family—that it might maintain itself incestuously, without reliance upon the legal conventions that turn otherwise unrelated persons into husband and wife—is to suggest the structural intimacy between nativism and modernism. Nativism, the social movement, will not, in other words, be presented here as the background of modernism, the aesthetic movement; rather, both nativism and modernism will be presented as efforts to work out the meaning of the commitment to identity—linguistic, national, cultural, racial—that I will argue is common to both.

So, while Quentin's joke, "Land of the kike home of the wop," makes one version of the nativist point—"America," as a congressman speaking in support of the immigration bill put it, "for Americans"[3]—his desire not only to commit incest but to commit incest by *saying* he committed incest makes another. And this extension of the interest in "purifying and keeping pure the blood of America" beyond Congress's desire to exclude "unassimilable aliens"[4] suggests not only the discursive range but the imaginative potential of nativist logic. "We have a great desire," Calvin Coolidge remarked, "to be supremely American,"[5] which is to say that, in nativist modernism, identity becomes an ambition as well as a description. Indeed, it is only this transformation of identity into the object of desire as well as its source that will make the dramas of nativism—the defense of identity, its loss, its repudiation, its rediscovery—possible. What we want, in other words, may be a function of what we are, but in order for us to want it, we cannot simply be it. Thus *The Sound and the Fury*'s insistence that "blood is blood" will be doubled by strategies for *making* blood be blood; the insistence that the word become the thing, that naming your sister be a way of having your sister, must be shadowed by the failure of the word to be the thing and by the disappearance of your sister.

This is why the only word that the languageless Benjy responds to is "caddie," which he hears as a proper name—Caddy—and which signifies to him not the presence but the disappearance of his sister, Caddy. Proper names are imagined in *The Sound and the Fury* as at least ideally linked to their referents so that, for example, changing Benjy's name from Maury can be imagined as a good thing for Benjy's Uncle Maury, who will no longer be linguistically linked to an idiot, and a bad thing for Benjy, who will no longer be called by the name that is really his. "Folks don't have no luck, changing names" (36), says Dilsey. And since names are further imagined not only as uniquely designating a single person but as inseparable from that person—"long after" she's "forgot," Dilsey says, "Dilsey" will still be her name, and when her name is read in "the Book," all she'll have to do is say "Ise here" (36)—the word "caddie" appears to Benjy less as the use than as the misuse of her name; uttered on the land that was sold to pay for her wedding, it marks not the fact that she's "here" but the fact that she's *not* here. Which is why, hearing the word that he understands only as a name, and hearing the name as a reference to the absence rather than the presence of the person named, Benjy starts bellowing. And he can only be calmed by another sign for Caddy, the "satin slipper" she wore on her wedding day, a sign that signifies Caddy more satisfactorily than her name since, understood as virtually a part of her, it comes closer to making her in fact present, "here."

The Reverend Shegog's sermon addresses this issue most obviously in its central assertion: "I got the recollection and the blood of the Lamb" (175). What it means to have this recollection and to have it through the blood of the Lamb has, of course, been a central issue in Christian theology. Does the bread and wine eaten and drunk "in remembrance" of Jesus *symbolize* Jesus (and thus remember him while acknowledging his absence) or does it *embody* him ("This is my body") (and thus remember him by making him present)? Is it like a word that functions in the absence of the referent or like a name that is supposed to mark the referent's presence or, even better, like a slipper, which can be imagined actually to make at least a little of the referent present? In the Reverend Shegog's sermon, through which the reverend himself "sees de blastin', blindin' sight" (177) and makes his hearers see it also, language appears to achieve the identity of word and thing that Caddy's slipper foreshadows.

The delivery of the sermon also makes a version of this point. Beginning in a voice that is "level," "cold," and "inflectionless," the minister ends in a voice that is "as different as day and dark from his former tone" (175). This new voice has "a sad, timbrous quality like an alto horn" and, in a description that seems to allude to the sermons of the Reverend Dimmesdale in Hawthorne's *The Scarlet Letter* (whose "vocal organ," like "other music," "breathed passion and pathos . . . in a tongue native to the human heart"),[6] the Reverend Shegog's voice sinks into the "hearts" of his audience, "speaking there again" until "there was not even a voice but instead their hearts were speaking to one another in chanting measures beyond the need for words" (176). Just as, in *The Scarlet Letter*, the "heart's native tongue" conveys Dimmesdale's "feeling" by embodying it rather than meaning it—"The young pastor's voice was tremulously sweet, rich, deep, and broken. The feeling that it so evidently manifested, rather than the direct purport of the words, caused it to vibrate within all hearts . . ." (53)—so, in *The Sound and the Fury*, the musical quality of the Reverend Shegog's voice produces its effect without recourse to the conventional symbols of meaning. Indeed, it is by making "words" unnecessary that the "chanting measures" in which his heart and the hearts of his congregation speak testify to the fact that he and they have been brought "face to face" (177) with Jesus.

Hawthorne imagines that words are not only unnecessary but also potentially dangerous; because they are a "grosser medium" than sound, they have the potential to "clog" the "spiritual sense" (172). So Dimmesdale's wordless eloquence shows how "etherealized by spirit" he has become, and his audience's wordless response—it "absolutely babbled" (175)—shows how truly they have understood him. The voice of the Reverend Shegog repeats this identification with the spirit and reproduces the Dimmesdale effect; "succubus like," it "consume[s]" his "body" (175) and elicits from his audience a series of prolonged "Mmmmmmmm-mmmmmmmmmm"'s (176) that match the babbling of Dimmesdale's congregation. The sermon's topic, the Eucharistic identity of sign and referent, is thus doubled by its formal repudiation of those conventions that, acknowledging the gap between sign and referent, are ordinarily understood to make meaning possible. If the word in Hawthorne must be etherealized in order to let the "spiritual" meaning come through, the word in Faulkner must be eliminated in order to let the thing itself appear. The Reverend Shegog's language "beyond the need for words" repeats the language of the Eucharist which, by making words things, makes them, as words, unnecessary: once the sign becomes the thing it need no longer function as a sign.[7]

But this commitment to transubstantiation achieves its most explicit articulation in the effort to save Caddy for the Compsons, to "isolate her out of the loud world" (107). Quentin's claim—*I have committed incest I said*" (49)—is an attempt through language to substitute the blood ties of family for the affective and/or legal ties of love and marriage. It picks up the linguistic fantasy of the word becoming the thing—"if I could tell you we did it would have been so"—and deploys it on behalf both of a Benjy-style preference for natural signs (the slipper instead of the word) and of Quentin's own commitment to replacing husbands and lovers with brothers—"and then the others wouldn't be so and then the world would roar away" (108). This is what it means for Quentin to call the little Italian girl he picks up "sister," and it is also what it means for the first word that the Reverend Shegog speaks in his transformed voice to be "Brethren." The linguistic fantasy of meaning without conventions turns out to be emblematic of a more thoroughgoing effort to empty the world of all non-natural relations. Every chapter in *The Sound and the Fury* involves the effort to replace arbitrary or social relations with natural ones, which is to say that every chapter imagines the disappearance of the sister, Caddy, as the introduction of the arbitrary, and so every chapter involves some attempt to keep her from going or to imagine her brought back.

Thus even Jason, who (unlike Benjy) has never slept with Caddy and (unlike Quentin) has never said he slept with Caddy, indeed who hates Caddy, nevertheless finds himself in the position of articulating the rationale of the commitment to Caddy. Lured into the woods and left stranded with a flat tire by Caddy's daughter, Quentin, and her boyfriend from the carnival, Jason can't believe that she would let her "own uncle be laughed at by a man that would wear a red tie" (146). The point is not that there is any affection between Jason and Quentin—"Let's forget for awhile how I feel toward you and you feel toward me . . ." (146)—but that kinship makes affection irrelevant—"I just wouldn't do you this way. I wouldn't do you this way no matter what you had done to me. Because like I say blood is blood and you can't get around it" (146). Who Quentin is should count more than how she feels and should thus determine what she does; "blood is blood" expresses the priority of identity over any other category of assessment and makes clear the position of the family as bearer of what I will call identitarian claims.

It is this position that I mean to emphasize here and that I regard as crucial in the development of American modernism. My point is not that the family as such is an object of interest in *The Sound and the Fury*; even less is it that the psychological relations among the members of the family are the object of interest. Rather, by insisting on the importance of family in *The Sound and the Fury*, I mean to suggest the way in which newly revised categories of collective identity—and, in particular, of collective *national* identity—began in the 1920s to occupy what I will argue was a central position in American culture, which is to say, first, in the idea of what an American was and, second, in the idea of what a culture was.[8] The significance of the family is that it was in terms of familial relations (as opposed, say, to economic relations or regional or even generational relations) that the new structures of identity were articulated. *America, A Family Matter* was the title of Charles W. Gould's nativist polemic of 1922. And, although Horace Kallen's *Culture and Democracy in the United States* (1924) was directed against nativism, Kallen shared Gould's model of national identity; according to him, the very idea of "nationality" was "familial in its essence."[9]

Thus, even though *The Sound and the Fury* may, at first blush, seem an extreme and even perverse instance of the defense of the family, both its strategies and its goals are, in fact, typical of American writing in the '20s. The long first section of Willa Cather's *The Professor's House* (1925) is called "The Family," and it is entirely animated by the impossible vision of Rosamond St. Peter saved for her father and sister by having married Tom Outland, who was "like an older brother," instead of the "foreign" Louie Marsellus.[10] By the same token, it's "family life" (130) that is invoked by Tom Buchanan in his attempt to keep Daisy from Jay Gatsby, and if *The Great Gatsby* (1925) seems, like Daisy herself, to be "pretty cynical" about "family life and family institutions," it's worth remembering that the "natural intimacy" between Tom and Daisy proves in the end more resistant than anything in Cather or Faulkner to the threat, embodied in Gatsby, of what Tom thinks of as miscegenation.[11] And even in a novel where no one is related to anyone else, like Hemingway's *The Sun Also Rises* (1926), the defining characteristic of familial identity—"breeding"—here transformed into the defining characteristic of the Hemingway aesthetic—*afición*—operates to reproduce the structure of *The Professor's House* and *The Great Gatsby*: Brett, like Daisy from Gatsby and Rosamond from Louie, must be saved from Robert Cohn.

What's wrong with Cohn is, put negatively, that he has no breeding, no *afición*, or, put positively, that he's Jewish. In this, of course, he is like Marsellus, whose "foreign" status is racial, and he is not unlike Gatsby who, although he differs from the Buchanans (and from Nick Carraway) in belonging to a different class, is persistently understood by them as belonging to something more like a different race; this is why he provokes in Tom diatribes against "intermarriage between black and white" (130). Indeed, in *The Sound and the Fury* Faulkner contrives to mark even Quentin's otherwise anonymous man in the red tie as racially other; this is what it means for him to be one of the show people who take money from the farmers without, Jason thinks, giving anything in return. Having "brought nothing to the town" (118), they occupy the same position in Jason's imagination as the cotton speculators in New York, the "dam eastern jews" who "trim the suckers" on the market and leave the farmer himself with nothing but "a red neck and the hump in his back" (116). "I have nothing against the jews as an individual," Jason says, "It's just the race. You'll admit that they produce nothing" (116). Blood is blood; by way of his nonproductivity, the man with the red tie turns out to occupy the position of the Jew, and keeping women *in* the family turns out to be identical to keeping them *from* the Jews.

What's at stake in the desire to keep someone in the family is thus the sense that what is outside the family is also outside the race. In *America, A Family Matter*, Gould argued that, forcing our children to "rub shoulders" with "strangers and foreigners," we were robbing them of their "heritage."[12] He urged not only that immigration be restricted—as it would be in the Johnson-Reed Immigration Act of 1924[13]—but that all naturalization laws be repealed. Immigrants, he thought, could never be successfully "Americanized" since the qualities that constituted the American could "not be taught"; they were functions instead of "birth, breeding," "they must come to us with the mother's milk, the baby's lisping questions, and grow with our nerves and thews and sinews until they become part and parcel of our very being" (163). The point, then, of identifying as a Jew the "stranger" who wants to marry into your family is to identify as American the family he wants to marry into, which is to say, to transform American identity from the sort of thing that could be acquired (through naturalization) into the sort of thing that had to be inherited (from one's parents).[14] Insofar as the family becomes the site of national identity, nationality becomes an effect of racial identity.

These transformations are, in an important if not an absolute sense, inventions of the '20s. The major writers of the Progressive period—London, Dreiser, Wharton—were comparatively indifferent to questions of both racial and national identity. Dreiser's *An American Tragedy* (published in 1925 but articulating a set of preoccupations that had been put in place some fifteen years earlier) looks in certain respects strikingly similar to texts like *The Great Gatsby* and *The Professor's House*: Clyde Griffiths, like Gatsby and Marsellus, is an outsider, eager to be accepted by Lycurgus society and seeking that acceptance through his relations with one of its daughters. But where Cather's Marsellus wants to join the family, Clyde already belongs to it (it's because he's a Griffiths that he's come to work in his uncle's factory), so the *object* of Marsellus's desire is the *condition* of Clyde's: Clyde wants "a better collar, a nicer shirt, finer shoes . . . a swell overcoat like some boys had";[15] Louie wants to be "related" to the professor's "sons" (165), those books on the Spanish adventurers in the new world, which play in *The Professor's House* the role played by the eyes of the Dutch sailors in the famous last pages of *The Great Gatsby*. "American" in *An American Tragedy* means a certain set of social and economic conditions that make the desire for nicer shirts unprecedentedly powerful; Gatsby and Louie Marsellus have all the nice shirts they need—what they want is something that seems to them more plausibly married than bought. In these texts, "American" designates not a set of social and economic conditions but an identity that exists prior to and independent of those conditions.

This transformation in the meaning of "American" proceeds necessarily in tandem with a transformation in the meaning of contrastive terms, like "Jew." In a text like Sinclair Lewis's *Babbitt*—published in 1922 but still committed to the logic of naturalization—the term "Jew" is so utterly deracinated that, even when used by Jews, it has almost no racial meaning. The Jewish Sidney Finkelstein, insisting that "in the long run," it always pays to buy the most expensive goods, admits that "if a fellow wants to be a Jew about it, he can get cheap junk" and acknowledges that "the Old Folks"—"they live in one of these hick towns up-state and they simply can't get into the way a city fellow's mind works, and then, of course, they're Jews"—would "lie right down and die" if they knew the price he'd paid for a new top for his car.[16] Since Sidney is himself Jewish, the "Old Folks" are, "of course," "Jews." But since Sidney is not himself "a Jew," the Old Folks' being Jewish isn't really enough to make them "Jews": Sidney *isn't* a Jew because he buys the best and the Old Folks *are* Jews because they are shocked by how much he spends. The economic meaning of the term is so removed from its racial roots that you don't have to be Jewish to be a Jew and being Jewish isn't enough to make you one. In a text like *The Sound and the Fury*, however, although "Jew" continues to have an economic meaning (Jews are identified with people like the carnival men who "produce nothing"), that meaning is put back into contact with its racial roots. If the alternative to being a Jew in *Babbitt* is being someone who spends freely, the alternative to being a Jew in *The Sound and the Fury* is being an "American." And this reconfiguration of the Jew transcends politics as well as and for the same reasons that it transcends economics. "I've known some Jews that were fine citizens," Jason tells the drummer with whom he drinks a Coca-Cola. " 'You might be one yourself . . .' 'No,' he says, 'I'm an American' " (116). Citizenship, like money, can be earned; for the new nativists, appalled by immigrants who, as Lothrop Stoddard put it, had become "American citizens but not Americans,"[17] "American" could no more be a simple political term than "Jew" could be a simple economic one.

But the comparison of these texts of the '20s to the major literary texts of the Progressive period (and to those texts like *Babbitt* and *An American Tragedy* that continue the Progressive problematic into the '20s) both over- and underemphasizes their originality. It overemphasizes their originality by ignoring an important body of Progressive literature that, unlike the works of Dreiser, Wharton, et al., *was* deeply concerned with questions of racial and national identity: the plantation novels of writers like Thomas Nelson Page and the radical racist novels of writers like Thomas Dixon. And it underemphasizes their originality in the same way, for only against the background of these earlier attempts to imagine through race an American national identity can the particular contribution of nativist modernism be understood. In Dixon, for example, the family represents a threat to rather than (as for Gould) the site of racial "purity," since what seemed to Dixon the omnipresence of the mulatto counted as a continual demonstration of the fact that one family could be made up of two races. Dixon's effort, then, is to replace family ties with racial ones and, since the only races he recognized were black and white, he was prepared to welcome as exemplary candidates for American citizenship those "aliens" who, twenty years later, would count as threats to the American family. In fact, insofar as its horror of "amalgamation" with any blacks was utterly compatible with its enthusiastically assimilationist attitude toward all whites, Progressive racism was foundational for the projects of "Americanization" that '20s racism existed to combat. The Jew in Dixon's *Trilogy of Reconstruction* is a negrophobic American hero, a supporter of the Klan who looks forward in dialect to the day when a "monumendt" to its leader will be erected in "de public squvare."[18]

Not all Progressives, of course, were as keen on Jews as Dixon; most, probably, were in some degree anti-Semitic. But, in contrast to the situation in the '20s, anti-Semitism played only a minor role in Progressive racism; indeed, part of the originality of '20s nativist modernism consists in its promotion of anti-Semitism (and of various related ethnic prejudices) from what Hannah Arendt called a form of "social discrimination" into something like what she called "a political argument."[19] And, as a political argument, anti-Semitism could play its role in nativism not only by going beyond but sometimes by abandoning altogether its socially discriminatory or prejudicial tendencies. This is surely one thing meant by Jason's remark that he's got nothing against "the jews as an individual . . . It's just the race." Twenties' nativism made anti-Semitism an element of American cultural citizenship and therefore an essential aspect of American identity regardless of how one felt personally about individual Jews, just as—in a slightly more eccentric fashion—Faulkner's version of that nativism made incest an element of Americanism regardless of how attracted one might be to one's brother or sister. In *The Sound and the Fury*, the logic of Jason's response to the man with the red tie and to the "dam eastern jews" is the logic also of Benjy's preference for slippers over words and of Quentin's claim to have slept with Caddy and of the Reverend Shegog's Christian transformation of a congregation of (to him) strangers into "Breddren and sistuhn" (176).[20]

At the same time, however, this rewriting of both race and nation as family corresponded to two important shifts in racial logic, one that emphasized not the inferiority of "alien" races but their "difference," and a second that began to represent difference in cultural instead of political (and in addition to) racial terms. These transformations will be analyzed at length in what follows, but they can be exhibited economically in Gino Speranza's description (in *Race or Nation*, 1925) of "the Jew" as someone who "can, of course, be politically a citizen of any state to which he gives his political allegiance," but who "holds tenaciously to his racial and special culture."[21] In Speranza, racial identity is disconnected from political citizenship and connected instead to "culture," and racial hierarchy is transformed into racial pluralism. Just as Anglo-Saxons, according to Speranza, think of their own "racial 'point of view' " not as "better or finer than that of the stocks of our newer immigration," but as "*different*" (52), so "the Jew" insists on his difference and declines to "assimilate." Indeed, from Speranza's point of view, what will seem disconcerting about a text like *The Professor's House* will not be the St. Peters' desire to keep the Jew out but the Jew's uncharacteristic desire to get in. And, in a series of texts, from Anzia Yezierska's *Bread Givers* (1925) to Oliver La Farge's *Laughing Boy* (1929), the refusal of the ethnic alien to become American will be increasingly crucial. In fact, this ethnic response to nativism finds expression even in *The Sound and the Fury*, tangentially in the Italian Julio's emergence as a figure for Quentin in defense of his sister against Quentin, more centrally in the Easter sermon. For as the Reverend Shegog turns his congregation into his family, and as his "cold inflectionless" articulacy becomes the inarticulate spiritual voice of hearts chanting to one another "beyond the need for words," Faulkner describes him as ceasing to sound "like a white man" (175) and beginning to sound "negroid" (176). The disappearance of the white man's voice and its replacement by "negroid" "intonation" and "pronunciation" marks an essential step in the process of what the "Cultural Pluralist" Kallen called "dissimilation" (114); in the presence of his racial family, repudiating the intonations of assimilation, the dissimilated Negro emerges.[22]

But if, as we have seen, the family is the essential form of nativist identity, it is also, as we have also begun to see, a form that is essentially flawed.

The marriages that keep it alive at the same time destroy it; even before Caddy's and Quentin's betrayals, the Compsons are threatened by the necessary presence among them of the Bascombs. Indeed, one of the novel's projects is to take the two Compsons who are in some way identified as Bascombs (Benjy, who is named originally after Uncle Maury Bascomb, and Jason, who is "a Bascomb" "despite" his "name" [110]) and make them into Compsons, changing Benjy's name and drawing Jason into a repetition of Quentin's effort to keep Caddy. But Caddy and Quentin aren't saved from the loud world; the unenforceability of the incestuous imperative makes the technology of biological reproduction simultaneously the technology of miscegenated contamination. Thus one alternative to incest as a strategy for keeping the blood uncontaminated is sterility. Writers like Cather and Zane Grey redeploy the nineteenth-century stereotype of "the vanishing race," celebrating the supposed disappearance of the Indian as a mark of his racial integrity—better death than "cross-breeding."[23] And this is what it means for Benjy to be not only (like Jake Barnes in *The Sun Also Rises*) a "gelding," but more precisely, as Jason puts it (and as Jake, I will argue, also is), "the Great American Gelding" (158). Because writers like Lothrop Stoddard in *The Rising Tide of Color* were impressed by the "reckless procreation" (234) of the non-Nordic races, the comparative sterility of Nordics constituted both a problem—they were committing "racial suicide"—and a solution—their low birthrate testified to the irreducibility of their difference from the non-Nordics. From this standpoint, Benjy's inability to procreate is a sign of his native Americanness, matched only by Jason's *refusal* to procreate and by Quentin's desire for there to be no such thing as procreation—what Quentin wants is to imagine himself not as castrated but as born without genitalia: "It's not not having them. It's never to have had them . . ." (71). *The Sound and the Fury* represents the Compsons as Cather's Indians, committed above all to their own "purity" and thus—since "Purity is a negative state and therefore contrary to nature" (71)—to their own disappearance. Blood is blood, but—because blood is blood—blood isn't enough.

Another nativist alternative to utopian incest is homosexuality. This is most obvious in the "Powhatan's Daughter" section of Hart Crane's *The Bridge* (1930), where the origin of American identity is located in a sexual dance between the white poet and an Indian chief, which—because the chief, Maquokeeta, has replaced the "wanton" Pocahontas—makes that American origin simultaneously the scene of "the extinction of the Indian."[24] Crane's Pocahontas is the ancestress of Caddy and Brett Ashley, and the poet's homosexuality is a kind of compensation for her promiscuity, as Jake's impotence is for Brett's. Indeed, the mention of Jake's "accident" in *The Sun Also Rises* immediately triggers Bill Gorton's declaration of affection for Jake—"I'm fonder of you than anybody on earth"—which in turn opens up the question of the homosexual—"I couldn't tell you that in New York. It'd mean I was a faggot."[25] But the point in Hemingway is not that Bill or Jake really is homosexual; when the hotelier Montoya smiles at Jake "as though there were something lewd about the[ir] secret to outsiders," something that it "would not do to expose" to "people who would not understand" (130), that something is *afición*, not homosexuality. Hence it is the easy substitutability of what I will characterize as the racial discourse of *afición* (Cohn doesn't have it) for the discourse of homosexuality that I mean to stress here, as well as the interchangeability of both the aficionado and the homosexual with the castrato. All these figures can be equally (if differently) mobilized as blood supplements, as strategies for insisting upon a race-based model of identity when more literal strategies for preserving it have failed.

Much of what follows in this book will be an attempt to elaborate the claims made above and, in so doing, to show that the great American modernist texts of the '20s must be understood as deeply committed to the nativist project of racializing the American. At the same time, however, I want to argue that the most important result of this effort, a result toward which the ingenuities of incest, impotence, and homosexuality count only as a series of rehearsals, was the perfection not of racial identity but of what would come to be called cultural identity. Another way to put this would be to say that the emergence of race as the crucial marker of modern identity was accompanied almost from the start by an acknowledgment of the limitations of race as a bearer of identity—it is these limitations that the technologies of blood supplementation were designed to overcome. In the end, however, the most effective of these technologies would be one that could proclaim itself in opposition to as well as in defense of race. Culture, put forward as a way of preserving the primacy of identity while avoiding the embarrassments of blood, would turn out to be much more effective than incest, impotence, and homosexuality as a way of reconceptualizing and thereby preserving the essential contours of racial identity.

It is in particular the pluralizing of culture, I will argue, that adapted it to a racial purpose. The commitment to pluralism—both racial and cultural—should probably be understood as nativism's most significant and distinctive contribution to the technology of racial identity in the United States. Pluralism is, in a sense, built into nativism since the essence of nativism is its preference for the native exclusively on the grounds of its being native. As Lothrop Stoddard reminded his readers in *Re-Forging America* (1927), the defense of American culture properly understood raised no "theoretical questions of 'superiority' or 'inferiority'": "The really important point is that even though America (abstractly considered) may not be nearly as good as we think it is, nevertheless it is *ours*. . . . That is the meat of the matter, and when we discuss immigration we had better stop theorizing about superiors and inferiors and get down to the bedrock of *difference*" (103). Stoddard had himself been a white supremacist; the argument of his first book, *The Rising Tide of Color Against White World-Supremacy* (1920), is parodically but accurately summarized by Tom Buchanan in *The Great Gatsby*: "It's up to us, who are the dominant race, to watch out or these other races will have control of us" (13). But by 1927 he had begun to recognize that his racism did not require the assertion of Nordic superiority. My point here is not that he had entirely given up white supremacy but that his commitment to it had become, as Gatsby himself might have put it, "just personal." Although he remains both a racist and, to some extent, a white supremacist, his racism has been disarticulated from his white supremacism. Even if, he argues, "it could be conclusively shown that a certain stock was superior to us . . . we should still refuse to receive it, on grounds of self-preservation" (257–58). This is what it means for the "bedrock" to be "difference"; it is only for the pluralist that identity—the difference of oneself from others (and, as we have already begun to see, of oneself from oneself)—is absolutely crucial since only the pluralist, striving to see the different as neither better nor worse, must like it or dislike it on the basis of its difference alone.

And it is precisely this pluralism that transforms the substitution of culture for race into the preservation of race. For pluralism's programmatic hostility to universalism—its hostility to the idea that cultural practices be justified by appeals to what seems universally good or true—requires that such practices be justified instead by appeals to what seems locally good or true, which is to say, it invokes the identity of the group as the grounds for the justification of the group's practices. Thus, although the move from racial identity to cultural identity appears to replace essentialist criteria of identity (who we are) with performative criteria (what we do), the commitment to pluralism requires in fact that the question of who we are continue to be understood as prior to questions about what we do. Since, in pluralism, what we do can be justified only by reference to who we are, we must, in pluralism, begin by affirming who we are; it is only once we know who we are that we will be able to tell what we should do; it is only when we know which race we are that we can tell which culture is ours.[26] It is only, we might say, in pluralism, that the meaning of Americanism comes clear.

Dimmesdale's election sermon at the end of *The Scarlet Letter* is heard by Hester Prynne from outside the church so she can't make out the actual words—a good thing, says Hawthorne, since the words, "if more distinctly heard, might have been only a grosser medium, and have clogged the spiritual sense" (172). Dimmesdale turns the letter into the spirit by way of the voice. And not only is this process made visible also to his congregation inside the church, who see the holy "spirit" "descending upon him, and possessing him, and continually lifting him out of the written discourse that lay before him . . ." (176), it is thematized in the sermon itself which, discussing "the relation between the Deity and the communities of mankind, with a special reference to the New England which they were here planting in the wilderness," makes good on the Puritans' understanding of themselves as "a people amongst whom religion and law were almost identical" (41). Through Dimmesdale's voice, the letter of New England law becomes the spirit of New England religion. Inspiration in Faulkner—"I got de ricklickshun en de blood of de Lamb" (176)—also addresses the problem of community identity but in a form that is quite different from the essentially religious problem imagined in *The Scarlet Letter* or from the essentially political problem to which *The Scarlet Letter* imagines itself the solution. That political problem is, in a nation confronted with the imminent possibility of dissolution: What makes the nation one nation? What makes Americans Americans? In the "land of the kike home of the wop," the question of what makes Americans American is a real one but not exactly or, at least, not primarily, a political one. Jews, we recall, may be "fine citizens" without being Americans. So what is an American?

The nativist answer to that question—the invention of American identity as a cultural identity—involves a double gesture of disarticulation. Identity is disconnected first from citizenship, which is to say, from the rights and obligations conferred upon the subject by his or her legal status as a citizen of the nation-state. Wops and kikes can participate in

American elections, but being able to participate in American elections doesn't make them American. But if what seems to be at stake here is a move to culture as the determinant of identity, a move that is, to the nonpolitical beliefs and practices that constitute more vividly than one's political affiliations the everyday fabric of the subject's life, that move is definitively set aside by the second disarticulation, which is precisely the disconnection of one's culture from one's actual beliefs and practices. Pluralism makes this disconnection possible by *deriving* one's beliefs and practices *from* one's cultural identity instead of *equating* one's beliefs and practices *with* one's cultural identity. It thus produces the possibility of a discrepancy between the two; because your culture cannot simply be equated with whatever you actually do and believe, it now becomes something that can be lost or stolen, reclaimed or repudiated. It now makes sense to think of yourself as deprived of your culture or as trying to get back in touch with your culture or as turning your back on your culture.

If, then, the meaning of "American" is altered in nativist modernism, so too is the meaning of "culture," and it is these reciprocal alterations that are the ultimate subject of the pages that follow.

Nation or Empire?

THOMAS NELSON Page's *Red Rock* was published in 1898, the year in which the United States annexed Hawaii, went to war in Cuba, seized the Philippines from Spain, and emerged as an imperial power. Needless to say, *Red Rock*, actually written the year before these events took place and written about events that themselves had taken place some thirty years earlier, is unconcerned with Cuba or the Philippines. But it is not unconcerned with American imperialism; indeed, American imperialism and, above all, the resistance to it, is its main subject. *Red Rock* tells the story of a conquered people, of how they survived under occupation, and of how they eventually "reconquered" what it sometimes refers to as their "country" and sometimes as their "section." It is, in short, an anti-imperialist novel.

In the years immediately after its publication, a good many other similarly anti-imperialist novels appeared, most notably Thomas Dixon's *The Leopard's Spots* (1902) and *The Clansman* (1905).[27] Like *Red Rock*, they are set in the Reconstruction South and make no mention of Cuba or the

Philippines.[28] But they are nevertheless importantly marked by the anti-imperialist arguments that had been invoked against McKinley, in particular by the description of the campaign in the Philippines as "a war of conquest" and by the claim that the president had no authority to "govern any person anywhere outside the constitution":[29] "The constitution," insisted Chicago reformer Edwin Burritt Smith, "makes no provision for the forcible intervention by our government in the affairs of a people who do not form an integral part of our union." More important still, "To the extent we permit our chosen representatives to exercise arbitrary powers, *whether at home or abroad*, we allow them to sap and destroy representative government itself" (emphasis mine).[30] McKinley's commitment to governing the Philippines "without constitutional restraint" was thus seen as an attack not merely upon Filipino rights but upon American rights, upon "the very principles for the maintenance of which our fathers pledged their lives." Hence Lincoln, in *The Clansman*, asserting that his first postwar "duty is to reestablish the Constitution as our supreme law over every inch of our soil" (43), denies that the Civil War was "a war of conquest" (44)[31] and refuses to establish martial law or to enforce "Negro suffrage" in North Carolina: "The Constitution," he says, "grants to the National Government no power to regulate suffrage, and makes no provision for the control of 'conquered' provinces" (42). And hence his radical Republican enemy Stoneman (Thaddeus Stevens) wishes to make the "Negro" "the ruler" and condemns the Constitution as "the creation, both in letter and spirit, of the slaveholders of the South" (43).

Thus, although the major anti-imperialist literature of the turn of the century made no mention of the major imperialist adventures of the turn of the century, it did not fail to address the issues raised by those adventures. Rather it understood those issues as having essentially to do with the nature of American self-government and American citizenship. "Nation or Empire?" was the question posed by the anti-imperialists.[32] The return to Reconstruction for the answer to this question placed anti-imperialism at the heart of an emerging discourse of American racial and national identity. Texts like *Red Rock*, I will argue, sought to avoid the perils of empire by avoiding the perils of nationhood first; for Page and for the plantation tradition more generally, the South was a "region" rather than a political entity. In *Red Rock*, no government can quite be legitimate, and this refusal of legitimacy is connected with a comparative indifference to racial identity (signaled by a feudal identification with the Indian) and an insistence on the importance of the family. For Progressives like Dixon, however, citizenship in the "new nation," produced out of resistance to an "African" empire, became *essentially* racial; the legitimacy of the state (its identity as nation rather than empire) was guaranteed by its whiteness. This is why in *Red Rock*, where whiteness doesn't yet have any real meaning, the state cannot be legitimated—the choice there is between the illegitimate government and the "tribe."

Another way to put this is to say that in *Red Rock*, by what would come to be Progressive standards, no one is American. *Red Rock* is set in the old South, in a "region" without a name, referred to as "'the old County,' or, 'the Red Rock section,' or just, 'My country, sir.'" Its heroes are those "aristocrats" who, "subjected to the humiliation" of Reconstruction, eventually "reconquered their section and preserved the civilization of the Anglo-Saxon."[33] But where, in Dixon, the resistance to Reconstruction will involve not just reconquering the "section" but nationalizing it, making Southern anti-imperialism the basis for the new American nation, in Page the restoration of "the old County" to "the rule of its own citizens" (506) is really meant to be just that, a restoration; it's no accident that the "old patrician[s]" of the South use china presented to their "ancestors by Charles the Second" (284). And where, in Dixon, what Anglo-Saxon civilization will be saved from is "the Negro," in *Red Rock* it is saved from ambitious "clerks" and "overseers." "Anglo-Saxon" in Dixon will mean "white"; in *Red Rock*, it means aristocratic. *Red Rock*'s clerks and overseers derisively refer to Page's heroes as "Lords," but the point of the novel is to confirm this identification and to insist on its patriarchal accessories. Thus, in contrast to the social threat posed by the new class of ambitious white men, *Red Rock*'s blacks present no real racial threat and stand instead as a kind of bulwark against the new whites: "these quality-niggers," the scalawag overseer explains to the carpetbagger clerk, "are just as stuck up as their masters" (129).

The "quality-nigger's" quality derives from membership in a quality family, and it is the family that Page presents as the essential unit of Red Rock society. During the war, slaves behave "more like clansmen" (43), and after the war, they are insulted by the new offer of wages: "How much does you pay Miss Bessie?" (91) Mammy Krenda asks her former master, contemptuously analogizing the idea of his paying his mammy to the idea of his paying his wife. In the context of the contemporary critique of marriage as a kind of prostitution (in, say, Charlotte Gilman), this analogy made a feminist point; in *Red Rock*, however, its purpose is to emphasize that Negroes are "member[s] of the family" (92) and that, as such, they cannot be sold or bought—even from themselves. The surest signs of the overseer's degeneracy are his desire to divorce his wife and his history as a "nigger-trader," both understood as assaults on the family.

The transformation in race relations envisioned by Dixon requires the destruction of this essentially multiracial family; it calls for the elimination of the old "uncles" and "aunts" of the plantation tradition and a general rewriting of the childhood intimacies with blacks that were supposed to enable white Southerners to understand and appreciate them better. In *The Leopard's Spots*, the lonely Charlie Gaston finds a "playmate and partner in work" in the "ragged little waif" Dick, who attaches himself to the Gaston household and even helps to defend it against a "Negro uprising." In plantation versions of this story, Dick, sticking "doggedly to Charlie's heels" (99), would count as the loyal Negro in contrast to the new Negroes of Reconstruction and especially of the '90s.[34] In *The Leopard's Spots*, however, Dick disappears in the early '70s only to reappear some twenty years later as rapist and murderer of a young white girl. Gaston's attempt to save him from being burned alive is represented here as a feeble and ineffectual deviation from his own white-supremacist principles, and Dixon's account of the girl's death doubles the repudiation of the old attachments to blacks by refusing even to allow her to be buried by a black man. The girl's father spurns the grave dug by "old Uncle Reuben Worth" (376) ("the only negro present") and asks "a group of old soldier comrades" to dig him a new one. Comradeship with white soldiers severs the ties of affection with blacks. The transformation of the friendly little black boy into a savage murderer, a transformation that is revealed rather than explained by the novel since it takes place entirely offstage, is made to stand, precisely because it is unexplained, as a revelation of the truth about blacks. In Dixon, the brutality of the new Negro exposes as a lie the fidelity of the old one.

But this exposure has positive consequences because it is only by means of this confrontation with the new Negro that new ties of affection among whites can be made available: "In a moment the white race had fused into a homogeneous mass of love, sympathy, hate and revenge. The rich and the poor, the learned and the ignorant, the banker and the blacksmith, the great and the small, they were all one now" (368). This "fusion" involves to some extent the blurring of lines that might in other contexts seem to divide whites racially among themselves; thus the speech that wins Gaston the gubernatorial nomination characterizes his fellow North Carolinians as descended, "by the lineal heritage of blood"

(442), not only from the "Angle" and the "Saxon" but also from the "Roman," the "Spartan," and the "Celt." Out of several possible races, "fusion" creates one "white race." But, more important than the elision of potential ethnic differences is the elision of social and political ones. The revolt against Reconstruction succeeds when rebellion against "black rule" melts the South's "furious political passions" into "harmonious unity" by collapsing Whigs and Democrats, Unionists and Secessionists, into a "White Man's Party" arrayed against "the Black Man's Party." And when, in the '90s, faced with the new problem of the new gap between rich and poor, the old alliance seems exhausted and unable to stand for anything except "the stupid reiteration of the old slogan of white supremacy" (197), the threat of the new Negro manages to make even the old slogan new too. Listening to Gaston offer as the only plank of the Democratic platform a proclamation that "the hour has now come in our history to eliminate the Negro from our life and reestablish for all time the government of our fathers" (433–34), the veteran General Worth experiences both nostalgia for "the years of his own daring young manhood" and admiration for "this challenge of the modern world." The nostalgia is for the war and the struggle against Reconstruction—both of which Dixon understood as an attempt to unite the nation along racial lines; the admiration is for the renewal and extension of that attempt in the '90s, the effort to make out of that united nation what Dixon calls a "State."[35]

The target against which Dixon's racial "fusion" is directed is the political "fusion" that successfully united Populists and Republicans against Democrats in the North Carolina elections of 1894 and 1896, and the point of Dixon's "fusion" is to eliminate political differences among whites by transforming them into racial differences between whites and blacks. Politics "is a religion," according to Charlie Gaston; the "Government is the organized virtue of the community" and "the State is . . . the only organ through which the whole people can search for righteousness . . ." (281). What Dixon imagines here are something like the literal conditions of Progressive nonpartisanship, but what political theorists like Walter Lippmann and Herbert Croly hoped to find in bureaucratic technologies that would turn political issues (i.e., conflicts of political interest) into administrative issues (i.e., conflicts of expertise), Dixon finds in race. As long as there can be "but one issue, are you a White Man or a Negro?" (159), there can be no partisan divisions between citizens.[36] For the two parties, the Democratic "White Man's Party" and the Populist/Republican "Black Man's Party," represent not a division between citizens but the division between citizens and noncitizens.

It was "on account of the enfranchisement of the Negro," Gaston says, that "the people of the South had to go into politics" (280). The Negro left in slavery would have left the essentially prepolitical, prenational plantation intact. But—every crisis an opportunity—his enfranchisement brought Southerners into politics in the effort to make the South part of the nation. And now the effort to disfranchise him (an effort that succeeds in *The Leopard's Spots* and that succeeded also in the elections of 1898) makes possible the elevation of politics to a "search for righteousness." For the Progressive Croly's desire to "purify" politics[37] and Dixon's insistence on the "purity" (281) of the "State" both require that political differences be understood as moral ones. "The principle of democracy is virtue," wrote Croly, citing Montesquieu and Santayana; for democracy to succeed, the "citizen" must aspire to become a "saint" (454). The great triumphs of *The Leopard's Spots* are thus its translation of political fusion into racial "fusion," its representation of a debate between citizens as a debate over who can be a citizen, and its consequent identification of citizenship with "righteousness."

From this perspective, *Red Rock*, with its evocation of the prewar "family, black and white"[38] and its suspicion of the "Government," represents a certain resistance both to the emergence of race as the crucial marker of identity and to the commitment to the state that the primacy of race makes possible. In *The Clansman* racial ties replace familial ones; the Klan, dressed like "Sperits" (348) and depicted by Dixon as "the reincarnated souls of the Clansmen of Old Scotland" (2), embody a racial purity that transcends the family. Under a regime in which even a single, invisible drop of black blood made a man black, their sheets are whiter than anyone's skin.[39] But in *Red Rock*, the Klan's sheets are disparaged as a "disguise" for "blackguards and sneaks" (352), and the familial "clan," in its biological and aristocratic purity, is multiracial. More striking still, *Red Rock*'s repudiation of the Klan is articulated not as respect for the laws the Klan violates but as respect for the code of "honor" that is itself violated by the law. (Think of Judge Driscoll's horror in *Pudd'nhead Wilson* [1894] when he learns that Tom, instead of taking physical revenge for Count Luigi's "assault" on him, has "crawled to a court of law about it.")[40] In *Red Rock*, it is carpetbaggers who embody the law, walking about, literally, with copies of "The Statutes of the United States" clasped under their arms, whereas Southern gentlemen, black and white, are bound by "honor" not to betray each other to the "Government." In Dixon, however, both the forming of the Klan and its disbanding are attempts to replace blood and honor with law and order.

This is most obviously true in the last volume of the trilogy, *The Traitor* (1907), which, although it is sometimes described as Dixon's attempt to back away from the positions he had taken so strongly in the first two volumes, is, in fact, an extension rather than a repudiation of them. Its hero, John Graham, is the leader of the Klan in North Carolina and so of the resistance to the "African Government," but as the Klan degenerates and becomes increasingly identified with "lawlessness," he will become increasingly reluctant to participate in its activities and will eventually seek to disband it. When he is nonetheless arrested for murder (actually committed by a carpetbagger), he rejects the possibility of escape, proclaiming, "I'm done with lawlessness. . . . I've led a successful revolution . . . and now with silent lips I'll face my accusers" (266). But while it is true that rejection of escape is somewhat anomalous in Dixon, the rejection of lawlessness and the proclamation of the "successful revolution" suggest the ways in which *The Traitor* continues the commitments of its predecessors. For insofar as the real effort of these books is to replace an illegitimate ("African") state with a legitimate one, "lawlessness" can never be countenanced. Indeed, Graham's submission to and eventual redemption by authority is here contrasted to the refusal of authority embodied in the "African Government" itself. For that government—making the Klan illegal, suspending habeas corpus, proclaiming martial law in the South, and placing Graham's home "county of Independence under military government"—itself stands "in violation of the Constitution" (330). And Graham's threat to take his case all the way to the Supreme Court, "the last bulwark of American liberties," produces a hasty pardon from those "little politicians" who finally "do not dare to allow the Supreme Court to overwhelm them with infamy." The point, then, is that Graham's is the true commitment to "the process of the law" (61) and to the Constitution that is both the ultimate law of the land and the originating document of the state.[41]

In sum, anti-imperialism here becomes synonymous with a certain constitutionalism. Just as the enemy throughout the trilogy is the imperial "African," usurping the Constitution, the hero is inevitably a defender of the Constitution and a creature of the state. In Page, the "clan" was saved from the state (loyal blacks supporting honorable whites against the corrupt administrators of the "Statutes"); in Dixon, the state is saved by the Klan ("We have rescued our state from Negro rule," [53] Graham tells his fellow Klansmen). Or rather, since Dixon actually imagines no preexisting state to be saved from the empire by the Klan, the state is *constituted* or *prefigured* by the Klan, which offers racial identity as a kind of rehearsal for the collective identity required by the new modes of national citizenship. Making it white, Dixon distinguishes the nation from the family and chooses it over the empire, indeed, creates it out of resistance to the empire. His point, then, is not the defense of the white state but the creation of the state through whiteness.[42]

The Rising Tide

T HE CARRAWAYS are something of a clan" (2), Nick Carraway remarks in *The Great Gatsby*, and Nick's "something" marks a certain distance not only from the Ku Klux Klan but from the less ironic identification of themselves as members of "clan Cameron" (192) produced by the Southern heroes of *The Clansman*. It is worth remembering, however, that in 1924—the year *Gatsby* was written—Klan membership was at its all-time peak, and, in fact, the Klan's style of racism finds a nonironic spokesman in *Gatsby*'s Tom Buchanan explaining the argument of a book Fitzgerald calls *The Rise of the Colored Empires* by a man he calls Goddard: "The idea, [Tom says,] is that that we're Nordics. . . . And we've produced all the things that go to make civilization, [but that] if we don't look out the white race will be . . . utterly submerged [by] these other races" (13–14). The book Tom is speaking of was actually called *The Rising Tide of Color Against White World-Supremacy*, and its real author was Lothrop Stoddard, but Tom's paraphrase, though crude, is essentially accurate. According to Stoddard, the world's population was divided into five major races—brown, black, red, yellow, and white— which could themselves be divided into "sub-species"; whites, for example, could be broken down into Nordics, Alpines, and Mediterraneans. Stoddard's mission in *The Rising Tide* was to teach white men the importance of a "true race-consciousness" (309) before it was too late, before, that is, the white race was overrun by the coloreds and before American Nordics, in particular, were drowned by the immigrant "flood" of Mediterraneans.

Stoddard's racism, then, like Dixon's, was anti-imperialist (and, like Dixon's, it would eventually involve a fundamental reconception of the meaning of "American"). He "regretted" the opening of the Far East which, although it had been "hailed by white men with general approval," had had the unfortunate effect of dragging till then "reluctant races" into "the full stream of world affairs" (19). The war between Russia and Japan had subsequently demonstrated that whites were not invincible in battle, and the Great War—Stoddard called it the "White Civil War"—had inopportunely weakened the white race in its preparation for what he envisioned as the great racial conflict to come. For although a political map of the world in 1920 revealed what looked like worldwide white supremacy, a racial map (Stoddard provided both) revealed how tenuous this supremacy was: on the political map, for example, India looked white; on the racial map, it was brown. Rereading the political map of Western imperialism as the racial map of colored imperialism, Stoddard ingeniously reproduced Dixon's vision of white Americans as the victims of imperialism while at the same time inflating it to a vision of the entire white race victimized.[43] Hence the appropriateness of Fitzgerald's title, *The Rise of the Colored Empires*, for a book that thought of itself as anti-imperialist on an international scale, written against "the imperious urge of the colored world toward racial expansion" (10).

At the same time, however, Stoddard's thinking represented not just an extension but a significant alteration of the racist discourse of the turn of the century. To Stoddard, for instance, Jewish immigrants, "about as thoroughly 'alien' to America as it is possible to conceive" (*Re-Forging*, 130), represented the greatest threat to America and, in fact, to the very idea of America. Having never themselves "been a nation," and having known only the "national life" of their "hostile Polish or Russian neighbors," they "instinctively" hate "nationality" itself: "This explains why international and radical revolutionary theories have gained such a hold upon the Eastern Jewish element in America" (130–31). Dixon, however, admired Jews: "the Jew," he said, "is the greatest race of people God has ever created."[44] And, more striking still, a Jewish storekeeper named Sam Nicaroshinski plays a favorable part in *The Traitor*. When the captured clansman John Graham is led through the streets to be carried away to a federal penitentiary (in a chapter Dixon calls "The Day of Atonement"), it is Nicaroshinski who slips him a hundred dollars and whispers, "don't you vorry, me poy, ve'll puild a monumendt to you in de public squvare yedt" (328).

This difference between Stoddard and Dixon is by no means merely personal or idiosyncratic. Indeed, in Mary Antin's *The Promised Land* (1912), it is the very thing that makes Stoddard's Jews unfit for Americanization—their lack of a national identity—that makes them exemplary Americans. In Russia, according to Antin, Jews were "a people without a country";[45] the Jew in America, however, as exemplified by Antin herself, instantaneously becomes an American, writing poems in honor of George Washington and celebrating his birthday with her "Fellow Citizens." What makes this transformation possible is that, whereas Jewish assimilation in Russia required "apostasy" (to become a Russian the Jew had to become a Gentile), assimilation in America is national rather than religious. Hence for the Jew to become American in no way requires giving up one nation for another; on the contrary, it involves, as it does for Dixon's (in contrast to Page's) unreconstructed Southerners, their first experience of "a spirit of nationalism." Americanization in Antin, as her title suggests, is almost a kind of Zionism, insofar, at least, as Zionism is understood as the fulfillment of the "national expectations" of a people in "exile." *The Promised Land*, like the *Trilogy of Reconstruction*, tells the story of a people achieving nationality and becoming citizens, and Mary Antin—with her hatred for the czar—is a fitting compatriot of Sam Nicaroshinski, with his hatred for the "African empire."

In Stoddard, however, and by the 1920s more generally, Jews and other Eastern Europeans had been redefined as "Asiatics" or "Mediterraneans," and just as the identity between them and Nordics had come to look a lot more problematic, the difference between them and Africans had come to look a lot less fundamental. So, in *The Rising Tide*, non-Nordic whites have their own role to play in the rise of the colored empires, a point missed by Fitzgerald's Jordan Baker when, in response to a diatribe by Tom that begins by attacking Gatsby and ends by predicting "intermarriage between black and white" (130), she murmurs, "We're all white here." For Tom, as for Stoddard, Gatsby (né Gatz, with his Wolfsheim "gonnegtion") isn't quite white, and Tom's identification of him as in some sense black suggests the power of the expanded notion of the alien. Gatsby's love for Daisy seems to Tom the expression of something like the impulse to miscegenation, an impulse that Nick Carraway understands as "the following of a grail. [Gatsby] knew that Daisy was extraordinary, but he didn't realize just how extraordinary a 'nice' girl could be" (149). "Nice" here doesn't exactly mean "white," but it doesn't exactly not mean "white" either. It is a term—like "breeding"—that will serve as a kind of switching point where the Progressive novel's discourse of class will be turned into the postwar novel's discourse of race.

Comparing *The Great Gatsby* to Dreiser's *An American Tragedy*, we have already noted that when Fitzgerald's novel begins, Gatsby already has what Clyde Griffiths wants; insofar as class mobility involves transforming one's clothes, one's manners, one's friends, one's women, *The Great Gatsby* makes it almost magically easy. But Gatsby wants Daisy—the "grail"—which is to say that he wants something more or something else. The fact that he is, when they first meet, "penniless" hardly presents itself as an obstacle, partly because it can be concealed from Daisy, more importantly because it can be—and quickly is—overcome. The real problem is that he is "without a past" (149) and to get Daisy he must get a past. Thus Jimmy Gatz's efforts to improve himself, which begin in the Franklin-like scheduling of his present intended to produce the perfected Gatsby of his future ("study electricity, etc."), must themselves be transformed into efforts to reconstruct his past: "I was brought up in America but educated at Oxford, because all my ancestors have been educated there for many years. It is a family tradition" (65). And thus in his mind (and also, as it turns out, in hers) the key to winning Daisy back is precisely his ability to redescribe and so alter the past.[46] Urged by Gatsby to proclaim not only that she doesn't love Tom but that she never loved Tom, Daisy finally cries out, "Oh, you want too much. . . . I love you now—isn't that enough? I can't help what's past" (133). Loving him now, as Gatsby, Tom, and Daisy herself all instantaneously see, isn't enough precisely because it doesn't help what's past, it doesn't contribute to the project of rewriting that would give Gatsby a past and thus retroactively make him someone who could be "married" to Daisy.

The point here is not only that the desire for a different future has been transformed into the desire for a different past but that the meaning of that past has been rendered genealogical, a matter of "ancestors."[47] Tom's mistress Myrtle only married George Wilson because she made a mistake about his "breeding" (35); her friend Mrs. McKee "almost made a mistake too" but avoided it by marrying Chester instead of the "little kike" (34) who had been after her for years but who she knew was "below" her. These distinctions parody but also reproduce the quest for the "nice"; indeed, by representing the attraction of niceness in its vulgarized form as the attraction of breeding, they make it possible for niceness to count simultaneously as identical to breeding and as a reproach to the vulgarity of breeders. Hemingway's Robert Cohn (another "kike" [164], although he didn't become "race-conscious," Hemingway says, until he went to Princeton) says in *The Sun Also Rises* that Lady Ashley has "breeding" (38). Jake Barnes says in response to Cohn that she is "very nice." "Breeding" is the term used by people who don't really have any; "nice" is the term used by people who do.[48]

Cohn thinks that Brett has "a certain quality, a certain fineness"; "nice" is deployed by Hemingway against descriptions like that and, more generally, against the "abstract words" famously condemned in *A Farewell to Arms* (1929). "There were many words that you could not stand to hear," Hemingway writes, "and finally only the names of places had dignity."[49] "Nice" isn't the name of a place, but it is a name for people who come from a place as opposed to, say, Gatsby who—despite the family history designed to show that he is not "just some nobody"—really is "Mr. Nobody from Nowhere" (130).[50] Removing Fitzgerald's quotation marks, Hemingway installs "nice"—along with words like "good" and "true"—at the heart of a prose style that no longer needs the explicit vocabulary of race (e.g., "Nordic") to distinguish those who have breeding from those who don't, in the way that, say, Jake's concierge distinguishes between visitors who are not to be allowed up and visitors like Brett, who is "very nice," which is to say, "très, très gentille," which is to say, "of very good family" (52). "Nice" has its pedigree; indeed, pedigree is its pedigree. As a character in Fitzgerald's *The Beautiful and Damned* (1922) puts it, "if a person comes from a good family, they're always nice people."[51]

Robert Cohn, not a very good writer, doesn't "know how to describe" (38) the "quality" that Jake Barnes so easily finds a word for. To be nice—even better, to be able to *say* nice—is to identify yourself as neither Gatsby nor Cohn; the social point of Hemingway's prose style was relentlessly to enforce such distinctions: "Cohn made some remark about it being a very good example of something or other, I forget what. It seemed like a nice cathedral, nice and dim, like Spanish churches" (90). Racial inferiority is reproduced here as aesthetic failure. To be insufficiently "race-conscious," as Cohn had been before going to Princeton, was to be insufficiently alert to the difference between people who really were nice and people who just looked or acted nice. The war had encouraged such inattentiveness: Tom can't understand how Gatsby "got within a mile" of Daisy unless "he brought the groceries to the back door" (132); the answer, of course, is that Gatsby was wearing the "invisible cloak of his uniform" (149) so that Daisy couldn't see he was just Jimmy Gatz. Tom has to make what he calls a "small investigation" to clear up the confusion. Even Cohn "can be . . . nice" (101); in fact, Hemingway's obsessive commitment to distinguishing between Cohn and Jake only makes sense in the light of their being in some sense indistinguishable, a fact that the novel makes particularly vivid in their relations to Brett. But such similarities are definitively disrupted by the taxonomies of the bullfight and by the "oral spiritual examination" (132) Jake has to pass to prove that he has *aficion*. "Aficion is passion," Jake says: the difference between a bull-fighter with it and a bullfighter without it is that the one gives "real emotion" while the other gives "a fake emotional feeling" (168). The bullfighter with *aficion* in *The Sun Also Rises* is Romero, who is to an "imitation" like Marcial as Nick is to Gatsby or as Jake is to Robert Cohn: "He knew everything when he started. The others can't ever learn what he was born with" (168).

Aficion thus takes its place alongside niceness as another name for breeding. It may be "spiritual" but, like breeding, it is manifest in bodies; when aficionados see that Jake has it too, they put a hand on his shoulder: "It seemed as though they wanted to touch you to make it certain" (132). But this doesn't exactly mean that *aficion* can be reduced to breeding. For one thing, as we have already seen, the term "breeding," when applied to people, isn't itself very nice; Robert Cohn is reproved for using it to describe Brett, and when Brett herself urges Mike Campbell to "show a little breeding" (141) and behave better to Cohn, Mike answers her, "Breeding be damned. Who has any breeding anyway, except the bulls?" And, for another thing, even the bulls' breeding can't exactly be reduced to breeding. Only bulls have breeding, as Mike says, but as Mike also says, "bulls have no balls" (175, 176). Mike is drunk and he means to be insulting the bullfighter Brett is so attracted to, but there is an important sense in which Hemingway's identification of breeding with a literal in-ability to breed should be taken seriously, as should indeed the converse identification of literal breeding prowess with a lack of breeding.

"One thing's sure and nothing's surer," someone sings at Gatsby's house, "The rich get richer and the poor get—children" (96). Or, as the author of *The Passing of the Great Race*, Madison Grant, put it, "If we continue to allow [immigrants] to enter they will in time drive us out of our own land by mere force of breeding."[52] Grant and Stoddard both worried that, compared to the other races, whites were the "slowest breeders" (7), and Stoddard focused in particular on the sterilizing effect of immigration on whites: "There can be no question," he wrote later in the decade (after the Immigration Act of 1924 had ostensibly put an end to mass immigration), "that every low-grade alien who landed prevented a native American baby or a North European baby from ever being born" (*Re-Forging*, 167).[53] This contraceptive effect finds a weirdly literal echo in *The Sun Also Rises*, where the alien Cohn is the only one with children and where, more tellingly, he has an appropriately sterilizing impact on

Nordic types like his girlfriend Frances who, having "wasted two and a half years" (47) on Cohn, imagines that her childbearing opportunities have passed: "I never liked children much," she says, "but I don't want to think I'll never have them."

Frances, however, is hardly the most spectacular example in *The Sun Also Rises* of the inability to reproduce. Jake Barnes is. The Great War, according to Stoddard, was a breeding disaster for the white race since, in killing millions of Nordic soldiers at an age when they were "best adapted to fecundity," it had (like immigration) "prevented millions more from being born or conceived" (*Rising Tide*, 185, 184). Jake's war wound is often understood as a symbol for the Lost Generation's disillusion, but the testimony of writers like Stoddard and Grant gives new meaning to the wound and to the very term Lost Generation. War tends to "induce sterility," Stoddard writes (184); "You . . . have given more than your life," the Italian colonel tells Jake (31). The Great War, the "White Civil War," had induced sterility above all in members of the "Nordic race" since it was Nordic men who "went forth eagerly to battle" (Stoddard, *Rising Tide*, 183) while "the little brunet Mediterranean either stayed home or even when at the front showed less fighting spirit, took fewer chances, and oftener saved their skins"; "You, a *foreigner*, an *Englishman* . . . have given more than your life," the Italian colonel says. The war had thus "unquestionably left Europe much poorer in Nordic blood," or, as Madison Grant put it, "As in all wars since Roman times, from the breeding point of view, the little dark man is the winner" (quoted in *The Rising Tide*, 183). In *The Sun Also Rises* the little dark man is Robert Cohn (during the war he "stayed home" [Grant] and "had three children" [Hemingway]), and one might say that Jake's war wound is simultaneously a consequence of the war and of unrestricted immigration since, as interpreted by the racial discourse of the '20s, immigration and the war were simply two aspects of the same phenomenon, the rising tide of color.

The Vanishing American

IMMIGRATION and the war had been so devastating, Stoddard thought, that in the "two short generations" between 1890 and 1920, "the Nordic native American" had "in many of our urban areas become almost extinct" (*Rising Tide*, 165). Stoddard himself made no explicit connection between the disappearance of "the big, blond man" from the streets of New York and the disappearance of the Indian from the prairie, but the rhetoric of racial extinction in America was, of course, the rhetoric of the vanishing American. To think of Nordics as a vanishing race was inevitably to identify them with the Indians and, in minds more imaginative than Stoddard's, this identification could involve a deeper kinship. Willa Cather's Tom Outland—who is contrasted by Cather to the Jew Louie Marsellus and who heroically volunteers for and is killed in the war—thinks of the "extinct" (202) Anasazi Indians as his "ancestors" (242).[54]

Cather wrote *The Professor's House* in 1924, a year which, because of the passage of the Immigration Act, Stoddard called "one of the decisive dates of American history" (*Re-Forging*, 192), and a year which also saw—one week later—the passage of the considerably less celebrated Indian Citizenship Act. The significance of the Immigration Act, of course, was not only that it brought to an end the tradition of unrestricted European immigration but that it did so according to the principle of "national origins."[55] Eligibility for American citizenship was now dependent upon ethnic identity. And, since the number of possible immigrants from any particular region was now linked first to the number of people living in America who had themselves been born in that region and, starting in 1927, to the number of Americans who could trace their "ancestry" back to that region, the Johnson Act required a "racial analysis" of the American population that, in effect, rewrote the map of the United States in the way that Stoddard's racial map of the world rewrote his political map. While it remained true that, say, Italian Americans and Swedish Americans were equally American, their Italianness and their Swedishness now took on a new significance since it was their ancestral identity (their identity as descendants of Swedes or Italians) as distinguished from their political identity (their identity as Americans) that would determine the access to American citizenship of future Italians and Swedes. Thus the Johnson Act's technology for making crucial the ancestry of those who might become American required that the ancestry of those who already were American be made crucial also.

But if the purpose of the Johnson Act was officially to exclude groups of people from citizenship, the purpose of the Indian Citizenship Act was just the opposite. Throughout the nineteenth and early twentieth centuries, Indians had been anomalies with respect to American citizenship, regarded first as citizens of their tribes and then, with the passage of the Dawes Act of 1887, as potential citizens of the United States.[56] Indian potential for citizenship was identified with the ability to adopt "the habits of civilized life" (174), and Indian policy was increasingly directed at "the absorption of the Indians into our national life, not as Indians, but as American citizens" (177). Thus a series of government initiatives, from the Lacey Act of 1907 (authorizing the secretary of the interior to grant individual Indians individual control of their "pro rata share" [210] of tribal funds) through the Sells "Declaration" of 1917 (authorizing a series of measures designed to "speedily achieve" the "ultimate absorption of the Indian race into the body politic of the Nation" [214–15]) to the Citizenship for World War I Veterans Act of 1919 (authorizing citizenship for every veteran who "desires" [215] it) encouraged the normalization of the Indians' status as citizens. And the Citizenship Act of 1924, declaring "all noncitizen Indians born within the territorial limits of the United States . . . to be citizens of the United States" (218) represented the triumphant end of this process. Where the Johnson Act identified the racial groups which would be prevented, ideally, from becoming American, the Citizenship Act celebrated that racial group which, ideally, had succeeded.

In fact, however, the Citizenship Act of 1924 did not mark anything like the successful culmination of the policy of assimilation; in fact, the policy of assimilation failed: as the Indian hero of Zane Grey's *The Rainbow Trail* (1915) puts it, "the white man's ways and his life and his God are not the Indian's. They never can be."[57] Instead of being absorbed into the body politic, Indians were increasingly relegated to "a peripheral role in society."[58] And from this perspective, the Citizenship Act could seem at best a futile gesture, at worst a cynical acknowledgment of the ultimate irrelevance of citizenship to the Indians' predicament.

But the discrepancy between the status envisioned for them by the Citizenship Act and the actual social status of the Indians should not be understood to exhaust the meaning of that act. The perceived impossibility of assimilating large numbers of Eastern European immigrants had led to the erection in the Johnson Act of barriers to citizenship; the actual failure to assimilate the Indians led through the Citizenship Act to citizenship. Undoubtedly, as Robert F. Berkhofer points out, the Congress was more afraid of "millions of Southern and Eastern Europeans" than of "a few hundred thousand pacified Indians."[59] In any event, however, the sense in which these two acts were opposed—one designed to exclude, the other to include—is less striking than the sense in which they were complementary: they were both designed to keep people from *becoming* citizens. The Johnson Act guaranteed that aliens would not become citizens by putting a halt to mass immigration; the Citizenship Act guaranteed that Indians would not become citizens by declaring that they already were citizens. Both acts, that is, participated in a recasting of American citizenship, changing it from a status that could be achieved through one's own actions (immigrating, becoming "civilized," getting "naturalized") to a status that could better be understood as inherited.[60] "America," as we have already seen Charles W. Gould describe it in his racist tract of 1922, was "A Family Matter," and the only way to keep the family strong was to "utterly reject . . . foreigners" (4). American traditions, Gould wrote, "cannot be taught, they must come to us with the mother's milk . . . and grow with our nerves and thews and sinews until they become part and parcel of our very being" (163). "Repeal our naturalization laws," Gould urged his readers, "secure our children and our children's children in their legitimate birthright" (165).

This is what it means for Tom Outland to think of the Indians who had inhabited the Blue Mesa as his "ancestors" and to describe the "relics" they left behind as "the pots and pans that belonged to my poor grandmothers" (243). And it is why Roddy Blake's selling those relics (to a German, to pay for Tom's college education) leads Tom to compare him to Dreyfus: "You've gone and sold them to a country that's got plenty of relics of its own. You've gone and sold your country's secrets, like Dreyfus" (242–43). Claiming descent from Indians, Tom is committing himself to the conception of American identity embodied in the Johnson Act and, comparing Roddy to Dreyfus, Tom is committing himself to an understanding of political disloyalty as racial betrayal. The issue, in other words, is what it means to be American, a point that Roddy, despite his feeling "away out of my depth," makes clear when he characterizes Tom's speech as a "Fourth of July talk" (245). Giving a *real* "Fourth of July talk" to the National Education Association in 1924, Calvin Coolidge had cited the Johnson Act as one of his administration's chief accomplishments in the effort, as he put it, to help "America . . . remain American" (28); identifying his own "national origin" as Indian, Tom suggests the meaning of remaining—rather than becoming—American.

This difference is figured even in the choice of holiday on which it is celebrated. The speech that Charlie Gaston (in *The Leopard's Spots*) calls the "biggest" of his life is a "Memorial day oration" (207). Memorial Day, increasingly an artifact of the reaction against Reconstruction, had been created in 1868 to honor Civil War dead on both sides, and, insofar as the Civil War was understood by Progressives to have made the birth of the new nation possible, Memorial Day counted as a kind of Progressive July 4.[61] The Civil War, replacing class and sectional differences between whites with racial differences between whites and blacks, had made what Dixon called the "ideal Union" possible. And because (under Jim Crow) no black person could become a citizen, any white person could:[62] for whites, becoming American required nothing more or less than learning to identify oneself as an American, as opposed to a Northerner or a Southerner, an Italian or a Jew.

Citizenship is imagined here as something that can be (except for blacks) and must be (even for whites) achieved, a matter of ideology rather than birthplace. Cather's early short story "The Namesake" (1907) makes this point by imagining its hero, a sculptor distinguished above all by his relation to America ("He seemed, almost more than any other one living man, to mean all of it—from ocean to ocean")[63] as both an immigrant and an expatriate. Born in Italy, living in France, his only American experience is a two-year visit to his aunt's house in the suburbs of Pittsburgh, and even here, he "never" feels "at home" (175); the one thing American that inspires in him a "sense of kinship" is a portrait of the namesake, his uncle, "killed in one of the big battles of Sixty-four" (171). And it is this attraction to the uncle that results in his Americanization.

From interrogating the local veterans about the circumstances of his uncle's death, he progresses to reading books about the Civil War and searching the house for the dead hero's memorabilia. The culmination of all this is an exceptionally intense Memorial Day on which, sent by his aunt to fetch the flag from the attic, he discovers an old trunk containing, among other things, a copy of the *Aeneid* with his "own name" written on the front flyleaf and written again, along with a drawing and inscription, on the back flyleaf. The drawing is of "the Federal flag" (178) and the inscription—"Oh, say, can you see by the dawn's early light / What so proudly we hailed at the twilight's last gleaming"—is from "The Star-Spangled Banner," which would not achieve any official status until ten years after Cather's writing (by executive order of Dixon's graduate school classmate, Woodrow Wilson) but which here, unofficially, makes the immigrant-expatriate feel, "for the first time," "the pull of race and blood and kindred" (179).[64] After this he goes back to Paris and starts producing the "monuments" to "the heroes of the Civil War" and the sculptures on American topics ("his *Scout*, his *Pioneer*, his *Gold Seekers*" [170]) that make his artistic career.

In Dixon, the Civil War makes American national identity possible; in

Cather, Civil War literature performs the same function. "The Namesake" is essentially a story about assimilation, about a "citizenship" which, although it is linked to "race and blood and kindred," is more a matter of "experience" than of heredity.[65] Where Dixon's heroes become Americans (instead of Northerners or Southerners) by fighting in the war, Cather's hero becomes American (instead of French or Italian) by reading about his uncle fighting in it. The fact that his "citizenship" is, as he himself puts it, "somewhat belated" (170) marks the sense in which he can be said to have acquired rather than inherited it, or rather it marks the transformation of an inheritance into an achievement. This is precisely what, according to Dixon, the Civil War was all about, the transformation of the Founding Fathers' legacy into their grandchildren's political creation; that's why *The Birth of a Nation* (made, of course, from Dixon's *The Clansman*) was called *The Birth of a Nation*.[66] Cather, by invoking "The Star-Spangled Banner" on behalf of the Civil War dead, helps to transform the almost-Revolutionary song of 1812 into the national anthem of 1917.

For Dixon, racism was crucial to the reinvention of the American state; only by freeing themselves from slavery, destroying their familial bonds to blacks, and intermarrying with their racial kinsmen from across the Mason-Dixon line could whites become Americans. But antiblack racism plays no role in "The Namesake"; my point in comparing Cather to Dixon is only to suggest that her concern in "The Namesake" with the question of American identity involves the characteristic Progressive understanding of that identity as essentially political, reenabled by the Civil War as the refounding of the American nation. But the celebration of July 4 on Blue Mesa is different from the celebration of Memorial Day in "The Namesake."[67] Although the Johnson Act had been a great victory, Coolidge told the National Education Association, "acts of legislation" were, in the end, of only secondary importance. Real progress toward "increased National freedom" (23) depended not on the "interposition of the government" but on "the genius of the people themselves" (13). And for an appreciation of this "genius"—for a more "intense" study of our "heritage"—we needed to go beyond the Civil War and beyond even the Revolutionary War to "the events which brought about the settlement of our own land" (38).

Stoddard was so enthusiastic about this project that (not content with thinking of the Great War as "the White Civil War") he took to calling the Revolution "the Anglo-Saxon Civil War" (*Re-Forging*, 19), and he began to think of it as the beginning of America's racial problems. It was the period "which *preceded* the beginning of national life" (italics mine) that now seemed to him the "basic fact in American history" (3), and, although Fitzgerald, of course, makes fun of Stoddard, the famous ending of *The Great Gatsby*—with its transformation of Nick's eyes into the "Dutch sailors' eyes" seeing once again the "vanished trees" of the "fresh, green breast of the new world" (182)—is as true to Coolidge's exhortation to "search out and think the thoughts of those who established our institutions" (56) as Stoddard could have wished. The sting of the irony Nick directs at his own family's conception of itself as a "clan"—priding itself (à la Dixon) on its distinguished Scots ancestry but tracing its actual prosperity to an immigrant who (contra Dixon) bought his way out of service in the Civil War—is removed by the post-Progressive repudiation of the foundational importance of the war and by the transformation of American identity from an achievement into a heritage. By the same token, Professor St. Peter's *Spanish Adventurers in North America* is an exercise in "purely cultural studies" designed precisely to provide the "more accurate knowledge of the causes and events which brought about the settlement of our own land and which went into the formation of its institutions" (38) that Coolidge and Stoddard hoped would help America "remain American." Indeed, given Madison Grant's claim that "The splendid conquistadores ["splendid" is also the word Louie uses to describe the professor's books on the conquistadors—"your splendid Spanish-adventurer sons"] of the New World were of Nordic type, but their pure stock did not long survive,"[68] the professor's scholarly project exemplifies a Nordicism even purer than Fitzgerald's invocation of the Dutch, about whose pure Nordic status some commentators had their doubts.[69]

But in *The Professor's House*, not even the Spanish explorers count as the originators of an American heritage; the episode in the "history" of his "country" (222) that concerns Tom Outland goes back to "before Columbus landed" (119). In this respect, Cather participates in a more general discussion of what was perceived to be a crisis in American culture or, more precisely, a crisis *of* culture. Coolidge is famous for minimizing the role of government and for insisting that the business of America was business, but in his frequent speeches on education he took a somewhat different line: "We do not need more government," he announced in 1923, "we need more culture" (74–75). And in the search for a source of and model for American culture, attention was increasingly focused on the American Indian. Indians were the exemplary instance of a society that could be understood as having a culture: thus Edward Sapir, writing on

"Culture, Genuine and Spurious" in the *American Journal of Sociology* (1924), characterized Indian salmon spearing as a "culturally higher type of activity" than the labor of a "telephone girl" or "mill hand" because it worked in "naturally with all the rest of the Indian's activities instead of standing out as a desert patch of merely economic effort in the whole of life."[70] For Sapir, the life of "the average participant in the civilization of a typical American Indian tribe" provided a model of "genuine culture," the experience of society as a "significant whole" (318), and of an individuality that avoids modern fragmentation because it both grows "organically" out of culture and contributes constructively to it: "A healthy national culture is never a passively accepted heritage from the past, but implies the creative participation of the members of the community." Sapir echoes Coolidge's insistence: "We did not acquire our position through our own individual efforts. We were born into it," and "it is only by intense application that the individual comes into the . . . possession of the heritage of civilization" (68). "It was possession," Tom says, when he begins "for the first time" to study "methodically" and "intelligently" (251) that summer on the mesa, and when he starts to see things that summer, also for "the first time," "as a whole" (250).

And the Indian is also understood as the exemplary instance of what it means no longer to have a culture. The "fragmentary existence" of the modern Indian—the "integrity of his tribe" destroyed and the "old cultural values" dead—leaves him, Sapir wrote, "with an uneasy sense of the loss of some vague and great good, some state of mind that he would be hard put to define but which gave him courage and joy . . ." (318). The "happiness unalloyed" that Tom experiences on the Blue Mesa is thus the recovery of Indian culture, which is to say, of the very idea of culture. Feeling toward the cliff dwellers the "filial piety" he is reading about in Virgil, he experiences "for the first time" what Sapir called "genuine" culture, the culture the Indians had had but lost, the culture that modern Americans were looking for, the culture that, according to Coolidge, would take the place of "government."

The transformation of the *Aeneid* from a poem about political identity—inscribed, in "The Namesake," with a "drawing" of the "federal flag"—into a poem about cultural identity—inscribed, in Tom's imagination, with the "picture" of the cliff dwellers' tower, "rising strong, with calmness and courage" (253)—marks in Cather the emergence of culture not only as an aspect of American identity but as one of its determinants. That, after all, was what the classics were for. "Modern civilization dates from Greece and Rome" (47), Coolidge said in an address before the annual meeting of the American Classical League at the University of Pennsylvania in 1921. As Greece and Rome had been "the inheritors of a civilization which had gone before" (47), we were now their "inheritors." Hence, in the effort to form a cultural in addition to a political identity, it was study of the classics rather than the Constitution that would promote (as had the Johnson Act) the modern American's desire "to be supremely American" (56). The answer to the question, "What are the fundamental things that young Americans should be taught?" was "Greek and Latin literature" (44–45).

Coolidge's word for cultural identity was "character" and his interest in education was a consequence of his view that the "first great duty" of education was "the formation of character, which is the result of heredity and training" (51–52). What the Johnson Act (keeping out, among others, the descendants of the Greeks and Romans) would contribute to the heredity side of American character formation, a classical education (studying the literature of the ancestors whose descendants the Johnson Act was excluding) would contribute to the training side. Indeed, insofar as Greek and Latin civilization was itself our inheritance (the civilization ours was descended from), our training could be understood not only to supplement but to double our heredity. More striking still, since we had no biological relation to Greece or Rome (and since the point of the Johnson Act was to make sure that we would continue to have no biological relation to them) our training could be understood not only as doubling but as constituting our heredity; it is only our education in our origins that guarantees that those origins will indeed be ours. "Culture is the product of a continuing effort," Coolidge told the classicists; "The education of the race is never accomplished" (49). The education of the race can never be accomplished because it is only education that makes the race. Our descent from the Greeks and Romans in Coolidge parallels Tom Outland's descent from the Indians in Cather, and the classical education Tom gets among the cliff dwellers exemplifies the "instruction in the classics" that Coolidge hoped would one day "be the portion of every American" (57). In Coolidge and Cather both, identity is a function of inheritance, but what gets inherited is not just a biology, it's a culture.

It is what will prove to be this extraordinarily fruitful equivocation about inheritance that makes the American Indian—conceived at the same time as biologically unrelated to and as an ancestor of boys like Tom Outland (who is a "stray" and has "no family" but whose cliff-dweller "grandmothers" owned the "pots and pans" that Roddy sells to the Germans)—play so crucial a role in the developing idea of cultural identity. The "utterly exterminated" tribe of *The Professor's House* and the tribe "without culture" that exterminated them represent, because the one biologically disappeared and the other culturally never existed, the possibility of an identity that, insofar as it is neither simply biological nor simply environmental, can be properly cultural. Neither by blood as such nor through education as such can Tom come into "possession" of himself, but only through a process of what is essentially acculturation, a process imaginable only as a kind of education which is simultaneously a kind of blood affiliation. If Tom had really been related to Indians or if he'd grown up speaking Latin around the house, this process would have been impossible. So although Coolidge had protested that Latin and Greek weren't really "dead languages," in fact, it was only because they *were* dead that they could assume the status of cultural standards. If the Italian immigrants disembarking at Ellis Island had spoken Latin, Coolidge wouldn't have urged the schools to teach it any more than Cather would have had Tom read it: a truly "living" language could not be an object of "purely cultural study." And if the Indians had not been perceived as vanishing, they could not have become the exemplary instance of what it meant to have a culture. "The sun of the Indian's day is setting," an old chief tells Nophaie, the hero of Zane Grey's *The Vanishing American* (1925).[71] It is because the Indian's sun was perceived as setting that he could become, I want to argue, a kind of paradigm for increasingly powerful American notions of ethnic identity and eventually for the idea of an ethnicity that could be threatened or defended, repudiated or reclaimed.[72]

Grey's Nophaie is a Navajo, raised among whites and now returned to his tribe; with "an Indian body and white man's mind" (94), he represents a synergetic combination of the means by which the vanishing Indian was supposed to vanish: cultural assimilation and biological obliteration. Raised among whites, he loves a white woman and, because he cannot marry her and will not (loving a member of an "alien" "race" [14]) marry a woman of his own race, he sees that he is "the last of his family and he would never have a child" (114). In the version of *The Vanishing American* published by Harper & Brothers in 1925, this turns out to be literally true: offended by the prospect of an Indian man marrying a white woman (the reverse was more acceptable), Harper & Brothers had required Grey to make changes in the original serial (published in the *Ladies' Home Journal* in 1922) that resulted in Nophaie dying unwed under what Grey's son Loren rightly calls "quite mysterious and really illogical circumstances" (vii).[73] But even in the uncensored version, where Nophaie ends up marrying white Marian after all, the spirit of his prediction, his representation of himself as "the last of his family," comes true. For, in marrying Marian, he tells her, "I shall be absorbed by you—by your love—by your children. . . ." Imagining their children as her children (and himself as her), Nophaie treats assimilation exactly as if it were a form of instead of an alternative to biological extinction, and approves it—"It is well" (342). Whether responding to racist demands or rejecting them, Grey made sure that the Indian vanished.

But Grey's title is not "The Vanishing Race" (the title of Curtis's famous photograph) or "The Vanishing Indian," it is *The Vanishing American*. And if, from the standpoint of assimilationism, this makes a certain sense—since it was in ceasing to be an Indian that the Indian would become an American—it makes even more sense from the standpoint of the hostility to assimilation that we have seen at work in Cather and that finds an important expression also in Grey. For *The Vanishing American*'s villains are the missionaries who preach to the Indians that by adopting "the white man's way, his clothes, his work, his talk, his life, and his God" they will become "white in heart" (183). In Indians like Nophaie, whose "soul" has "as much right to its inheritance of ideals and faith as any white man's" (103–4), these teachings produce a "spiritual catastrophe." But the war, which in fact dealt a major blow to the project of assimilating the immigrant ("The war virtually swept from the American consciousness the old belief in unrestricted immigration"),[74] in *The Vanishing American* deals a major blow to the project of assimilating the Indian. That is, like the Indian Citizenship Act, it renders the project of assimilation impossible because unnecessary. For the war reveals the missionaries as themselves *less American* than the Indians. Grey's missionaries are "all German" (213); "their forefathers," as an old Navajo chief puts it, "belonged to that wicked people who practice war. They are not American. They are not friends of the Indian" (227–28). And the Indian, by contrast and "by every right and law and heritage," is "the first and best blood of America." In *The Vanishing American*, then, the opposition between Indian and white is transformed into an opposition between American and German.[75] Offered the opportunity to enlist, Nophaie immediately volunteers. "I will go," he says, "I am an American" (224).[76]

But the neat trick of representing the Germans as the ancestral enemies of the Indians (and it is a German who buys the Indian relics that by rights, Tom Outland thinks, should be in the Smithsonian) pales by comparison to the truly astonishing rearrangement of ancestry that the war makes possible. Attempting to persuade his fellow tribesmen to enlist, Nophaie gives what Grey calls "a trenchant statement of his own stand": "Nophaie will go to war. He will fight for the English, who are forefathers of Americans. Nophaie and all the Nopahs are the first of Americans. He will fight for them" (229). If the Indians are the first Americans and the Americans are descended from the English, then the English become the "forefathers" of the Indians and the Indians going off to fight for them are fighting as Americans for their ancestors and against the ancestors of the un-American missionaries. Or, to put this from the standpoint not of the Indians *about* whom Grey was writing but of the white Americans *for* whom he was writing, if the Indians are the "first Americans," then the Americans now going off to war are descended from them; the Indians, whose forefathers are the English, are themselves the forefathers of the Americans. Volunteering to fight and so proving themselves as American as the white man, they make it possible for the white man to become their descendant and so to become as American as the Indian.[77]

A Family Matter

THE READERS of *The Vanishing American* are thus understood to bear the same relation to the Indians that Tom Outland does.[78] And when Nophaie vanishes at *The Vanishing American's* end, he is only following in the footsteps of the cliff dwellers whose extinction counts as a crucial aspect of their legacy. In *The Professor's House*, one's ancestors cannot actually be members of one's family, and the reason for this is that, although it is the family that provides the indispensable model for the new conception of American identity—for the transmission of "traditions" that "must come to us with the mother's milk"—the inability to maintain the purity to which the theorists of racial integrity were committed is at the same time the very essence of family life. "Blood is blood," Jason Compson says, but the family which gives meaning to that tautology must also compromise it: Compsons are also Bascombs. Which is only to say, as Jason also says, "A woman'll do anything," where "anything" is always one thing, whether it's Caddie with Dalton Ames,

Brett with Robert Cohn, Daisy with Jay Gatsby, or Rosamond St. Peter with Louie Marsellus.

The structural identity of these novels, the fact that each is orchestrated around the defense of or attack upon what Fitzgerald—describing the relation between Tom and Daisy—calls a "natural intimacy," testifies to the power of the familial model. Faulkner, as a famous anecdote has it, had responded to a Hollywood producer's desire for something new in the way of a "boy meets girl" story by proposing to make the boy and girl brother and sister; Caddie's "intimacy" with her brothers is literally "natural" just because they are her brothers: she and they belong to the same family. Tom and Daisy, whose "intimacy" is not literally "natural," are nonetheless treated by the text as something more than a married couple; Fitzgerald describes them at one point as belonging together to "a rather distinguished secret society" (18). But the meaning of their relationship is made clearer by the fact that Nick and Daisy are "cousins" and by the fact that there is one "natural" category that unites the three of them and Jordan Baker too: " 'The idea [Tom says] is that we're Nordics. I am, and you are, and you are, and—' After an infinitesimal hesitation he included Daisy with a slight nod . . ." (14). The hesitation over Daisy reminds us of the feminine threat to racial purity in all these texts, a threat that can be figured characterologically as promiscuity (Brett) or vulgarity (Rosamond) but that must finally—since the exogamous requirements of marriage (that the woman leave her family) conflict with the endogamous requirements of the race (that the woman be kept in the family)—be understood as structural. Nick's kinship with Daisy solves this problem in *The Great Gatsby*; his Nordicism vouches for hers while at the same time establishing his identity with Tom and thus turning Tom's marriage to Daisy into a relation that both is and isn't incestuous. The point here is that the differences the novel works to establish between Tom and Nick (and to which the critical literature on *The Great Gatsby* is so committed) are in the end—to use Gatsby's phrase—"just personal" (152). Ironizing Tom's Nordicism, Nick nevertheless extends it; it is Nick, after all, who experiences for us "our identity with this country" (177), and it is Nick's translation of the "fresh, green breast of the new world" into the "vanished trees" that have "made way for Gatsby's house" that prefigures Stoddard's lament for "our vanished America," destroyed by a "Pluralistic America" (248). It is in this respect that the "natural intimacy" between Tom and Daisy is made truly natural. Because the difference between Tom and Nick is finally nothing more than the difference between Jason and

Quentin, the relations between Tom/Nick and Daisy should be understood on the model of the relations between Jason/Quentin and Caddie/Quentin.

Incest saves the family from marriage. Hemingway, returning some twenty years later to the mid-'20s as the setting for *The Garden of Eden*, would center his narrative on a couple whom "most people thought . . . were brother and sister until they said they were married."[79] One of the things that makes them look related is their tan, and a good portion of the novel is preoccupied with their desire to get more tan as a way of enhancing the similarity between them and insisting on their difference from everyone else: "I want every part of me dark . . . ," Catherine says, "and you'll be darker than an Indian and that takes us further away from other people" (38). The desire to be "dark"—"I wish I had some Indian blood," Catherine says (39)—is the desire to be brother and sister instead of husband and wife and thus to be, as Quentin says, "isolate[d] . . . from the loud world" (107) or, as Catherine says, "further away from other people."[80] Catherine's other way of asserting her identity with David is to get her hair cut like his, which makes her look like his "brother" (30) and which links her to Brett who, with "her hair brushed back like a boy's," "started all that" (22). Jake, of course, is neither Brett's sister nor her brother, but the missing part of his penis, which literalizes and thus replaces the incest taboo, requires him to treat her as if he were. "You are very nice people," Count Mippipopolous says to Brett and Jake; "Why don't you get married. . . ?" (61). The whole point of Jake's war wound is to save him and Brett from marriage.

This repudiation of marriage marks a change from the racial discourse of Dixonian progressivism. For Dixon, as we have already noted, the family presented an obstacle to rather than a vehicle of racial purity. Paternalist defenses of slavery, legitimating the relations between whites and blacks by appealing to the model of father and children and sanctioning (or at least overlooking) the actual paternal relations between white master/father and black slaves/children, had made the family the site of racial contamination. Thus, in a text like *The Clansman*, it is the relation between husband and wife *rather than* the relation between parent and child or brother and sister that constitutes the racial unit: "People have told me that your father and I are more alike than brother and sister of the same blood," his mother writes to the clansman; "In spirit I'm sure it's true" (118). Racial identity in Dixon is characteristically a function of "spirit" instead of blood, which is to say of marriage instead of the family: "those who love and live the sweet home-life for years grow alike in soul and body. . . ." (118). The achieved racial identity of "spirit" and "soul" trumps the inherited racial identity of "blood."

Or, rather, the inherited identity of blood is not yet regarded as properly racial. We have already seen how, in *The Leopard's Spots*, it is their Negrophobia that unites men first of different classes ("the rich and the poor") and then of different ethnicities (the "Saxon," the "Roman," the "Spartan," and the "Celt") into "one white race." As the contemporaneous novels of Ellen Glasgow suggest, membership in different families needed also to be transformed into membership in one race. Indeed, in *The Voice of the People* (1900), "race" itself is a term that oscillates between naming family and naming color.[81] When Nick Burr, whose family is so heterogeneous that it cannot count as a "race," makes love to her, the attracted but also appalled Eugenia Battle retreats into what Glasgow describes as the "shelter" of her "race" (208), a shelter whose "security" is enhanced rather than threatened by the presence of the faithful family retainer, Congo. "Race" here is a term that insists on the differences between white people. But when Nick Burr is nominated for governor, the ambition that made him hostile to his own family finds fulfillment in his new identification with the Anglo-Saxon "race" (239). "Race" here is a term that insists on the differences between whites and blacks.

What the movement of "race" in *The Voice of the People* traces is thus the process through which people cease thinking of themselves as belonging first of all to a family and begin thinking of themselves as having first of all a color. And this process is identified, as are the parallel processes in Dixon, with the rise of the "State" and the triumph of the "Law." Thus Nick's success is a consequence of his identification with the Founding Fathers of the Virginia democracy, Thomas Jefferson and Patrick Henry, and his disaffection from his own father: "I have tried to love my family, but I never did" (193), he tells Eugenia; "He was born a Democrat, he lives a Democrat, he will die a Democrat" (245), they say at the nominating convention. The lily-white Democratic Party confers upon Nick the race that blood could not. And he does indeed die a Democrat, the "guardian" of "laws," trying to prevent a lynching. This may seem paradoxical; after all, it's the lynching itself, not the attempt to prevent it, that produces whiteness in *The Leopard's Spots*. But *The Voice of the People*, like *The Traitor*, sees racial rage as only a first step. Dying for a "damned nigger" (334) whom he knows to be guilty but who must, he insists, "die by law" (321), Nick in no way compromises white rage; rather he transforms it into the emergence of a white "State."

In its identification of race and family, then, the racial discourse of the

'20s moves away from the political commitment—that is, the commitment to politics—of Progressive racism. It was this commitment to race as an essentially political category and to whiteness as the foundation of the new nation that had distinguished Dixonian racism from the plantation tradition's nostalgia for the Old South and for the pride in "blood" that animates writers like Page. The nativist turn to the family is thus in at least one sense a *re*turn to the family, and it is marked as such by the identification with the Indian that we have begun to see in Cather and Hemingway and that is prefigured in texts like Page's *Red Rock*.

Red Rock is named for the plantation, which gives its name also to the whole "region" that otherwise has no name and is called only "the old County" or "my country." I have suggested in "Nation or Empire?" that the refusal to give this "country" a name involves a refusal to understand it as part of a "nation," and even the etiology of the name Red Rock—the rock is supposed to have been made red by "the blood of the Indian chief" who killed the first settler's wife and was in turn killed by him—represents a kind of solidarity with those who, like the Confederacy, resist the nationalizing power of the United States. For if the "Lords" of Red Rock have always been "Indian-killer[s]" (that's what the first one was called and, at the end of the novel, that's what the last one is out west doing), they are also in a way Indians themselves: young Rupert is a "volunteer scout" (473), which is to say that although he fights Indians, he serves with that branch of the army that was made up mainly of Indians; and it is said of the Red Rock "aristocrats" generally that "they stick together like Indians," so that, the overseer complains to his carpetbagger ally, "if one of 'em got hurt, the whole tribe would come down on me like hornets" (206). To which the carpetbagger's reply, "We'll be more than a match for the whole tribe. Wait till I get in the Legislature; I'll pass some laws that will settle 'em," represents precisely the opposition (between family and state, as tribe and law) that Dixonian or Progressive racism sought to overcome.

But if identification with the Indian could function at the turn of the century as a *refusal* of American identity—in effect, as a refusal of American citizenship—it would come to function by the early 1920s as the *assertion* of an American identity that could be understood as going beyond citizenship. The Johnson Act had put at least a putative end to mass immigration but it had not, of course, solved the problem of the immigrants who were already here: aliens and their children with legal rights but also with a hostility to America "ranging all the way from a

slight distaste for certain aspects of American life to a deep seated, malev-
olent hatred of everything characteristically American" (Stoddard, *Re-
Forging*, 238); Stoddard called them, disparagingly, "New Americans":
they are "American citizens but not Americans." The Indian, embodying
an American identity that explicitly antedated his own legal citizenship,
could figure as an exemplary counterinstance to these aliens; where they
had become American citizens but had not become Americans, the Indian had been an American even before becoming an American citizen.

So if Page's Indians bespeak a certain uneasiness about the use of the
term "American," the new Indian of the '20s represents an extension of its
meaning. Perhaps the most powerful literary instance of this process is
the production of Tom Outland as the descendant of Anasazi cliff dwellers in *The Professor's House*, but Cather's earlier novel, *A Lost Lady* (1923),
provides an even clearer outline of how the old regionalist resistance to
the American state could begin to be transformed into the defense not of
that state but of an Americanism that transcended the state. The Indian-
identified "aristocratic" family that in Page resisted subsumption by the
Progressive American "nation" in Cather provides the technology enabling an Americanism that will go beyond the merely national citizenship that the state can offer. But to provide this technology the family
must itself be altered; it must in particular cease to be the site of a certain
indifference to racial difference ("the family black and white") and must
be made instead into the unequivocal source of racial difference.

In *A Lost Lady*, the family in question is Captain Forrester's, and Forrester himself is both a member of what Cather calls the "railroad aristocracy" and—through his status as one of the "pioneers" whose "dreams"
settled the West—an Indian.[82] "All our great West has been developed
from . . . dreams," Captain Forrester says, but his account of those dreams
(and of the disappearance of the aristocratic pioneers) culminates in a
"grunt" that Cather describes as "the lonely, defiant note that is so often
heard in the voices of old Indians" (55). In one sense, of course, this
identification is exceptionally misleading; after all, it was the pioneers
and railroad men who made the Indians disappear. But in Cather, as in
Page, killing Indians is no obstacle to being Indian, and the fact that the
pioneers are now themselves a vanishing race only confirms the identification. The "Old West had been settled by dreamers, great-hearted adventurers . . . a courteous brotherhood," but it is now "at the mercy of
men like Ivy Peters, who . . . never dared anything, never risked anything" (106). Ivy Peters makes his fortune by "cheat[ing] Indians" (124)

("He gets splendid land from the Indians some way, for next to nothing"), which is to say also, by exploiting men like Captain Forrester. And in this he is like Forrester's own partners who, after their bank has failed, refuse to "come up to the scratch and pay their losses like gentlemen" (90). "In my day," the captain's aristocratic lawyer exclaims, "the difference between a business man and a scoundrel was bigger than the difference between a white man and a nigger" (92). Now that the difference between businessmen and scoundrels is disappearing, the difference between white men and "niggers" must be preserved. The reason that Ivy Peters can't properly succeed Captain Forrester is that he's more like a "nigger" than he is like an Indian.

In *The Great Gatsby*, published two years after *A Lost Lady*, Gatsby's relation to Daisy seems, at least to Tom, a kind of miscegenation, a threat to the difference between white men and "niggers." Fitzgerald had read and admired *A Lost Lady* while working on *Gatsby* and subsequently wrote Cather a famous note, apologizing for what he described as an act of "apparent plagiarism," an unintentional similarity between descriptions of Mrs. Forrester and Daisy. How similar the descriptions actually are is open to question,[83] but the connection—with respect to miscegenation—between the captain's wife, Marian, and Daisy Buchanan is real enough. Though married to an aristocrat, Marian reveals herself, in sleeping with Ivy Peters, to be nothing but "a common woman" (170). What gets "betrayed" by this affair is not exactly the captain, since he's dead, but the "quality" the captain and Mrs. Forrester herself supposedly embodied. This is what makes it, like Daisy's affair with Jimmy Gatz, a kind of miscegenation. Mrs. Forrester is untrue to something more than her husband: "she was not willing to immolate herself, like the widow of all these great men, and die with the pioneer period to which she belonged" (169). The great men, like Indians, had died rather than adjust to changing conditions; Mrs. Forrester "preferred life on any terms." She is like an Indian who has somehow consented to change; what she betrays is not so much a husband as a race.

The racial meaning of this betrayal is clarified by the substitution two years later in *The Professor's House* of the Jewish Louie Marsellus for the merely unscrupulous Ivy Peters (as well as by Gatsby's association with Meyer Wolfsheim and Brett Ashley's affair with Robert Cohn). Marian Forrester's affair with Ivy Peters counts as a kind of miscegenation, one might say, not only because he's like a "nigger" but also because he's a proto-Jew. At the same time, then, that *A Lost Lady* asserts the importance of the difference between the "white man" and the "nigger," it begins to rewrite that difference as the difference between an Indian and a Jew. And this rewriting can hardly be read as the adjustment of an older racist structure to new racial tensions: for one thing, racial conflict between Indians and Jews was hardly a social phenomenon of even observable magnitude; and, for another, the older racist structure is not perpetuated with a new content, rather it is altered. For the new valorization of the Indian points toward that interest in the essentially *prenational* (i.e., pre-Revolutionary or, in Dixonian terms, pre–Civil War) America that we have already begun to find everywhere in the '20s from Cather to Coolidge (the end of *Gatsby* is, perhaps, the most obvious example) and that repudiates the political nationalism of the Progressives: Americanism would now be understood as something more than and different from the American citizenship that so many aliens had so easily achieved.

Indeed the substitution of the Jew for the "nigger" makes the point even more strongly. When, in Dixon, the outlaw remnants of the disbanded Klan set out to raid "old Sam Nicaroshinski, the Jew storekeeper, and rob 'im ter-night," the act of robbery as such is a sure sign of the "new" Klan's renegade status, its identification with the "lawlessness" that in *The Traitor* is essentially "African." But robbing a Jew is even more damning, for if the Jew in the '20s will be a problematic figure for the Klan, the Jew in Dixon is a fellow revolutionary: "A refugee from Poland, his instinctive sympathies had always been with the oppressed people of the South . . ." (107). The Jew has a place in the anti-African revolutionary American state that he will not have in American culture. For in 1924, the Jew's "instinctive sympathies" make him not an anti-imperialist Southerner, but "a Jew." The Jew is "by primal instinct a Jew," according to Dr. H. W. Evans, the Imperial Wizard of the Klan; he is "a stranger to the emotion of patriotism as the Anglo-Saxon feels it."[84] Patriotism, as the Anglo-Saxon has come to feel it, will involve something beyond mere allegiance to the state, something more like the "filial piety" (251) that Tom Outland comes to feel on Blue Mesa. Where Mary Antin (in 1912) achieves what she calls "possession" of her America by realizing at school what it means for her and George Washington to be "Fellow Citizens" (224), Tom achieves what he calls "possession" (251) of his America by reaching beyond the origin of "the Republic" and beyond citizenship to descent from his cliff-dwelling "ancestors."

Mary Antin, "born an alien," becomes a "citizen" (341). The Jew in *The Professor's House* is born a citizen but remains "foreign"; the professor is surprised that his wife "would adopt anyone so foreign into the family circle" (78). Tom Outland, by contrast, was "like an older brother" to the girls; marrying him would have been marrying someone who was already "almost a member of the family" (173). When Rosamond marries Louie instead, the professor's other daughter, Kitty, to whom Rosie has been "a kind of ideal" (86), is "done with her sister . . . all at once" (89). Married to a "stranger," Rosie is lost from the family; the family's regret is that, if it hadn't been for Marsellus, "we might have kept Rosie . . . in the family, for ourselves" (87). In *The Professor's House*, the prohibition of incest (enforced by Tom's death in the war) threatens to make any continuation of the family simultaneously a threat to its purity; what prompts St. Peter's final despair is a telegram announcing Rosie's pregnancy and so "the advent of a young Marsellus" (273). If St. Peters give birth to Marselluses, then the technology of reproduction is also the technology of contamination: "When a man had lovely children in his house . . . why couldn't he keep them?" the professor wonders; "Was there no way but Medea's?" (126).

One way—not Medea's—of saving the family from itself is by making it exclusively male. The "happy family" on the winter range next to Blue Mesa consists of Tom, Rodney, and their English housekeeper, Henry. And in *A Lost Lady*, the all-male family functions almost as a kind of ideal. When the novel begins, Niel Herbert's mother is dead; he lives shabbily with his father and Cousin Sadie, hating "to have any one come to see them" (30) and clinging, first in his imagination and then in reality, to his "bachelor" uncle, Judge Pommeroy. The judge, then, is his true family, and when Niel, "glad to be rid of his cousin and her inconsequential housewifery" (33), resolves to be a bachelor himself eventually and sets up "monastic" housekeeping in his uncle's quarters, what Cather seems to propose (as if heterosexuality as such were a form of miscegenation) is a vision of the family as a series of bachelors, independent of and so unthreatened by the deracinating potential of femininity.

Whether or not Cather's all-male families should be understood as homosexual families is a nice question, but there can be little doubt about the attraction of both the all-male and the homosexual as a solution to the problem of heterosexuality, which is to say, as an emblem of the nonreproductive family.[85] In *The Bridge*, for example, Crane's efforts to capture "the Myth of America" (*Letters*, 305) revolve around the figure of a Pocahontas whose "wanton" heterosexuality makes it necessary for her to be replaced in "The Dance" by "her kin, her chieftain lover," Maquokeeta.[86] Both Crane's interest in "possessing the Indian and his world as a cultural factor" (*Letters*, 307) and his easy translation of the wanton Pocahontas into the "halfbreed" "squaw" of "Indiana"—a product and thus a carrier of miscegenation—are characteristic of nativist literature, as is the appeal to relations between men (mainly Maquokeeta and the poet, but think also of Rip Van Winkle and the other "ancient men— wifeless or runaway" [18] of "Powhatan's Daughter") as a way of carrying on *The Bridge*'s "redskin dynasties" without recourse to women. But in Crane these relations are unequivocally homosexual; in fact, as Jared Gardner has shown, at a time when a newly public homophobia was casting the homosexual as a threat to American life, Crane's identification of the Indian and the homosexual represented an ideological defense of homosexuality.[87] *The Bridge* eroticizes the relations between men that in Cather serve as the model for a purified Americanism, which is to say that it deploys homosexuality on behalf of nativism and, in so doing, legiti- mates the homosexual as the figure for a purified American identity.

If, in other words, the purely American family must be the nonrepro- ductive family, and if the nonreproductive family is the homosexual fam- ily, then the purest American is the homosexual. Indeed, insofar as homo- sexual desire is identified in *The Bridge* as desire for Indians, the founding moment of American identity is conceived to be doubly secured—it's as if Captain Forrester had married an Indian man instead of an inevitably lost white lady. And "Indiana"—which derives the moment of the son Larry's going off to sea from what his mother describes as the moment in which she met the eyes ("strange for an Indian's," "not black,") of the "homeless squaw" (28) and, she tells him, while the squaw "cradled a babe's body," "I held you up"—goes one step further, transforming the desire for Indians into descent from Indians. For Larry's "blue eyes" link him to his dead father ("you're the only one with eyes like him—/ Kentucky bred!" [29]) and, through his mother's gaze, to the squaw's "not black" eyes, so that the suggestion that the squaw's baby is dead allows Larry to be understood as a substitute for him and allows the fact that he, *unlike* his brothers and sisters by his mother's second husband and *like* both his father and his mother, is "Kentucky bred" to be understood as an analog for the native identity that could only be inherited from the Indian. If in "The Dance," Crane said, he became "identified with the Indian and his world . . . as a cultural factor," (*Letters*, 307) "Indiana" makes that identification literal: sleeping with Indians is imagined as a way of being an Indian.

The homosexual family and the incestuous family thus emerge as par- allel technologies in the effort to prevent half-breeds, and there are mo- ments when these technologies are invoked simultaneously. This is what it means for Catherine and David to have the same haircuts in *The Garden of Eden* and for Catherine in bed to penetrate him so that "you can't tell who is who" (25). In *The Garden of Eden*, the incestuous couple and the homosexual couple are made identical; being husband and wife is transformed into being "brother and sister" (12), and being brother and sister is transformed into "being brothers" (29).[88] But *The Garden of Eden* was written some thirty years after *The Bridge*, *The Professor's House*, et al., and in it the discourse of purity appears almost completely as a discourse of perversity, attractive but destructive and transposed into an almost entirely psychological register. The presentation of the incestuous and the homosexual is managed differently in the nativist writing of the '20s where the stakes are more national than personal, which is to say, where the ultimate question is always the "half-breed."

This is most striking in a text like *The Vanishing American*, which, insofar as it is committed to the romance between the Indian Nophaie and the white Marian, seems to be explicitly committed to the production of half-breeds but which also, as we have already seen, will understand the union of Nophaie and Marian as the device through which white children are made the descendants of Indian parents. The homosexual appears here in Marian's appreciation of the West as a place that is "virile" but not heterosexual. When a missionary looks at her with "admiration" (30), she is appalled, but the white trader, Withers, is allowed the sexual expression that the missionaries aren't insofar as he first mistakes her (in her new Western outfit) for a boy. What appalls Marian—the "look" that she hates and that she never meets "twice" (31)—is the look of heterosexual desire, but Withers mistakes her for a "boy," calls her "Johnny," and thus converts the repulsive "admiration" of the missionaries into a "frank admiration" that Marian finds "pleasing" (53). Educated by Withers's desire and by her response to it, Marian now looks forward to meeting Nophaie dressed in her new "masculine garb." "Feminine apparel," she thinks, would be "out of place" in the West. It is dressed as a boy that Nophaie will "find her attractive"; it is out of the relation between two boys that children who are not half-breeds will somehow be produced.

By the same token, the meaning of a truly heterosexual relation between Indian and white is displaced in *The Vanishing American* onto an affair between a young Indian girl named Gekin Yashi and one of the desiring missionaries. Gekin Yashi is in love with Nophaie, but Nophaie declares that he can love her only "as a brother" (138), and it is, of course, precisely this insistence on the fraternal relation that identifies Nophaie and Gekin Yashi as a version of Tom and Rosamond or Jake and Brett and that makes the missionary a version of Louie Marsellus or Robert Cohn. The "advent of a young Marsellus" precipitates the professor's attempted suicide; the birth of a "half white" baby (293) kills Gekin Yashi. For although she (and the baby) actually die of influenza, it is miscegenation that the novel represents as having killed her: "By God, every white man who has wronged an Indian girl should see Gekin Yashi *now!*" (294) Withers says over her corpse.

The incestuous and the homosexual couple, then, are impossible ideals in *The Vanishing American*'s effort to meet the contradictory but complementary demands of American identity. These demands are contradictory because that identity requires both whites and Indians to be racially pure—no "half-breeds"—and because it requires Indians to be understood as the ancestors of whites—a genealogy impossible without the half-breed. They are complementary because the whole point of claiming descent from Indians is to guarantee racial purity against descent from aliens. So neither the contradiction nor the complementarity can be sacrificed, and it is in the attempt to preserve them both that Nophaie will be married to Marian—guaranteeing their children Indian ancestors—and that his marriage will, as I noted earlier, be represented as the disappearance of the Indian—guaranteeing that the children won't be half-breeds.[89] Nophaie's last words to Marian are, "They are vanishing— vanishing. My Nopahs! . . . And I too—Nophaie, the warrior. In the end I shall be absorbed by you—by your love—by your children. . . . It is well!" (342). Making this marriage less the union between Nophaie and Marian than the absorption of Nophaie by Marian and understanding the children it will produce not as theirs but as hers, *The Vanishing American* turns the clash between whites and Indians into the derivation of whites from Indians.[90]

But the virgin birth of Nophaie's white children and the absorption of Nophaie by Marian find only an unsatisfactory parallel in *The Professor's House*, where Rosamond instead of absorbing Louie has been absorbed by him: "She's become Louie" (86). Unable to "keep" his children, even in Medea's way, the professor imagines himself instead as a "boy" who never had them: "he had never married, never been a father" (265); unable to keep his children, the professor becomes a child, and he identifies the child he has become as his "original, unmodified" (263) "self" (267).[91] Reproduction is saved from contamination by being transformed into a kind of regression. And the object of that regression is, like the cliff dwellers, a "primitive" (265), and, again like the cliff dwellers, subject to "extinction" (282). Indeed, it is only the promise of this extinction that guarantees the boy's originality; it is the vanishing of the Indian that authenticates the identity of his descendants: Nophaie's children, Tom Outland.

Which is only to say that, in *The Professor's House* as well as in *The Vanishing American*, the only good Indian is a dead Indian. In Washington, looking to the "Government" for help with his "relics," Tom is sent first to the Indian commissioner and then, after being informed that the commission's business is "with living Indians, not dead ones" (226), to the Smithsonian, where they also—albeit for different reasons—turn out not to "care much about dead and gone Indians" (235). Tom, however, has no interest in living Indians; he mentions them only once to compare the men's "contemptible" habit of helping to shop for their wives' clothes to the practice of the pathetic Washington bureaucrat Bixby, and the paradigm of a man who shops with women is, of course, Louie, who chooses all his wife's clothes. "A man . . . could get from his daughter a peculiar kind of hurt," Mrs. St. Peter thinks, "one of the cruelest that flesh is heir to" (155). The professor gets his from Rosamond on a "shopping expedition" to Chicago where, required to stand in for Louie, he realizes not merely that he has lost Rosamond but that, losing her to Louie, he runs the risk, like Rosamond herself, of "becoming Louie." It is to avoid becoming Louie (a Washington bureaucrat, a living Indian, a Jew) that, in the end, he imagines his "original" "self" not only dead but (like the cliff dwellers) extinct. So the only good Indian is not so much dead as "vanished"; if the Jews have their way, Lothrop Stoddard predicted, "in place of our vanished America" we will have "a racial crazy-quilt" (*Re-Forging*, 248–49). The extinguished family is thus added to the incestuous family and the homosexual one as a repository of the "American"; the fact that it has "vanished" counts as the proof that it is "ours."

The First American

AGAINST the anticipation of a vanished America and the lament for vanishing Americans, Jean Toomer worked in 1920 and 1921 on a poem called "The First American."[92] Identifying himself as someone with "Scotch, Welsh, German, English, French, Dutch, Spanish" and "some dark" "blood," either "Negro" or "Negro and Indian,"[93] Toomer declined to think of himself as either black or white and so, with respect to the publication in 1923 of *Cane*, refused to "feature" himself as a "Negro."[94] Like the mulattoes whom Joel Williamson has called "the new people, new not just in the surface way of a new physical type, but new in the vital way of constituting a new culture that is both African and European, each transformed in America and married to one another,"[95] Toomer thought of himself as belonging to a new race and of his writing as the effort to achieve "a spiritual fusion analogous to the fact of racial inter-mingling."[96] The "racial crazy-quilt" that Stoddard predicted would be the end of America Toomer hoped would be its beginning.

In fact, however, the very idea of "racial intermingling" or, to be more precise, the idea that there was something distinctive about the progeny of such intermingling, was itself threatened with extinction. Nineteen-twenty would be the last year the category "mulatto" appeared in the census and, even as early as 1900, in the novel from which Williamson gets the term "new people," the mulatto is under siege. We are not "an old family, or a rich family, or a distinguished family," says the hero of Charles W. Chesnutt's *The House Behind the Cedars* (1900) to his sister Rowena's suitor, "we have no connections of which you could boast, and no relatives to whom we should be glad to introduce you. You must take us for ourselves alone—we are new people."[97] Williamson regards the term "new people" as "beautifully fitting" since it expresses the newness of a culture produced by the marriage of European and African. But the point of John Warwick's remarks to George Tryon is to conceal his African heritage, not to express it. Warwick and his sister are passing, and the description of them as "people of no family" (58) is meant to hide their unforgivably problematic racial identity beneath the veil of a forgivably problematic class identity. By confessing that his "ancestry" is not aristocratic, Warwick avoids acknowledging that it is not all white. And when Tryon responds to Warwick's confession with one of his own—*his* "family secret" is that a great-great-grandfather was "hanged, drawn, and quartered for stealing cattle across the Scottish border" (57)—he only demonstrates how well Warwick's deception has worked, how well the question of racial origin has been disguised as a question of class origin. We have already seen (in Glasgow's *The Voice of the People* and Dixon's *The Trilogy of Reconstruction*) how the Progressive commitment to racial difference was accompanied by a certain hostility to class difference. Claiming to be "new people," the Warwicks seek to benefit from this new indifference to class while rescuing themselves from the newly intensified interest in race.

But *The House Behind the Cedars* will not allow the true, racial nature of the Warwicks' "secret" to go undisclosed. On the contrary, not only is it revealed, but the very critique of class difference on which Warwick's confession depends is shown to be itself dependent on the emergence of the racial difference he conceals. In Chesnutt, as in Dixon and Glasgow, class difference can be repudiated only if racial difference is insisted upon. Thus Chesnutt subjects the idea of class difference—the idea that differences in class can matter—to a sustained criticism from the standpoint of race. In fact, the novel makes class difference into a thing of the past, and, by keying the survival of the mulatto to the survival of class difference, it also makes the mulatto into a thing of the past. In this sense, the mulattoes are precisely not *new* people; in *The House Behind the Cedars*, they are becoming extinct.

Their heyday is, in fact, imagined by Chesnutt as having been before the war, when some free mulattoes "attained to a considerable degree of prosperity and dreamed of a still brighter future" until "the growing tyranny of the slave power crushed their hopes and crowded the free people back upon the black mass just beneath them" (105). But if the increasingly hysterical defense of slavery in the years before the war undermined the distinction between free mulattoes and black slaves, emancipation threatens it even further. With the "black mass" now as "free" as the "free people" ("since the slaves had been freed, was not one negro as good as another?" [117]), the class differences between free mulatto and black slave survive only insofar as they are memorialized in color—"bright" versus "dark" (141)—and the difference in color is no longer accorded the status of a difference in race. Thus, although *The House Behind the Cedars* begins in a world of black, white, and mulatto, it ends in black and white. George Tryon repudiates Rowena because she's not white, and Rowena vows to stick in the future with her "own people" (121); in the end, she even recognizes that the only man who has loved her truly is "dark" Frank, a man with skin so brown the "high yallers" won't let him cross their threshold. And Frank himself, who hasn't dared to think of the "ivory"-complexioned (47) Rowena, comes to acknowledge what the text calls (only partly in irony) the "deeper wisdom" of white people who "regarded Rena and himself as very much alike" (188).

The intermediate shades of color that commemorate "racial intermingling" and that would be taken by Toomer to inaugurate the new American are in Chesnutt already beginning to fade and to appear only as the afterimage of class differences made obsolete by emancipation. That's why, in Chesnutt's free mulattoes and even more in the characters of his contemporary Pauline Hopkins, we see the hopeful but temporary emergence of a renewed and transformed commitment to "the family black and white" of the plantation. As products of miscegenation, the fair-skinned heroes and heroines of *The House Behind the Cedars* and of the novels Hopkins published in *The Colored American Magazine* represent what for a brief while will look like the possibility of a breakdown of difference between black and white. Although Hazel Carby plausibly writes that Hopkins's response to white racist "accusations that miscegenation was the inmost desire of the darker races" was "to reconstruct miscegenation as white male rape and to deny that the black community wanted intermarriage,"[98] in fact, both in Hopkins's *Hagar's Daughter* (1901–2) and her *Winona* (1902), miscegenation as white male rape is displaced onto the slave past and redescribed in the narrative present as the expression of white male virtue. Indeed, in *Hagar's Daughter*, the willingness of a white man to marry a black woman becomes the supreme test of what Chesnutt would call white "liberality," a test that one white man, Ellis Enson, eventually passes and that another, Cuthbert Sumner, taken temporarily aback by the revelation that his "dazzling fair" Jewel (her "beauty was of the Saxon type")[99] is actually an octoroon, fails. Hesitating before his "good angel" (282) triumphs, Sumner finds that Jewel has departed for "the Continent" where she will soon die of "Roman fever," as much a victim of his uncertain social judgment as Daisy Miller was of Frederick Winterbourne's.

Whether or not Hopkins intended the comparison, the continuity between the kinds of social calibrations imagined by Henry James and the kind imagined by Hopkins is clear; in *Hagar's Daughter*, the question of whether a white man can marry an octoroon is understood as no different in kind from the question of whether a "gentleman" can marry a young woman from a newly rich and hence "vulgar" family. Indeed, as we have already begun to see, Chesnutt makes a significant, albeit failed, gesture in this direction in *The House Behind the Cedars*. What he calls George Tryon's "liberality" is "not a mere form of words": had Rena's "people been simply poor and of low estate," he would have "sacrificed convention for love" (97); it is precisely this liberality that the characterization "new people" is designed to evoke. But the discovery that "new" means "black" is too much for Tryon's liberality; it is "the one objection" that he cannot "overlook." In *The House Behind the Cedars*, in other words, the objection of racial difference begins to achieve a new order of magnitude, whereas in *Hagar's Daughter*, it remains an objection like another, one that can and

should be overlooked, just as Winterbourne could have, and should
have, overlooked Daisy's bad breeding.[100]

In fact, at a stage in his career more nearly contemporaneous with
Hopkins and Chesnutt, James does imagine the overlooking of exactly
this objection: Maisie's father (in *What Maisie Knew* [1897]) gets involved
with a woman identified as "the brown lady."[101] But where it may plausibly be argued that Winterbourne's refusal to involve himself with Daisy is
regarded in *Daisy Miller* as a mistake, it is absolutely clear that Beale
Farange's willingness to involve himself with "the brown lady" in *What
Maisie Knew* is an even bigger mistake. And James's explicit disapproval
of "the brown lady," however minor a character she turns out to be, may
perhaps be understood as one of those casual but telling racial references
that, Kenneth Warren has argued, articulate James's position with respect
to "the prevailing climate of race relations in late nineteenth-century
America" and especially with respect to "the nation's general acquies-
cence to laws mandating the separation of races in American public
spaces."[102] Insofar as realist writers like James depicted the United States
as a society in which the distinction between public and private space
was under continual siege, Warren argues, they indirectly supported the
segregationist argument that "social equality" was the deeper meaning
and would be the inevitable outcome of "political equality." Writers less
committed to realism's social vision, like the Southern liberal George
Washington Cable, could not share the realists' sense of urgency. For
them, association with blacks on "trains, ships, and streetcars did not
constitute a 'social relation' and hence did not challenge communal
norms regarding marriage, the family, and education"; "Civil equality," as
Warren puts it, "did not presume social equality" (40). In the world of
literary realism, however, a world where, as depicted in James's *The American Scene* (1907), private spaces consist of rooms without doors and
public spaces are the sites of unexpected "intimacies," the defense of
civil equality could hardly seem as inconsequential as writers like Cable
claimed. Thus, for example, the distaste James expresses for the "intimate
presence of the Negro"[103] marks one of the "troubling links between"
realism's "treatment of ethnicity and race and the nation's general ac-
quiescence to laws mandating the separation of races in American public
spaces" (38).

But if, from one standpoint, this fear of intimacy with "the Negro"
suggests James's complicity with the new racism, from another standpoint, it suggests his inability to recognize the potential of that racism as

an organizing principle of social life. For the "intimate presence of the Negro" counts in James only as an extreme instance of those intimacies that modern life makes everywhere inevitable. Thus Maisie's initial encounter with "the brown lady" takes place as one of a series of embarrassing public encounters between her natural parents and their new lovers on the one side and the ex-wives and ex-husbands who have replaced them on the other, and her description of her father's new lover as "almost black" is glossed with the observation that "They're always hideous . . . the vulgarest of the vulgar" (125). It is, in other words, as an instance of vulgarity rather than of race-mixing that the relation between Beale Farange and "the brown lady" shocks; it marks what appears in James as a general breakdown of social distinction. To learn to see it as race-mixing *instead of* vulgarity will be to reinvent a principle of social distinction.

James's problem in this regard is not so much that he's racist but that, like Cable, he isn't quite racist enough. In "The Freedman's Case in Equity" (1884), Cable had remarked with astonishment that "the average Southern white passenger" in "the average Southern railway coach" finds "less offense in the presence of a profane, boisterous, or unclean white person than in that of a quiet well-behaved colored man or woman."[104] But, of course, it was precisely because offensiveness could be racialized that inoffensiveness could be legislated; no law at the turn of the century could keep the vulgar from imposing themselves upon the genteel, but insofar as gentility could be effaced by whiteness and vulgarity by blackness, an entire social system could be erected on laws that kept blacks from imposing themselves on whites. When, in *The Clansman*, "two big negro troopers" walk into a hotel, go up to the watercooler and drink "ostentatiously, thrusting their thick lips coated with filth far into the cocoanut dipper" (355), the intolerable and inescapable "intimacies" of life in what James, in *The American Scene*, called a society epitomized by its hotels ("one is verily tempted to ask if the hotel-spirit may not just *be* the American spirit" [102]) are transformed into the equally intolerable but remediable intimacies of "racial intermingling." The troopers' next act is to make advances to a white woman, and they are promptly shot dead by a Klan sympathizer. If James was appalled by the threat in America to class difference and by the disappearance of the "gentleman," the ambition of Progressive racism was, as we have already seen, to replace class difference with racial difference, and the triumph of segregation would be to replace the gentleman with the white man.

Strictly speaking, then, James must be understood as indifferent to miscegenation, which is to say, as insufficiently alert to racism's potential as a technology of social organization. Overly attached not so much to "the old discrimination in favor of the private life" (*American Scene*, 102–3) as to the class structures that provided the grounds for that discrimination, he was unable to imagine the new forms of privacy that the new discrimination would make available. The inability, or what would be in writers like Chesnutt and Hopkins the *refusal*, to see miscegenation as the source of social breakdown is thus accompanied by an essentially structural allegiance to the class mythologies of gentility. That's why Chesnutt's Rena is named Rowena; that's why the father of Hopkins's Winona is an English nobleman who, unjustly accused of murder, flees to the United States where he lives like an Indian, calls himself White Eagle, marries "a handsome mulattress" (290), and is himself eventually murdered. "He was a gentleman," as one character puts it, "But he never breathed a word what he was, an' he kept away from his equals—meanin' white men" (311). The replacement of class by race in America makes every white man the equal of an English "gentleman," so the unwillingness to accept such equality is expressed as the unwillingness to be white.[105] Living in a "mixed community of Anglo-Saxons, Indians and Negroes," White Eagle's family—in particular, his daughter—embodies the disappearance of "the dividing line supposed to be a natural barrier between the whites and the dark-skinned race" (287). And Winona's eventual marriage to another English gentleman, accompanied by her return to England and to her rightful place as the "beautiful representative of an ancient family" (435), guarantees the victory of the miscegenated aristocracy. Where "the unwashed Democracy of Missouri" (382) would assert itself by stealing Winona into slavery and lynching the gentleman who tried to rescue her, English gentility asserts itself by restoring the slave to her noble family and to a "home" where "caste prejudice" could not reach and where even a Negro, if he is an aristocrat, can be "a man among men" (434).[106]

If for Chesnutt the promise of miscegenation was the promise of the mulatto as a disruptive supplement to the racial binaries of black and white, for Hopkins the promise of miscegenation is the promise of the disappearance of racial difference—which is to say, of race itself—altogether. This disappearance is emblematized most distinctly in her account of John Brown's "great family of fugitives" living together in "trusting brotherhood" (373) and following "God's commands in the words of Holy Writ: 'He hath made of one blood all the nations of the earth'" (374).

Acts 17:26 was an exceptionally popular text among African American preachers in the nineteenth century, and it was crucial also to Hopkins, who quotes it frequently and who derived from it the title of the last of her *Magazine* novels, *Of One Blood*.[107] But, just as in Chesnutt the promise of miscegenation cannot be kept and the "bright" mulatto must make common cause with the "dark" Negro, so in *Of One Blood* (1902–3) the fair-skinned products of miscegenation are rendered increasingly black and one blood is turned into two.

"The slogan of the hour is 'Keep the Negro down!'" Hopkins writes, "but who is clear enough in vision to decide who hath black blood and who hath it not?" (607). Put this way, the question is an epistemological one but, of course, the real question raised by the citation from Acts is *ontological*: If "all nations" are made "of one blood," how can anyone have "black blood" and anyone else not have it? One possible answer is that no one can, that there is no such thing as black blood or white blood, or at least that, given the history of black and white "amalgamation" (535) in North America, there is no such thing as black or white blood anymore: "No man can draw the dividing line between the two races, for they are both of one blood" (607). On this account, the mulatto marks the disappearance of racial identity, and the "white" skin of Hopkins's central characters is an emblem of the disappearance of "the color line" in the face of the universal "brotherhood" (590) that writers like Dixon imagined blacks to desire. But *Of One Blood*'s amazing Gothic plot—the (apparently white) hero's (apparently white) bride turns out to be his (black) sister; the (apparently white) best friend who seduces her turns out to be his (and so, her other) (black) brother—puts a new twist both on brotherhood and on the claim that Hopkins's protagonists are "all of one blood." Hero, heroine, and villain all bear a birthmark that, despite their whiteness, "proves" their "race" and "descent" (555) from ancient kings of Ethiopia and that guarantees a racial identity no amount of miscegenation can obscure. Their indistinguishability from whites in color turns out only to accent their absolute distinction in race.

For Hopkins, then, the family romance involves the discovery of an identity that survives "amalgamation with other races" (535), an African identity that remains pure despite the fact that "on the American continent," as a character in her long novel *Contending Forces* (1900) remarks, "there is no such thing as an unmixed black," no one who can "trace an unmixed flow of African blood."[108] *Of One Blood* makes such a survival possible by its commitment to "spiritualistic phenomena" (444), to a world in which the dead communicate with the living and those with "the power" (443) cross from one world to the other. Hopkins's doctor-hero has discovered "by research" that "life is not dependent upon organic function as a principle" (468), and he has "inherited" from his mother the "mysticism" and "occult powers" that, transcending the organic, connect him to the "race of African kings": "the mystic within him . . . was a dreamlike devotion to the spirit that had swayed his ancestors" (558). The organic language of identity by "descent" is here invoked on behalf of a nonorganic, "spiritual" identity; what you inherit from your mother is not biological but the "principle" that supersedes biology. Racial purity, for Hopkins as for Dixon, thus requires the transubstantiation of "blood" into "spirit"; biologically corrupted by two hundred and fifty years of compulsory miscegenation, the black race can "conserve" itself only by repudiating biological principles of identity and insisting on "a new principle," "an idea." Amalgamation destroys races; "Ideas only save races."[109] If, then, in *Hagar's Daughter* and *Winona*, the predominance of the mulatto expresses Hopkins's hostility to racial difference, in *Of One Blood* it expresses her commitment to it, to an idea of racial identity that can be rescued from the overwhelming fact of "racial intermingling" ("there were in my heredity the following strains," Toomer said, "Scotch, Welsh, German, English, French, Dutch, Spanish . . . Negro and Indian") only because it is an idea, the black version of the white soul. The white skin of the mulatto "race woman" embodies a blackness that black skin cannot, in itself, record; it is the sheet she wears to face down the Klansman in his.

In both Chesnutt and Hopkins, then, the mulatto is absorbed into the "Negro." What "racial intermingling" produces will finally count as black; neither Chesnutt's vision of a "new" race nor Hopkins's more radical vision of no race will stand. And, although both these visions would play an important role in the racial discourse of Progressivism, the "fusion of all races"[110] imagined by the apostles of the melting pot would characteristically exclude—either as a constitutive principle or as a strategic omission—the African American. So in Dixon, as we have already seen, the ability of the Jew to become an American depends upon his whiteness, which is to say, upon his difference from blacks, and in Israel Zangwill's *The Melting-Pot*, it is "all the races of *Europe*" (33)[111] who are characteristically imagined "melting and re-forming" to produce "the real American." Thus Toomer's "First American" is simultaneously paradigmatic of Progressive racial discourse and an anomaly: like Dixon and

Zangwill, Toomer is committed to assimilation; unlike them, he imagines that even "dark blood" can be assimilated.

But Toomer, of course, is writing some fifteen to twenty years after Hopkins, Chesnutt, Dixon, and Zangwill, at a moment when, as we have already begun to see, the idea of the American and the idea of the melting pot are coming to seem mutually exclusive. Nativism generalizes the hostility to miscegenation between black and white; it is now the unassimilability of "dark blood" rather than the heretofore easy assimilation of the "European races" that will emerge as paradigmatic. Hence, if the fantasy of miscegenation dominates *Cane*, it does so in a way that makes Toomer's goal of a "spiritual fusion analogous to the fact of racial intermingling" (128) seem not merely difficult to attain but impossible, since the desired analogy between "racial intermingling" and "spiritual fusion" will more often appear as an oxymoron, or since the intermingling—the fact of miscegenation—will be treated not as the fusion of two races but as the destruction of one by the other.

In the poem "Portrait in Georgia," for example, which begins "Hair—braided chestnut,/coiled like a lyncher's rope" and ends "And her slim body, white as the ash/of black flesh after flame,"[112] not only does the desire of a black man for a white woman culminate in violence, the very possibility of that desire, the difference between black and white that makes it possible, is imagined as the product of violence. The basic strategy of this poem is to take the highly conventionalized effort to find analogues for a woman's body ("My love is like a red, red rose") and to twist it by finding those analogues first in the apparatus of a lynching—her "braided chestnut" hair is "coiled like a lyncher's rope," her eyes are "fagots"—and second in the results of a lynching—her lips are "old scars, or the first red blisters." The description of *her* body is simultaneously the narrative of the destruction of *his* body, which is to say that the description of the black man's love for the white woman is simultaneously the description of the destruction of the black man by his love for the white woman.

But in its description of her whiteness, the poem also complicates our sense of the woman's position in this narrative. On the one hand, her whiteness is the reason for (and hence a cause of) his being burned. On the other hand, her whiteness is explicitly described as a consequence of the burning: "And her slim body, white as the ash/of black flesh after flame." The simile suggests that whiteness is produced by (rather than produces) the burning of black flesh, and thus suggests a certain skepticism about the portrayal of lynching as an attempt to defend whiteness. In this poem, lynching establishes (rather than enforces) racial difference—black flesh is burned in order to make a white body. What begins as a narrative of the attempt to preserve racial difference turns out to be a narrative of the origins of racial difference, a narrative in which white bodies are depicted as the consequence of violence against black bodies. This violence against these black bodies is itself a consequence of their own desire, not exactly for white bodies—since, in the terms of the poem, white bodies don't exist until the desire not for them but for something like them has been punished—but for what must be instead the idea of or fantasy of white bodies. Thus lynching no longer attempts to enforce the taboo against "racial intermingling"; it actualizes the racial difference that makes the intermingling possible.

If we read this account of the violent origins of racial difference as a critique of racial difference, then "Portrait in Georgia" should probably be understood as a kind of prelude to "The First American," the poem that would express the idea that the "racial intermingling" of melting-pot America was eliminating old racial differences and creating a new "American" race, embodied to begin with in Toomer himself. It was this belief that, as we have already noted, led Toomer to refuse to allow himself to be "featured" as a "Negro" in the advertising for Cane. At the same time, however, the poem belies the "harmony" with which the various racial strands were supposed to mingle in Toomer's new American and, as we have seen, it imagines the Negro's loss of blackness as a violent insult to his body, even (perhaps especially) if the insult is self-inflicted. So it may be that the poem does, after all, express a certain commitment to racial difference and to "the Negro group." For, despite his conviction that the "pure Negro" (like the Indian and like Madison Grant's "Great Race") was "passing" from the American scene, the Washington, D.C.-bred Toomer described his 1921 encounter with black life in Sparta, Georgia, as eliciting response from "a deep part" of his "nature" that had hitherto been "repressed," as if the Americanness of the first American had been achieved only by the sacrifice of his blackness. The literary ambition of "giving the Negro to himself" that he announced in a letter to Sherwood Anderson in 1922,[113] an ambition that ran significantly counter to the desire to create a new race, had thus found a personal parallel in the trip south that gave the Negro to Toomer. More striking still, it had already found expression in a section of Cane written before he went to Georgia, where a man with a "red-brown face" and a racial heritage that reflects Toomer's own is turned into a "nigger" (72).

"Bona and Paul" is said to be based on a romance between Toomer and a young woman that was wrecked by rumors that he was really black at a time when he was identifying himself as white; whatever its biographical antecedents, the story certainly narrates the circulation of just such rumors about Paul: "He is a nigger . . . don't all the dorm girls say so?" (72). But it isn't at all clear that the relationship in the story is destroyed by these rumors—"That's why I love" him, Bona thinks. Furthermore, the alternative to being black in the story is not exactly being white. Even whites like Paul's "red-blooded Norwegian friend" (75), Art, aren't simply white; Art is a "pale purple facsimile of a red-blooded Norwegian," and the general proliferation of colors in the story tends to be identified with the way surfaces can change color: white turning "crimson" from effort or embarrassment, gray turning "lavender" (73) in the sunset, Paul's own "dark" skin turning "rosy" (77) with desire. What's being sporadically imagined here is not simply an alternative to being either "nigger" or "white," but an alternative that, by disconnecting color from race and insisting on the priority of color over race, problematizes race by making it available only in "facsimile."[114]

At the same time, however, the story insists not only that the color of Paul's skin be racialized by the "dorm girls" but also that Paul experience this racialization as the truth about himself. The question people ask about him—"What is he, a Spaniard, an Indian, an Italian, a Mexican, a Hindu, or a Japanese?"—produces knowledge as well as "pain": "Suddenly he knew that people saw, not attractiveness in his dark skin, but difference. Their stares, giving him to himself, filled something long empty within him, and were like green blades sprouting in his consciousness" (76–77). The "stares" that transform "attractiveness" into "difference," "giving" Paul "to himself," begin the process, envisaged in the letter to Anderson, of "giving the Negro to himself." Not only do they restore color to its status as a necessary (and necessarily misleading) sign of race, they rescue race itself and install it as the "cloudy, but real" center of identity. In filling "something long empty within him," Paul's new experience of his racial identity reconstitutes his previous experience as a form of passing. Both the sustained effort to imagine oneself belonging to a new American race and the occasional effort to imagine oneself belonging to no race at all are retroactively turned into the effort to conceal—even from oneself—one's "real" race.

The first American is thus the last mulatto, but instead of becoming American by being mulatto he becomes American by ceasing to be mulatto. The commitment to purity embodied in Cather's and Stoddard's

vanishing Americans—they vanish because they refuse "intermingling"—
is, in other words, retroactively deployed on the products of "intermingling": mulattoes vanish by being made black. Thus the desire not to
produce mulattoes is fulfilled by the assertion that there are no such
things as mulattoes. And the discovery that there are no mulattoes marks
the literally definitive defeat of the melting pot.

Difference Not Inferiority

T HE RESISTANCE to what Stoddard called "a mulatto America" (Re-
Forging, 282) could thus be mounted from both sides of the color
line; for instance, the Jew whose hopes for a "Pluralistic America"
embodied the racial "crazy-quilt" that Stoddard feared had as his own
goal an America where "Italians and Jews and Yankees and Irishmen"
(185) would resist "Americanization" and freely express their different
"national inheritances" (195). Horace Kallen's arguments in Culture and
Democracy in the United States (1924) were more directly opposed to
Progressive assimilationists than to nativists like Stoddard, whose own
conceptions of American identity were also founded, as we have already
seen, on the repudiation of assimilationism and Americanization. And,
since Kallen understood the identity of the "culturally autonomous,"
"self-sustaining" "ethnic group[s]" he wished to preserve to be "ances-
trally determined" (123), it makes no sense, as several scholars have
pointed out, to see Kallen's pluralism as opposed to racism.[115] In fact, as
Werner Sollors in particular has shown, Kallen's famous defense of Alain
Locke against some Americans "mean-spirited enough to draw the color-
line" at Oxford, an event that Kallen himself cited as the origin of "Cultural Pluralism," strikingly reveals his own racism: "I have neither respect
nor liking for [Locke's] race," Kallen wrote his former teacher, Barrett
Wendell; he apparently based his support of Locke on the fact that he "is a
Harvard man and as such he has a definite claim on me."[116] So it seems
clear that Kallen's pluralism, as Sollors puts it, "did not have any room for
Afro-Americans."[117] But it would be a mistake also to understand Kallen's
pluralism as a less intense or vestigial version of Progressive racism. For
the real point here is not that pluralists, like their opponents, were racists; it is that the metamorphosis of Progressive racism into pluralist
racism produced a crucial change in its meaning. Pluralism, one might
say, essentialized racism.

Kallen and Stoddard both were committed above all to difference. Polemicizing against the Progressive racist E. A. Ross in 1915, Kallen wrote that what "troubles Mr. Ross and so many other American citizens of British stock is not really inequality; what troubles them is *difference*" (115). Whether or not Kallen was accurate in his assessment of Ross (Ross's commitment to white supremacy appears to have been sincere), Kallen's own sense that difference was what mattered placed him at the cutting edge of nativism. As Stoddard would put it in 1927: "No theoretical questions of 'superiority' or 'inferiority' need be raised. . . . The really important point is that even though America (abstractly considered) may not be nearly as good as we think it is, nevertheless it is *ours*. . . . That is the meat of the matter, and when we discuss immigration we had better stop theorizing about superiors and inferiors and get down to the bedrock of *difference*" (103). Although the commitment to white (or, at least, Nordic) supremacy was explicit in *The Rising Tide of Color* (1920), and although Stoddard may well have continued to believe that Nordics were in fact superior to others, by the time of *Re-Forging America*, Stoddard's racism had been crucially disarticulated from his white supremacism. Dixon's Progressive racism had been fundamentally committed to the inferiority of the Negro and to the necessity of controlling what one of his Klansmen calls "black barbarians . . . with the intelligence of children and the instincts of savages" (*The Clansman*, 289). Nativism in the '20s required no such commitment and on occasion the new Klan explicitly repudiated white supremacism. "Difference Not Inferiority" was its slogan; "Ku Kluxism," as an Indiana Klansman put it, "cherishes no hostility to Catholics, Jews, negroes or foreigners as such"; "its implications are not those of inferiority, but those of difference."[118]

It should not be thought, however, that the declared absence of "hostility" and the commitment to difference represent any diminution of racism. After all, the numerous whippings and occasional lynchings carried out by the Klan in the early '20s make it clear that a good deal of racial hostility continued to be felt. But, even setting these incidents aside, the commitment to difference itself represents a theoretical intensification rather than diminution of racism, an intensification that has nothing to do with feelings of tolerance or intolerance toward other races and everything to do with the conceptual apparatus of pluralist racism.[119] For the Dixonian commitment to white supremacy and so to a hierarchical ranking of the races required a common scale of measurement between them and could thus be seen to undermine the rationale for preferring difference to superiority. For example, Frank H. Hankins, a critic of pluralism, argued that, since racial identity consisted in a set of "distinctive hereditary traits"[120] distributed within each race on a bell-shaped curve, there was, on the one hand, no "discontinuity" between the races and, on the other hand, no equality. There could be no discontinuity because all the traits of all the races could be plotted somewhere along the curve, hence racial differences were necessarily "not those of kind but those of degree; not those of quality but of quantity."[121] There could be no equality because if the distribution of traits in one race exactly matched the distribution in another, there would be no grounds for distinguishing between the two races. Hankins's denial that racial differences are differences "of kind" thus amounts to an insistence on racial inequality—if there are races, they must be unequal. And, by the same token, the pluralist denial of racial inequality amounts to an insistence that, since they can't be "of degree," racial differences must be "of kind." Pluralism requires the assertion of differences in "quality," not just "quantity."[122] Where Hankins's commitment to white supremacy required that races be different from each other only insofar as one had more or less of what the others also had, the antisupremacist or pluralist commitment to difference without hierarchy made races essentially different rather than more or less like each other. It was only, in other words, the pluralist denial of hierarchy that made possible the escape from the common scale and the emergence of an unmeasurable and hence incomparable racial essence.

"Can we assimilate the Negro?" (291) one of Dixon's Klansmen asks. The answer, because of the Negro's "animal" inferiority is, of course, no, but everyone else in Dixon is assimilable. Indeed, his effort to present the post-Reconstruction South as a prefiguration of the Progressive nation leads Dixon to suggest that the "power of assimilation has always been a mark of Southern genius" (*The Clansman*, 276). Yankees and, as we have seen, even Jews can be mobilized as white men. But if, in Dixon, equality means assimilability, in nativism it means just the opposite. Although "few well-informed Americans to-day consider the Chinese or Japanese as 'inferiors,'" Stoddard remarks, these same "well-informed Americans are almost as much a unit against free intercourse with Chinese and Japanese as they are against intermarriage with Mexican peons or negroes . . ." (*Re-Forging*, 259). This is what it means for "difference" to be "bedrock." Only the pluralist, ultimately unconcerned with whether the different is either better or worse, must judge on the basis of difference as such. In pluralism one prefers one's own race not because it is superior but because it is one's own.[123]

Progressive racism was nationalist, concerned with eliminating sectional differences and deploying racial identity on behalf of both the nation and the state. It was hierarchical and assimilationist: white supremacy made possible the Americanization of the immigrant. Dixon represented the Civil War as the creation of a new united nation and the revolt against Reconstruction as the creation of a new citizenry. Nativism, by contrast, was plural and anti-assimilationist. World War I was its (white) Civil War, and what that war had created was not a new nation but a new awakening to "racial realities" (*Re-Forging*, 175). It would be a mistake, however, to think that these changes took place neatly or all at once. As late as 1927, for example, the poet Stephen Vincent Benét could choose the Civil War as his subject for an American epic, and as late as 1928, the critic Henry Seidel Canby could praise Benét for being (along with Sinclair Lewis) the first American writer "concerned with the great theme of a national life."[124] Indeed, it was precisely Benét's treatment of the war that marked for Canby his originality. According to Canby, a true understanding of the Civil War had not been possible until the Great War because it took the Great War to make us see that the Civil War had been the first truly "modern" war, modern in the sense that it was "a people's war." Previous treatments of the Civil War, Canby wrote, had been "content either with odes on the North and paeans on the South, or with local color sketches like Stephen Crane's *The Red Badge of Courage*" (x). In other words, from the standpoint of what Canby praises as the "intense nationalism" of *John Brown's Body*, previous treatments had been insufficiently *national*, devoted, almost as if the war had never taken place, to one side or the other ("odes on the North and paeans on the South") or, if not actually taking sides between the two regions, to the idea of regionalism itself (*The Red Badge of Courage* as "local color"). For Canby, then, Benét is the first truly national writer because he is the first to see what the Civil War created, the first to see the Civil War as the origin of the American nation.

There is, of course, an important sense in which this claim is obviously false: the whole point of the Civil War for a writer like Dixon was that, freeing racism from slavery, it dissolved the sectional differences between North and South and replaced them with the racial difference between black and white, thus making possible the transsectional, white nation. But there are important ways also in which Canby's sense of the novelty, if not exactly the originality, of *John Brown's Body* is appropriate. For one thing, as we have already noted, the major writers of the Progressive period—Dreiser, Wharton, London—were comparatively indifferent to the question of American national identity: even in Dreiser's masterpiece of the postwar period, *An American Tragedy*, "American" signifies a certain set of social and economic conditions rather than a political entity or cultural heritage. It is as if, during the period when industrial America was devoted to assimilating and "Americanizing" its immigrants as quickly and thoroughly as possible, only those confronted with what seemed to them the unassimilable "Negro" were compelled to produce an account of the constitutive boundaries of the American. It is from this standpoint that books like *The Leopard's Spots* and *The Clansman*—without any literary merit or, for that matter, any real literary ambition—can count as rehearsals for the major literary achievements of Cather, Fitzgerald, Hemingway, and Faulkner.

And for another thing, in addition to the fact that Benét's literary ambitions are closer to Cather's than to Dixon's, there are important differences between *John Brown's Body* and its nationalist predecessors. If, for Dixon (and even for Canby), the alternative to "American" is sectional—Northern or Southern, "local"—for Benét it is "foreign" ("This flesh was seeded from no foreign grain/But Pennsylvania and Kentucky wheat" [7]) or "alien" ("To strive at last, against an alien proof"). The "American thing" (5) in Benét is not the state that subsumes local differences and that (as embodied in the various Progressive projects of Americanization) converts aliens into Americans; it is the "native" ("As native as the shape of Navajo quivers" [3]) that insists on its difference from the "alien." Benét's nationalism, in other words, is a kind of (tolerant) nativism, committed not to turning the alien into an American but to distinguishing between the alien and the American. And this anti-Progressive anti-Americanization shows up even in his treatment of racial difference: "Oh, blackskinned epic, epic with the black spear,/I cannot sing you, having too white a heart . . ." (308). Canby says (amazingly) that Benét's "Negroes are the truest I know in American poetry" (xiv), but Benét's essentially pluralistic nationalism commits him more truly to denying that he can represent the Negro at all than to representing him well.[125] The discovery of "the American thing" thus appears most certainly in the assertion of what the "American Muse" *can't* sing: the Negro, the alien. The inability of the American muse to sing it is the proof that she's American.

It is, in other words, as nationalism turns into nativism that it becomes also a kind of pluralism. From the standpoint of the "native," this must involve the repudiation of any attempt to blur differences, which is to say, the repudiation of any effort of Americanization, since Americanization is no longer understood as the alien's attempt to become a citizen but instead as his or her attempt to join the family. Tom Outland could marry the professor's daughter because Tom is already imagined as his son (incestuous marriages bring no one into the family). But marriage to Louie Marsellus compromises the family; indeed, it compromises two families. For Louie's desire to become Tom Outland's brother ("I never think of him as a rival," Louie tells the professor, "I think of him as a brother, an adored and gifted brother" [166]) is at the same time an eagerness to abandon the brother he already has and with whom he is to attend a Marsellus "family reunion"; the professor remarks that "with very little encouragement," Louie "would have sent his brother on alone and remained in Chicago with his wife and father-in-law" (151). And if the nativist's nightmare Jew is the one who wants to marry his daughter, his dream Jew is too "inflexibly segregative" to have any interest in her. The Jew is, by "deliberate election," "unassimilable," remarks the Klan's Dr. H. W. Evans; "He rejects intermarriage" (*Is the Ku Klux Klan Constructive or Destructive?*, 14). A thoroughgoing pluralism would put Louie Marsellus's father in the same position as the professor, in opposition to a marriage that will eliminate differences rather than preserve them.

Of course, the self-appointed spokesman for the Jew here is the Imperial Wizard of the Ku Klux Klan and, when asked to comment on these remarks, Israel Zangwill disputed him, claiming that intermarriage of Jews with Gentiles was frequent, more frequent than intermarriage of "protestants with Catholics" (32). But it's hardly as if nativist pluralism went unarticulated among Jews. Anzia Yezierska's *Bread Givers*, for example (published, like *The Great Gatsby* and *The Professor's House*, in 1925), presents itself as a first-person narrative of the attempt to assimilate, almost as if a suitably reconfigured *Professor's House* had been written from the standpoint of a lower-class Louie Marsellus. But the central conflict is not between assimilating aliens and Americans who unjustly reject them, it is between Sara, whose desire to become one of the "real Americans"[126] is so intense that successful Americanization seems to her the equivalent of being "changed into a person" (237), and her father, whose embodiment of the Jewish "race" is so absolute that he seems to his family "an ancient prophet that had just stepped out of the Bible" (125).

Insofar as Sara is like a "pioneer," compared by a sympathetic dean at her "real American" college to his own "grandmother" contending with the "wilderness" (232), her father, Reb Smolinski, is an Indian: "In a world where all is changed, he alone remained unchanged—as tragically isolate as the rocks" (296). From this standpoint, from the Jewish as opposed to the American standpoint, Sara is less like Louie Marsellus than like the woman he marries, the professor's daughter Rosamond; as Rosie betrays her family by marrying a Jew, Sara wants to marry "an American-born man" (66). And her father, Reb Smolinski, is like the professor; indeed, to reproduce in *Bread Givers* not just the thematic but the *affective* structure of *The Professor's House*, one need only imagine it written from the point of view of Reb Smolinski: *The Rabbi's House*. But the goal here, of course, is not simply to find ways of mapping these two texts onto each other; it is to suggest instead (in part, through such a mapping) that the nativist's vanishing Indian could function simultaneously as the alien's vanishing Jew: assimilation could be repudiated from both sides.[127]

The opposition between "Indian" and "Jew," between Tom Outland and Louie Marsellus, is not in this way undone, it is just, like the *Bread Givers* imagined above, reconfigured. The Indian who in Cather (and Grey and Crane) embodies the nativist American is made instead to embody the nativist ethnic and in both positions resists assimilation. This is made most explicit in Oliver La Farge's *Laughing Boy* (1929), where the Indians really are Indians and the "foreigners" or "aliens" are the Americans. La Farge's Slim Girl (like Grey's Carlisle Indian, Nophaie) has been sent to an American-run school and the Navajos think of her as no longer Navajo: "She is a school-girl. . . . She is not of the People any more, she is American."[128] But where *The Vanishing American* works to narrativize the opposition between Indian and American so that, by the text's end, the Indian can melt into the American, becoming not his antagonist but his ancestor, *Laughing Boy* insists on the antagonism. Nophaie marries an American but Slim Girl, having been seduced and prostituted by Americans, turns the act of prostitution into an act of war—when she returns from sleeping with her American, she has the "look," La Farge says, "of a man who has just killed and scalped a hated enemy" (88)—and seeks to restore herself to the Navajos by marrying one: "he was the means of returning to the good things of the Navajo, the good things of life" (109). Thus where the Indians in *The Vanishing American*, as in *The Professor's House*, are foundational for a distinctly *American* cultural identity, in *Laughing Boy* they have become a culture of their own, no longer deployed in opposition to the ethnics but as one of them.

In *Laughing Boy*, then, the structure of nativism is repeated but rotated. The "alien"[129] (Louie Marsellus, Robert Cohn, Jimmy Gatz) is turned into an American called George. More striking, although the alien's desire to join the family is reversed (George wants to make Slim Girl "a superior American" [135]), that desire in its original form is relocated in Slim Girl herself, whose only goal is to find "her way back to her people" (45), and it is legitimated by the fact that Slim Girl is, after all, a Navajo—when Laughing Boy calls her "little sister," he is identifying the quality that, from the nativist standpoint, redeems their marriage. Slim Girl's genealogical ambition is to have children who are "all Navajo" (46) but, with its own evidence of her (miscegenetic) promiscuity, the novel is more inclined to follow the rules of nativist reproduction: the child she has by an American is born dead, and it is only as she herself dies, barren, that she can imagine her*self* "all Navajo"—"The Americans spoiled me for a Navajo life, but I shall die a Navajo now" (177). The Navajos had replaced the cliff dwellers as the great civilization of the Southwest but, in Slim Girl and Laughing Boy, they become the cliff dwellers, testifying with their extinction to their purity.

In *Bread Givers*, however, the return of the daughter is managed in a slightly different manner. Determined to become an "*Americanerin*" and to marry an American, Sara falls in love with the principal of her school, who is, on the one hand, Americanized enough to be able to correct her English pronunciation ("sing," not "sing-gg") but who, on the other hand, comes from a village in Poland only a few miles from hers: "*Landsleute—* countrymen!" (277) Sara and Hugo exclaim to each other in recognition of this coincidence. "He was the Old World. I was the New," Sara says of her father and herself, but marriage to the principal will have the effect of reconciling Sara to the Old World and to her father too; Hugo will ask her father to teach him Hebrew and will welcome the old man into their home. The marriage that was supposed to remove Sara from her father's house returns her to it; it is as if Rosie had married Tom Outland after all.[130]

"You and I, we are of one blood" (278), Hugo tells Sara, inadvertently quoting the familiar verse from Acts that we have seen so widely circulated. Paul's universalism and its antiracist implications are treated with contempt by Dixon: when *The Clansman's* Lincoln insists that "The Nation cannot . . . exist half white and half black," the miscegenetic Stoneman responds ("with a sneer"), "Yet 'God hath made of one blood all races'" (47). But Yezierska's *Bread Givers* follows Hopkins, revising rather than repudiating "of one blood," transforming the universal into the particular and rewriting the critique of racial identity as the commitment to racial identity. "I thought that in America we were all lost," Yezierska's Rabbi says; "Jewishness is no Jewishness. Children are no children" (293). Through the restoration of the child to her father, Jewishness is made Jewishness again; the claim to one blood becomes the claim to difference.

My Country, Right or Wrong

ROBERT COHN was once middleweight boxing champion of Princeton. Do not think that I am very much impressed by that as a boxing title, but it meant a lot to Cohn" (3). The first two sentences of *The Sun Also Rises* are devoted to enforcing the distinction between Jake and Cohn, and its third sentence makes sure that the distinction be understood as something more than a question of sophistication about sports: the reason that his boxing prowess meant so much to Cohn is that it helped to "counteract the feeling of inferiority and shyness he had felt at being treated as a Jew at Princeton." Cohn's failure to appreciate the true meaning of his title is thus identified with his being made "race-conscious," and both the failure and the new consciousness, as I have noted earlier, are connected to the many failures of appreciation that mark Cohn's relations with Jake, from his inability to respond appropriately to cathedrals to his turning "green" at the bullfight when he'd only worried about being "bored"—"Does Cohn look bored?" Jake asks his friend Bill Gorton; "That kike!" Bill replies (164). Hemingway's insistence on these distinctions would seem like ludicrous overkill if it weren't made necessary by the fact that, as noted earlier, Jake and Cohn are in certain respects so much alike, a fact that the novel makes particularly vivid in their relations to Brett—if, after all, Cohn follows Brett around "like a poor bloody steer" (142), it's Jake's footsteps he's treading in.

What attracts Cohn to Brett is "a certain quality, a certain fineness" that Jake dispatches with the same response he makes to the pedantry about cathedrals: "She's very nice" (38). But the deployment here of "nice" against "fine" and "straight" is complicated by the fact that words like "fine" (e.g., "The pastureland was green and there were fine trees . . ." [87]) and especially "straight" play a crucial role in Jake's own vocabulary; it's the fact that Romero's work is "straight and pure and natural in line" (167) that distinguishes it from the "false aesthetics" of the "commercial" bullfighters. Romero's bullfighting gives "real emotion," as opposed to the "fake emotional feeling" given by his competitors, even by Belmonte, who is now nothing but "an imitation of himself." Jake's prose, the prose of "nice," "straight," and "pure," is "real"; Cohn's appropriation of that vocabulary establishes the way in which we are to understand his similarity to Jake: it is the similarity of the "imitation" to the real thing. (It's as if Cohn's real point in following Brett around like a steer is to become more like Jake.)

In bullfighting, this reality is called *afición*, and, even though Americans are thought at best to be able to "simulate" (132) it, Jake has it. In writing, it is the vocabulary of experience, of words which serve not to represent the experience but to testify to its authenticity. (Hugh Kenner describes Hemingway as the "recorder of authenticities.")[131] Thus, although the usual procedure of *The Sun Also Rises* is to translate French dialogue into idiomatic English, it is sometimes translated with a bizarre literality (as in the concierge's reference to Brett as "a species of woman" [32]) and sometimes not translated at all (as in the concierge's later description of Brett as "gentille" [52]). These strategies have differently disruptive impacts on the realism of the representation—one by making her say what she *really* said, the other by making her say something that nobody has *ever* said—but they both bear witness to the reality of Jake's having heard her, to the authenticity of his experience of her French.[132]

But the point here is not simply that the impulse toward realism pushes Hemingway beyond realism, or even that the commitment to authenticity turns out to conflict with the conventions of realistic representation. For the effort to achieve phenomenological authenticity goes beyond both realism and the critique of realism. What I mean by this is just that phenomenological authenticity finds its semiotic parallel in linguistic untranslatability: the literality of "species of woman" speaks to the failure of translation; "très très gentille" simply refuses translation. The meaning of these signs is understood as essentially linked to the particular form of their signifiers. From this standpoint, an idiomatic translation of *"espèce de femme"* could only be understood as seeking to disguise this fact, whereas the insistence on "très très gentille" unabashedly proclaims it. Thus the claim of authenticity for the writer's experience asserts at the same time the primacy of the sign's materiality.

This movement recapitulates two familiar (if often opposed) accounts of modernism, one emphasizing the primacy of experience, the other the primacy of language. But my point here is not just to emphasize the compatibility of the commitments to experience and to the materiality of the sign. For in Hemingway, both these commitments are put to work in the effort to separate the "imitation" from the "real," Cohn from Jake. "There is no Spanish word for bull-fight" (173), Jake remarks, which is to say that the aesthetic of sincerity embodied in the bullfight is simultaneously an aesthetic of untranslatability. What we call a bullfight cannot properly be translated into Spanish, and what Spaniards call what we call a bullfight is not properly translated by "bullfight." The meaning of this link between experience and language is made explicit by the contemptuous response to Cohn's telegram informing Jake and Bill Gorton of his plans: "The telegram was in Spanish: 'Vengo Jueves Cohn.' I handed it to Bill. 'What does the word Cohn mean?' he asked?" (127). The joke is precipitated by Cohn's writing in Spanish when everyone else writes in English and when, by contrast to Jake, he can't really speak Spanish. But its point depends upon the fact that names are like bullfights: there are no words for them in other languages. So Cohn's writing in Spanish is treated as an attempt to translate what cannot be translated, by speaking Spanish to try to make himself "one of us" and by treating his name as if it could be translated to try to disguise who he really is. Bill's response ends up, in other words, presenting the telegram as if it were an effort of assimilation—as if Cohn's speaking Spanish were to be understood on the model of Jews' speaking English and as if his identifying himself as the author of a Spanish sentence were to be understood as his attempt to anglicize a Jewish name.[133]

The untranslatability of a "word" like Cohn, the fact that, as Hemingway presents it, "Cohn" always names just one thing and what it names is who he is, reminds us, on the one hand, of Dilsey's remark about Benjy (né Maury) Compson—"Folks don't have no luck, changing names" (74) —and may begin to suggest, on the other hand, the attraction to words as things that is such a familiar component of modernist poetry. For if rigidly linking a word to its referent is one way of insisting on the impossibility of substituting one word for another, then privileging the word over its referent is another; insofar as our interest is in the word itself rather than in what it signifies, we cannot replace it with another word that will seem to us to signify the same thing. From this standpoint, *The Sound and the Fury*'s commitment to the word that will be the thing it names is matched rather than contradicted by the perhaps more characteristic modernist commitment to the word that achieves what William Carlos Williams called its "reality" by transcending rather than being the thing it names. Indeed, it was precisely this commitment to "the reality of

the word" that Williams was prepared in 1929 to describe as the "base" of
"modernism," meaning by "reality" "the materials of letters" which are
"real" and which "supersede in themselves all ideas, facts, movements
which they may under other circumstances be asked to signify."[134]

The manuscript Williams put together in 1928 and 1929 under the title
The Embodiment of Knowledge testifies in prose to the intensity of his
desire to make poems that would in fact count as objects rather than
signs—"words," "not symbols" (18). But the ambition to make such poems
is already visible in *Spring and All* (1923), and especially in that collection's first poem, which is also its most explicit response to the publication the year before of what Williams would call in his *Autobiography* "the
great catastrophe to our letters," Eliot's *The Waste Land*.[135] Williams identified what he regarded as the failure of *The Waste Land* with what he
called "plagiarism," by which he meant not the copying of other poems
but the copying of "reality." *Spring and All* attacks the "traditionalists of
plagiarism" by replacing the copy of reality with "reality itself," by making
"the writing have reality."[136] It is crucial, for example, that versions of the
words "spring," "and," and "all" are distributed through the opening description of "the waste," "brown with dried weeds, standing and fallen/
patches of standing water/the scattering of tall trees/All along the road"
(183). "Fallen," "tall," "all," and, elsewhere, "small" and even "hospital"
repeat the "reality" of "all," an effect that is even more striking with the
repetition of "standing" (which produces both "and" and a version of
"spring"), then "scattering" and later "upstanding" and "spring" itself.
This deployment of "ing" takes up quite literally the distinctive partici-
ples of *The Waste Land*'s opening lines ("breeding," "mixing," "stirring") in
an effort not only to free the words of what Williams contemptuously
called "the pleasing wraiths of former masteries"[137] but also to assert the
primacy of the "materials" demanded by "modernism." Although "By the
road to the contagious hospital" is invariably praised for its precise description of the landscape, there is an important sense in which what
these lines do above all is produce the presence on the page of "and," "all,"
and "ing."[138] "The thing that saves your work," Pound had written Williams six years earlier, "is *opacity*";[139] it is the "opacity" of Williams's
words that makes their "reality" *as* words visible. The reproach to Eliot in
Spring and All requires this opacity in order that the "reality" of words like
"spring" be made prior to their "meaning."

But Pound went on in the same letter to tell Williams that "Opacity is
NOT an American quality," when, in fact, as *Spring and All* begins to

suggest and as *The Embodiment of Knowledge* would make entirely clear, a materialist poetics was beginning to occupy in Williams precisely the place not only of a modern but also of a distinctively American aesthetic. The "first American poet" (Poe), Williams writes in *Spring and All*, "had to be a man of great separation" (198). In one sense, this is simply a remark (in the tradition of James on Hawthorne) about the difficulty of producing literature in what Williams characterizes as the "crudely repressive environment" of the United States in the nineteenth century. But "separation" is a term of art for Williams; it designates the position of the "independent" (207) painting or poem: "It is not a matter of 'representation' . . . but of separate existence" (204).[140] Thus the qualities that Williams thinks of as "typically American" in Poe—his "reality," his "completeness"—are the very qualities that characterize for him the material or "modernist" work of art: it "separates" (207), it has its own "reality" (206), it is "complete" (207).

And this conjunction is not in Williams a merely contingent one, by which I mean it is not merely the case that the qualities he admires in poetry also happen to be qualities that he thinks of as characteristically American as opposed, say, to characteristically French or English. Rather the criteria of poetic ambition in Williams are indistinguishable from the conditions of national identity as he and others understood them. "We have a great desire to be supremely American" (56), Calvin Coolidge had told the Annual Meeting of the American Classical League in 1921. Insofar as the point of the poem in Williams is to be itself (rather than to represent some other thing), and insofar as the self the poem must be is American, the poetic goal is what Williams calls "the American thing." This is insisted upon by the title page to *The Embodiment of Knowledge*, which juxtaposes the epigraphs "The book as a whole is a whole" and "My country, right or wrong." The wholeness of the book is the mark of its existence as a "separate," "complete," "independent" entity; it is the primacy of this autonomy that Williams means to emphasize when he calls the writing he admires "pure" and distinguishes it from writing which has compromised its independence: "There is pure writing and writing which is made to be the horse of any one who has a burden to carry" (117). The commitment to country "right or wrong" is produced according to the same logic; by eliminating the appeal to any external criteria of justification (i.e., rightness or wrongness), it makes one's identity into one's justification. The material poetic of embodiment is matched by the desire "to embody America" (47).[141]

Furthermore, Williams's commitment to "pure writing"—to identity as such—is explicitly linked to what he himself calls "pluralism," the principle that since "every individual, every place, every opportunity of thought is both favored and limited by its emplacement in time and place," the "old cultures" of Europe "can never, without our history, our blood or climate, our time of flowering in history—can never be the same as we" (149–50). The point here is that "reality" is "plural" (150), different for different cultures, and it is this assertion of difference rather than any claim to superiority that, as we began to see in the previous section, lies at the heart of nativist logic. Thus Gino Speranza in *Race or Nation* (1925) denies that "what is excellent . . . for one people is necessarily excellent . . . for a totally different people. . . . What is important," he says, "is to see and stress the fact that there is a difference" (107). And even Stoddard, who in 1920 had produced detailed rankings of racial quality, maintains in 1927 that "No theoretical questions of 'superiority' or 'inferiority' need be raised" (*Re-Forging*, 101). This is the meaning, after all, of "My country, right or wrong"; the attachment to country, irrespective of rightness and wrongness, affirms the primacy of identity over any other category of assessment. Hence, whether or not Stoddard had personally given up his belief in white supremacy, he had, as we have already seen, disarticulated it from his opposition to immigration: "The really important point is that even though America (abstractly considered) may not be nearly as good as we think it is, nevertheless it is *ours* . . ." (102).

What's striking here about Stoddard's effort to set aside his ethnocentrism—his bracketing the question of whether America is really as good as we think it is—is not that he in fact gets rid of the ethnocentrism but that he recognizes its irrelevance to his nativism, or rather, that he recognizes that the power of nativism depends upon its pluralism, its transcendence of questions about superiority and inferiority. The point of suspending the question of America's goodness is to make clear the fact that our attachment to it is based only on our identity with it; even if, Stoddard says, "it could be conclusively shown that a certain stock was superior to us in some ways . . . we should still refuse to receive it, on grounds of self-preservation" (257–58). Where the assertion of racial superiority requires a primary commitment to certain universal values (the ones according to which some races are deemed superior and some inferior) and thus a merely secondary commitment to whichever race happens to rank the highest, the denial of the relevance of superiority and inferiority makes the race as such into the cathected object. This is what it means for

Americans to want not to be supremely good or supremely powerful or supremely rich but "supremely American."

It's in this context not only that miscegenation, the breaking down of difference, becomes the privileged sex crime of nativist modernism (and incest, the insistence on identity, becomes its privileged form of sexual expression) but also that assimilation, the great desideratum of Progressive social policy, becomes a threat both to those who would assimilate and to those who would be assimilated. Nativist writers derided the ideal of the "melting pot" and the projects of "Americanization" developed to produce it. No "environmental influence," wrote the "cultural pluralist" Horace Kallen, can take "different races" and "remold them into an indifferent sameness."[142] Thus, according to Speranza, even a "people" as "fine and loyal" as the Mexicans of the Southwest could only remain "culturally and historically unadapted and ill at ease in the body-politic of the republic" (64). The "lesson" of New Mexico "to our 'Americanizers' and our theorists," Speranza thought, was that "racial characteristics"—"especially those subtler qualities of mind and character which profoundly differentiate the culture and the spirit of one people from those of another"—"do not die out" (31).

Of course, Speranza and Kallen had different affective relations to this lesson (Kallen hopefully anticipating a "national fellowship of cultural diversities" [32], Speranza fearfully anticipating the same thing), but the difference in affect presupposes the shared commitment to the identity through time of "racial characteristics"; if New Mexico is a "tragic example" of the failure of assimilation, it is also a triumphant tribute to the refusal of assimilation. In New Mexico, as Willa Cather put it in *Death Comes for the Archbishop* (1927), "The Mexicans were always Mexicans, the Indians were always Indians."[143] Indeed, in the context of a novel explicitly concerned with the possibility of transforming people—that is, after all, what the missionary Father Latour has come to New Mexico for—the persistence of race marks the point beyond which no transformation is possible. Replacing Americanization with conversion, Cather will imagine the Catholic Church as an institution committed to preserving rather than obliterating Speranza's subtle differences "of mind and character." Set in a moment before the problem of Americanization had even been conceived, the novel depicts conversion as the solution to that problem.

It is for this reason that the problem of identity dominates *Death Comes for the Archbishop*, whether in the form of Father Vaillant's ship-of-

Theseus-like wagon, "repaired so often and so extensively that long before he abandoned it there was none of the original structure left" (258),
or in the thematically more central form of the missionaries' inability to
get the Indians to give up "their own beliefs" (135). Or rather, it is for this
reason that identity in *Death Comes for the Archbishop* never actually
registers as a problem; after all, the trick of the ship of Theseus, as Hobbes
presented it, is that the gradual replacement of even every piece doesn't
really seem to raise an identity problem until it is revealed that all the
discarded pieces have been used to assemble another ship—which one is
the ship of Theseus? In Cather, Father Vaillant's wagon has no competitors so it is left standing as an example of how identity can be maintained
in the face of the eventual disappearance of all the materials which
seemed to constitute it. And, more importantly, Catholicism doesn't seem
finally to be in competition with what the bishop approvingly describes
as the Indians' "veneration for [their] old customs" (135). When a trader
tells him, "he might make good Catholics among the Indians, but he
would never separate them from their own beliefs" (135) the point seems
to be that there is no necessary contradiction between being a good
Catholic and clinging to one's own beliefs. "The Mexicans were always
Mexicans, the Indians were always Indians"; the point of Father Latour's
Catholicism seems to be that it encourages rather than disputes this
maintenance of identity.[144]

As we know, the bishop's equanimity in the face of New Mexican
cultural differences was not shared by all observers. Speranza, admiring
the "native people" of New Mexico as a "people with old traditions and
customs, and a civilization of their own" (64), nevertheless regarded
them as "a deeply tragic example" of the impossibility of making good
American citizens out of aliens. The tragedy consists not in the New
Mexicans' refusal to accept American rule; on the contrary, not only have
they accepted it, they have been, by Speranza's own admission, "splen-
didly loyal to the stars and stripes" which they have "stoutly defended on
every occasion" (64). The tragedy consists rather in the inability of New
Mexico's natives to adapt "culturally and historically" to "American institutions"; despite their political loyalty and precisely because of their
veneration for "old traditions and customs," they constitute "an unas-
similated and culturally alien element" "in our midst" (64).

Speranza separates politics from "culture" as Cather separates religion
from "beliefs"; the point in each case is to imagine a form of identity
immune to the transformations of Americanization or conversion. The

missionary bishop's relation to his Indian guide Jacinto is in this respect exemplary: "The Bishop seldom questioned Jacinto about his thoughts or beliefs. He didn't think it polite and he believed it to be useless. There was no way in which he could transfer his own memories of European civilization into the Indian mind, and he was quite willing to believe that behind Jacinto there was a long tradition, a story of experience, which no language could translate to him" (92). It is the representation of European civilization as existing in the bishop's memory and the representation of Indian tradition as Jacinto's experience that elevate the impolite to the useless. For insofar as European civilization is imagined as something one remembers instead of as something one learns, it is clearly impossible to "transfer" it; Jacinto might conceivably learn about European civilization but he will never remember it. And insofar as the Indian's long tradition is identified as a story of experience, the bishop can have, in principle, no access to it; even if meanings are translatable, experiences surely are not. This is what it means for identity to be displayed in *Death Comes for the Archbishop* as a problem that has been solved. If to belong to a culture you must be able to encounter it in the form of memory, as a tradition that is already yours, then no one can ever cease to belong to his or her culture or begin to belong to some other culture. The assimilating ambitions of, say, the Jew Louie Marsellus in *The Professor's House* (or of Jimmy Gatz in *The Great Gatsby* or Robert Cohn in *The Sun Also Rises*) are imagined in *Death Comes to the Archbishop* as ontological absurdities.

In this respect, at least, *Death Comes for the Archbishop* represents an advance over *The Professor's House*. Insofar as struggles like the professor's to defend his family are abandoned in *Death Comes for the Archbishop*, that is only because they have become unnecessary: there is no Rosamond St. Peter to try to rescue from miscegenation in *Death Comes for the Archbishop*. In fact, as Cather herself somewhat hyperbolically put it, *Death Comes for the Archbishop* is "a story with no woman in it but the Virgin Mary."[145] Removing temptation from the paths of the priesthood, Cather guarantees that the Europeans—like the Mexicans and the Indians—will always be Europeans.[146] Indeed she locates this principle of cultural self-identity through celibacy in the "story" of the Indian "experience" itself: the "life-force" of the "best" young men in the "tribe" is said to be "sapped" in the service of "a ceremonial fire" that is never "allowed to go out" (122). Thus their refusal to give up "their own beliefs" is killing the Indians, and the fact that they are "dying out" is the proof of their allegiance to "their own beliefs." This more or less conventional representation of the vanishing race is here transformed into the Indian's way of being "supremely" Indian.

But her commitment to the purified ontology of nativist identity finds perhaps its most explicit form in Cather's internal thematization of her own aesthetic. Amid the prologue's general discussion of "ancestry" and of the attributes of different nationalities ("the Germans classify, but the French arrange" [9]), a question is raised about the future Bishop's "intelligence in matters of art," about whether he has what the cardinal calls "a discerning eye." The relevance to missionary work of a good eye for pictures is not obvious to the bishop's supporters, but Cather's model for *Death Comes for the Archbishop* was at least partly pictorial, and Father Latour is explicitly made to articulate for her the meaning of the visual in the context of a narrative genre like the novel. The model was the frescoes of Puvis de Chavannes, which had long inspired her, Cather says, "to try something a little like that in prose; something without accent. . . ."[147] The point of eliminating accent is "to treat all human experiences" as if they are of "about the same importance," to minimize the significance of what she calls the "situation." This formal ambition seems to her to match the "mood" or "spirit" in which the historical models for Latour and Vaillant seem actually to have "accepted the accidents and hardships of a desert country" (*On Writing*, 10). More concretely, it finds expression in what she describes as the dying bishop's loss of "perspective in his memories" (*Death Comes for the Archbishop*, 290). This disappearance of "calendared time" turns the narrativized connection of past to present self into a "great picture," guaranteeing continuity through time by reimagining it as continuity in space. (In Puvis's art, this involved privileging allegorical or "decorative" values over those of narrative or drama.) Not only are the achievements of "European civilization" understood as one's "own memories," one's own memories are understood as continuing experiences: "He sat in the middle of his own consciousness; none of his former states of mind were lost or outgrown. They were all within reach of his hand . . ." (290).

"It is impossible for society to break with its past" (49), Coolidge had told the classicists; the "great picture" of the bishop's life makes this impossibility literal. The problem of securing one's identity in the past is solved by making the past continually present. Instead of "states of mind" succeeding each other, they are laid out next to each other, and the elimination of perspective guarantees that none will seem closer than any other. Cather is often and plausibly regarded as an exponent of "organic

unity," but the commitment here to unity goes beyond the organic because it denies the possibility of time and so of change; because nothing
can be "outgrown," nothing can grow. What this means at the level of plot
is that nothing leads to anything else. So, paradoxically, everything is
connected but anything can be disconnected, which is why, for example,
Cather thought that it would be easy to select parts of *Death Comes for the
Archbishop* to anthologize. Because no part of the narrative was subordi-
nated to any other part of the narrative, every part was equally a part of
the whole. But because every part was equally a part of the whole, any
part could be used as a whole.

The identity of the work of art is imagined here as the utopian form of
cultural identity, simultaneously determining the relation of the self to
the past (guaranteeing that Indians remain Indian) and the relation of the
self to the collective identity the past produces (guaranteeing, in effect,
that Indians be defined by their being Indians). Hence in Williams's version of this "memoriam to identity,"[148] "My country, right or wrong" is
accompanied not only by "The book as a whole is a whole" but also by
a dedication "TO MY BOYS—Wishing them luck" (*The Embodiment of
Knowledge*, 2). The dedication makes explicit what a poem like *Spring and
All*'s "The pure products of America/go crazy" suggests,[149] that the conception of identity built into the poetics of embodiment is essentially
genetic; what makes a poem a poem, for example, and not a piece of prose
is its "source" or "origin" (144–45). This is why Williams regards it as
"possible, even essential, that when poetry fails it does not become prose
but bad poetry" (145). It cannot "become" prose because neither prose nor
poetry can ever become anything different from what it already is. If
poetry, in order to be poetry, must come "from the source from which
poetry starts," if, in other words, the identity of the object is determined
by its origin, then nothing can ever be anything other than what it already
is. To treat prose as bad poetry would be to collapse the difference between two different things by treating them as if they were two more or
less good versions of the same thing. Insisting instead that each has "a
separate origin," Williams makes comparison between them odious by
making the difference between them "essential."

In *The Embodiment of Knowledge*, this principle, as we have already
seen, is generalized: "every individual, every place, every opportunity of
thought is both favored and limited by its emplacement in time and
place" (150). And "America is such a place. The old cultures *cannot*, can
never, without our history, our blood or climate, our time of flowering in

history—can never be the same as we" (150). Williams's name for this principle is "the pluralism of experience" (149). Modernism and pluralism necessarily accompany each other in Williams since the modernist commitment to the materiality of the poem requires above all that the poem be itself, which is to say that it locates the poem's value in its identity and so in its difference from anything else. Just as in nativism the goal of the American is to be American, in Williams's modernism the goal of the American poet is to produce American poetry. In this respect, Williams's polemic against Eliot and the "traditionalists of plagiarism" explicitly extends Poe's attack on "Longfellow and Other Plagiarists." Their plagiarism consists in a betrayal of originality—since they "copy" other poets—and a betrayal of materiality—since they "copy" "reality"— both of which are understood by Williams as betrayals of nationality, since by copying other poets they attach themselves to a tradition that is essentially European and by copying reality they refuse the obligation to embodiment that constitutes in nativism the very meaning of nationality. Poe, by contrast, is "original" (*In the American Grain*, 229) and "abstract" (230). His originality consists in the fact that for inspiration he goes not to England but "back to the ground"; his abstraction consists in the fact that what he does when he gets there is not copy it (no local color in Poe) but "clear" it (216). Getting rid of the "scenery . . . in order to let the real business of composition *show*" (230), Poe "was American" (226).

From this standpoint, what is striking about Williams's poetic is not its materialism—its commitment to the idea that the poem's identity consists in its material features—but its deployment of that materialism in the service of what should be called its *identitarianism*: its commitment to the idea that the success of the poem consists in the achievement of its identity.[150] Coolidge's characterization of Americans as desiring "to be supremely American" had great success with audiences beyond the classicists to whom he spoke in 1921: Speranza quotes it on the first page of *Race or Nation* and Stoddard makes it the cornerstone of a chapter on "The Will to National Unity" in *Re-Forging America*. Both these books attempt to rescue what they call "American culture" not simply by excluding aliens (the Congress and the Coolidge administration had already, they thought, accomplished that in the Immigration Act of 1924) but by urging their readers to appreciate the past and present glories of the American "heritage." "We are to-day evolving a whole series of distinctively 'American' forms which truly express the national spirit and which therefore possess creative feeling and beauty," Stoddard wrote;

"Thus culturally, as well as racially and spiritually, alienism is being slowly but surely mastered" (368).

Nativism's racial pluralism makes one's difference from others essential; nativism's cultural pluralism makes one's potential difference from oneself equally essential. Culture here provides the technology through which the fact that you are who you are can be doubled by the responsibility to be who you are. Stoddard's criterion of beauty is thus the true expression of "national spirit," a criterion that Williams makes more powerful by making formal; the poem will express America by embodying it. Transforming tautology (the poem is itself) into imperative (the poem must be itself), Williams produces for American poetry the project of American nativism: what we are (Americans), is what we must strive to be (American). The poem becomes what it is, in effect, not by expressing something else but by accepting that it can only express itself: "quite truly a work of art means nothing . . . but itself" (*The Embodiment of Knowledge*, 120).

It is from this perspective that Cohn's efforts to write in Spanish—the telegram—or, more pointedly, to talk like Jake—"fine," "straight"—look like a kind of passing and require the relentless and repeated outings that constitute so much of the plot of *The Sun Also Rises*. By the same token, Jake's own inclination to linguistic imitation (and, through that inclination, Hemingway's own prose style) is here subjected to a kind of exculpatory critique. "When you were with the English," Jake says, "you got into the habit of using English expressions in your thinking. The English spoken language—the upper classes anyway—must have fewer words than the Eskimo. Of course, I didn't know anything about the Eskimo. . . . Say the Cherokee" (149). The feature of Hemingway's prose style on which Jake most insists and which he deploys against Cohn—its laconic commitment to what Hugh Kenner calls "small full words"—is here imagined to derive from the English upper classes and then, as if recapitulating Zane Grey's nativist family tree ("The English are . . ."), from the American Indian.[151] Imitation can be redeemed but only if it is transformed into genealogy.

Thus also Williams derives Poe's "greatness" from Daniel Boone—"he turned his back and faced inland, to originality, with the identical gesture of a Boone" (*In the American Grain*, 226)—and derives Boone's "genius" from the Indian: "To Boone the Indian was his greatest master. Not for himself surely to be an Indian, though they eagerly sought to adopt him into their tribes, but the reverse: to be *himself* in a new world, Indianlike"

(137).[152] Poetry, in Williams, is, above all, "not 'like' anything" (*Spring and All*, 207); his writing is American not because it represents American subjects ("the Indians, the forests, the great natural beauty of the New World" [*In the American Grain*, 227]) but because it *is* American, it's made "of original fibre." In order to be "Indianlike," the writer must make no likenesses of Indians, he must devote himself to "WRITING." Thus Boone is most "Indianlike" when he refuses to become an Indian (refuses, in effect, the ontological assumptions of naturalization) and insists instead on "be[ing] himself," and Poe is most "Indianlike" when he refuses to write about Indians and insists instead on the poem "be[ing] itself": "Sometimes he used words so playfully his sentences seem to fly away from sense, the destructive!" (*In the American Grain*, 221). Poe is "abstract," hence "native"; the goal of a modernist poetic is to give the words themselves "reality," to write "like an Indian" (137).

The Psychology of Imitation

I N THE SECOND edition of her *American Rhythm* (1930; the first was published in 1923), Mary Austin identifies what she describes as "the growing interest of Americans in Amerind dancing" with the tendency toward "abstraction of movement" in modern "esthetic dancing" (67). Abstraction here plays the role of "opacity" in Williams. Such abstraction is easier in "the plastic arts," Austin thinks, because they "are not burdened, as literature often is, with the necessity of conveying a certain amount of information." It is this "burden" that Williams's "pure writing" refuses to assume ("There is pure writing and writing which is made to be the horse of any one who has a burden to carry" [*The Embodiment of Knowledge*, 117]), and it is striking in this context that the element of American verse that Austin herself singles out as distinctively American is rhythm, which she identifies, through its manifestations in the "human organism" (4) as the "physical basis of poetry" (8). What makes American poetry American, in other words, is not that it thematizes American subjects but that it has the physical qualities of American bodies. The modern poets Austin admires, resisting "Greek and Hebrew" models, "derive their impulses" from "our own aboriginals" (46); in a paradigmatically nativist gesture, Amy Lowell and Carl Sandburg are made the heirs of the Ojibway and the Chippewa.

Insofar as modernist abstraction could be understood to have a non-

European genealogy, however, it was more usually described as African than as Amerindian. African sculpture, in particular, seemed to have achieved a "plastic freedom" that went beyond anything accomplished in the West. In the West, as Albert Barnes put it, sculpture was "at all times complicated by the motive of representation, so that the arrangement of masses, of head, trunk and limbs, which would have made the most effective plastic ensemble, was rarely found. Literature, in other words, stood in the way of plastic form. With negro sculpture, the literary motive was absent and the artist strove to distribute his masses in accord with the requirements of a truly sculptural design."[153] For Barnes and for other critics, it was the explicit three-dimensionality of African sculpture that produced the effect of abstraction and hence of objects that were to be understood on their own terms rather than as imitations of other objects. Thus, in his influential anthology The New Negro (1925) (to which Barnes also contributed), Alain Locke praises the "abstract decorative forms" of African art and quotes Roger Fry on the "disconcerting vitality" of these forms, "the suggestion that they make of being not mere echoes of actual figures, but of possessing an inner life of their own."[154] African sculpture, like modernist poetry, insists on its own "reality."

For Locke, however, the new prestige of African art, its influence on Matisse, Picasso, Modigliani, and others, is a phenomenon complicated by the inability thus far of Negro artists to profit from it. In an essay called "The Legacy of the Ancestral Arts," he deplores the fact that Negro artists have lagged behind Europeans in discovering and asserting the value of African art, and he attributes this failure to what he calls "our timid and apologetic imitativeness and overburdening sense of cultural indebtedness" (256). While avant-garde Europeans have been mining African sculpture for "lesson[s] in simplicity and originality of expression," the "timid conventionalism" of the Negro has left him in thrall to "the most reactionary conventions in art" (262). It is only, then, by following the lead of the Europeans and turning his attention to Africa that the Negro can overcome his "imitativeness" and "conventionalism." And while this might seem paradoxical—Isn't Locke just asking the Negro to stop imitating reactionary Europeans and to start imitating progressive ones?—in fact, what Locke is imagining here is a way out of imitation altogether. For the Negro's relation to African sculpture will be significantly different from the European's relation to it. Where the European "inherit[s]" it by "tradition," the Negro is "bound to it by a sense of direct cultural kinship" (256). Thus in taking up his ancestral legacy, the Negro is not only not imitating the European, he is not imitating the African either; he is, in effect, being himself. Indeed, from this standpoint, what's paradoxical is the European's relation to African art: the "originality" that the European finds in African art is something that he can only imitate; the origin that the Negro finds there is his own.

In this account, the modernism of the Negro is a function of his racial identity,[155] or rather, of his ability to establish the right relation to his racial identity. Like Coolidge's Americans desiring to be "supremely American," the "New Negro's" aspiration to modernity generates a project out of a tautology. If, in other words, the New Negro was new insofar as he managed to be himself, the "Old Negro" was old because he hadn't quite managed to be himself. He had been instead a "myth," produced partly by whites and partly by the "protective social mimicry" (3) that his "psychology of imitation" (4) had deployed in response to whites. The project, then, of being oneself is given content by the Negro's historical propensity to imitation, a propensity that has, as Zora Neale Hurston puts it, given rise to the charge (repeated so often that it has "almost become a gospel") that "the Negro is lacking in originality."[156]

Locke's response to this charge was, as we have already seen, to deny the imitativeness at least of the New Negro: the project of being a New Negro involves the refusal of imitation. For Hurston, however, such a refusal is impossible. "The Negro, the world over, is famous as a mimic" (59), she writes in "Characteristics of Negro Expression." Her goal is not to deny the qualities that have produced this fame but instead to undo the opposition between imitation and originality, which is to say that she is concerned to assert the Negro's ability as a "mimic" while defending him from charges that he lacks "originality" and that he "imitates from a feeling of inferiority." The defense against the first charge is that all art is "mimicry"; if it doesn't "reflect" or "suggest anything in nature or human experience we turn away with a dull wonder in our hearts at why the thing was done" (159). From this standpoint, the Negro's ability as a mimic is just his ability as an artist and would seem to need no further defense. But the second charge—"that the Negro imitates from a feeling of inferiority"—suggests the insufficiency of the response that all art is imitation of nature. For what the Negro is accused of imitating here is not nature but "white civilization," so the Negro's claim to originality has to be established here in the face of what even Hurston acknowledges is a "group of Negroes who slavishly imitate" whites.

To accomplish this defense, Hurston invokes a set of class distinctions.

Locke, introducing *The New Negro*, had cited "class differentiation" (6) as
one of the factors rendering "traditional lines of opinion" about the Negro
"obsolete" (5); it is now "unjust" and "ridiculous," he argued, "to regard
and treat the Negro *en masse*" (6). But this argument could have at best a
problematic relation to the major claim of *The New Negro*, that "Negro
life" was now "seizing upon its first chances for group expression and
self-determination" (7): How can it no longer be right to regard the Negro
"*en masse*" at the very moment when "a great race-welding" has finally
made Negro "group expression" possible? Earlier, in, say, Du Bois, the
commitment to class difference had been accompanied by a certain skepticism about racial solidarity, a suspicion that upper-class blacks had
more in common with upper-class whites than with lower-class blacks;[157]
how could class difference be mobilized now to produce (rather than
undermine) the "group expression" of the New Negro?

Hurston answers this question by describing the differences between
classes as differences in racial identification: "The average Negro glories
in his ways. The highly educated Negro the same. The self-despisement
lies in a middle class who scorns to do or be anything Negro" (59). Racial
authenticity becomes the principle of class distinction. The Negro "farthest down" "likes his own things best"; it is this Negro whose mimicry
counts as original, because it is not of whites and because what it is of
("various animals," for example, i.e., nature) shows that he imitates "for
the love of it, and not because he wishes to be like the one imitated" (60).
(The status of this mimicry as autotelic imitation is what makes it "art.")
The middle-class Negro, however, "wears drab clothing, sits through a
boresome church service . . . , holds beauty contests, and otherwise apes
all the mediocrities of the white brother" (59). Hurston's idea is not that as
Negroes rise in class they become less Negro; on the contrary, it is only
the imitation of whites that identifies the middle class as a class. The
racial betrayal is understood here to produce rather than to reflect ad-
herence to the middle class, a point that is hammered home by the claim
that the "truly cultured Negro" "glories," like the "average Negro," in his
"ways": you don't need to be "average" to be authentically Negro but you
do need to be inauthentically Negro (imitation white) to be "middle
class."

But, of course, the very success of this effort to key class identity to
racial identification produces a problem: What, exactly, are the "highly
educated" Negro's ways? Does the "highly educated" Negro, like the
"average" one, imitate nature? If he does, how is he different from the
"average?" And, if he doesn't, what guarantees his authenticity? It is

essential to Hurston that the higher class not be collapsed into the bottom one (the "farthest down") because, if it were collapsed, there could be no reason for thinking of racial identity as prior to class identity. Any movement upward from "the farthest down" would, in other words, automatically count as movement away from the race and so, with racial identity and class identity exactly correlated, there would be no place for racial autonomy. And it is racial autonomy that, as we can now see, is the payoff for the New Negro's insistence on class difference. Where race and class are *not* precisely correlated, race achieves an identity of its own—this is why the breakup of the Negro "*en masse*" is actually a necessary condition rather than, as it first seemed, an unfortunate contradiction of the "great race-welding." It seemed like a contradiction because it seemed to threaten the unity of the "group"; in fact, however, breaking up *class* unity, it sets the stage for *race* unity.

So the problem is, on the one hand, if there is to be a Negro there need to be identifiably Negro "ways," and, on the other hand, if there is to be a Negro there needs to be more than one class of Negroes. And this is a *problem* because if there's more than one class but there's only one set of ways, it's difficult to see how the difference in class can be kept from becoming a difference in racial authenticity or, to put it the other way around, how the identity of race can be kept from becoming a mere identity of class. Hurston's solution to this problem is embodied in her own intellectual practice. Where the middle-class Negro rejects Negro "ways" with the "terrible rebuke," "That's just like a Nigger," the "truly cultured" Negro writer insists on writing "just like a Nigger." She cannot write *as* a "Nigger" because, in order to guarantee the autonomy of the "Negro," not all "Negroes" can be "Niggers." But she cannot write *like* a white since that would make her inauthentically middle class. In order to write *as* a Negro she must write "like" a "Nigger." This is what it means for Hurston to believe that "The Negro's universal mimicry is not so much a thing in itself as an evidence of something that permeates his entire self" (49). It is only mimicry that guarantees the Negro's existence as a Negro; imitation is, in Hurston, the condition of racial identity.

The point, then, of Hurston's discussion of the "truly cultured" is not simply to legitimate black intellectuals by connecting them to their racial base. For without the black intellectual there could be no racial base. The function of the "truly cultured" in Hurston is to escape the reduction of race to class implicit in the identification of "the Negro farthest down" with racial authenticity and in the description of the "middle-class Negro" as imitation white. Imitating the "farthest down," the "truly cultured" make racial autonomy (the irreducibility of race to class) possible and so make racial authenticity possible. The "Nigger" is thus the criterion of authenticity, but the "truly cultured" provide the technology of authenticity, since without the existence of the "truly cultured" making themselves "just like" the "Nigger," there would be no properly racial "Nigger" at all—the "Nigger" would just be the "farthest down" who, insofar as he improves himself socially and economically and educationally, ceases to be "Nigger" and becomes "imitation white."

Everything here depends on the distinction between just being "Nigger" and both being and imitating "Nigger," between being something and trying to be the thing one is. In Williams's nativist poetic, as we have seen, this effort of identity takes the form of a critique of representation where representation seems essential (i.e., in language); in the constitution of the "New Negro," it takes the form of an insistence on representation where representation seems supererogatory (i.e., the representation of one's own racial identity). (An analog for this would be someone who could "pass" but who chooses not to and is therefore required to represent in some way his or her otherwise invisible racial essence.)[158] With respect to a poetics of "Negro" rather than "American" identity, this demand for representation put an almost unbearable pressure on the lyric poem. Thus, in "The Negro in American Literature," William Stanley Braithwaite finds himself characterizing Paul Dunbar's dialect poems both as the "first authentic lyric utterance" of "Negro life"[159] (*The New Negro*, 37) and as "the end of a regime" rather than "the beginning of a tradition" (38), and this despite the fact that after Dunbar, "many versifiers appeared—all largely dominated by his successful dialect work." Dunbar's problem, according to Braithwaite, is that he "expressed a folk temperament, but not a race soul" (38), a judgment that Braithwaite himself leaves unexplained but that we can gloss through Hurston: the dialect poem seems to be rather than both to be and to represent "Nigger." The dialect poem thus represents a kind of trap, but one that was perhaps not as easily avoidable as Braithwaite seems to have thought. For the new poets whom Braithwaite praises (e.g., Fenton Johnson, Roscoe Jameson, Anne Spencer, and especially Claude McKay) manage to achieve what he calls a "poetry that is racial in substance" (38) only by making race their subject while speaking in a voice that sounds what he calls "the universal note, with the conscious background of the full heritage of English poetry." The alternative to "Nigger," in other words, seems to be "imitation white."

This, at least, is how Langston Hughes, the most talented of the "New Negro" poets, depicted the reaction against Dunbar in *Not Without Laughter* (1930), where the socially ambitious Tempy—who thinks "colored people" should "dress like white people, talk like white people, think like white people"—only tolerates Dunbar "on account of his fame" and condemns him because he wrote "so much in dialect and so often of the lower classes of colored people."[160] Tempy is contrasted in this book to her sister Harriet, a blues singer, and, of course, Hughes would frequently cast himself as a blues poet in poems that would count for him as equivalents of Dunbar's dialect poems. But his commitment to a poetry of racial identity could be asserted also in poems whose diction is that of the standard English to which Tempy aspires (like "The Negro Speaks of Rivers"), and, in fact, *Not Without Laughter* seems at least as committed to reconciling these two modes as it is to distinguishing between them. For although Hughes is as interested as Hurston in keying class differences between blacks to different ways of being black (committed, in other words, to understanding class identity as a relation to racial identity), he is, unlike Hurston, also committed to what amounts to a kind of collaboration between the classes that will "help the whole race" (303).

Thus the class difference embodied in the antagonism between the upwardly mobile Tempy and the family she leaves behind is imagined by her sister (as it might be by Hurston) as an effect of Tempy's attempt to imitate whites—"when niggers get up in the world, they act just like white folks" (41)—but by Tempy herself as an attempt to escape subservience to whites; where Harriet has been taught to admire Booker T. Washington, Tempy dismisses him as a "white folks' nigger" (245) and sings the praises of W. E. B. Du Bois instead. So, although each class defines itself in opposition to the other, each class defines itself also by its commitment to "the Negro," and the difference between their definitions is elided in the figure of their nephew Sandy, who reads Washington *and* Du Bois: " 'I guess they are both great men,' he thought" (245). Refusing to choose between the classes, Sandy embodies both their hopes for "the black race," mediating without dissolving the differences between Washington and Du Bois. In effect, he transforms them into the components of a racial identity that will not be reduced to a class position. And insofar as *Not Without Laughter*'s commitment to Sandy expresses Hughes's autobiographical commitment to the meaning of his own career, the poet becomes the vehicle for a racial identity that simultaneously defines and transcends class identity: defines it because each class thinks of itself as more truly black, transcends it because the blackness of each class is revealed through Sandy to be only a part of the blackness of "the whole race."

The story of Sandy's relation to his race is thus a variant of Hurston's account of the role played by the "truly cultured," the Negro intellectual, in the constitution of racial identity. It's different in that Sandy subsumes rather than simply repudiates the ambitions of the middle class, but it's perhaps more powerfully the same in that Sandy's aspiration to make "a great man" of himself embodies Hurston's aspiration through class difference to racial identity. And the fulfillment of this aspiration is demonstrated by Hughes not in anything that actually happens to Sandy in the novel but in the narrative voice that depicts the aspiration. Insofar as that narrative voice is not itself the voice of the Negro "farthest down" (it's not dialect, for example), it runs the risk of looking like imitation white. But insofar as that narrative voice is concerned to *imitate* the Negro "farthest down," to portray the speech and actions of those whom imitation whites call "Nigger," it achieves the condition of the "truly cultured," those whose racial identity consists not in simply being but in representing "Nigger." In effect, then, the narrative voice of the novel produces both the necessary discrepancy from and mimetic relation to the "Nigger" that in Hurston characterizes the emergence of a properly racial autonomy.

In this sense, the formal distinction between the representing and the represented voices of the novel is at the same time a genealogy, a fact that the novel insists upon in its commitment to Sandy's representation of his family and that it literalizes by making Sandy's father, Jimboy, the kind of blues singer out of whom the blues poet will emerge. So the story Sandy tells of his own genealogy—the story, in Locke's terms, of the emergence of the "New Negro" out of the "Old"—will at the same time be the means by which he establishes his own place in that genealogy, the means by which he both affiliates himself with and distinguishes himself from the "Nigger." Hurston's requirement that the "truly cultured" be inextricably linked but not identical to the "farthest down" invents a new position for the black intellectual, making him the key to racial identity by making him the heir to and thus the transmitter of a racial "legacy." Which is to say that the representational strategies of Not Without Laughter, strategies that find probably their greatest racial achievement in Hurston's own Their Eyes Were Watching God (1937), produce the conditions in which a "primitive" or "folk" culture can be transformed into a racial heritage.[161]

Another way to put this is to say that the great achievement of African

American intellectuals in the Harlem Renaissance was to invent a new answer to the longstanding question of the intellectual's relation to the masses. In Marxist terms, of course, this could only be a question about the class identification of intellectuals. Thus, in essentially the same time frame (1929–1935), Gramsci was articulating the distinction between "traditional" and "organic" intellectuals as a distinction between those intellectuals who understood themselves to belong to "an autonomous and independent social group," a group constituted without reference to social class, and those intellectuals who understood themselves to express a set of class interests and who therefore identified their position as intellectuals with "active participation" in the "practical life" of the class to which they belonged.[162] Hurston obviously understood herself to belong to the group about which she wrote but, as Hazel Carby has remarked, most "African-American intellectuals were generations removed from the 'folk' they tried to represent," and even those who weren't had, in the process of becoming intellectuals, left behind the world and the "people" described by Hurston and Hughes. Thus Carby criticizes Hurston for identifying herself "both as an intellectual and as a representative figure from the folk culture she reproduced and made authentic in her work"; as Carby points out, "asserting that she *was* both did not resolve the contradictions embedded in the social meaning of each category."[163]

But to put the point in this way is insufficiently to acknowledge what is original about writers like Hurston and Hughes: their transformation of folk culture into racial heritage, their rewriting of the people as the race, and so their deployment of racial identity as a category through which class difference can be articulated and by which class difference can be subsumed. It is race, not class, that connects the African American intellectual to the culture that, disconnected by the intellectual from the "folk," is thereby reconnected to the race. Where, for example, the sociologist Robert Park distinguished between the "folk culture" of "the Negro of the plantation" and the "blues" culture of the Negro "proletariat,"[164] Hurston and Hughes identified the two, not to deny the differences in class but to affirm, through the culture that transcended those differences, the priority of race. In Park's account, culture is a product of social and economic rather than racial considerations; in Hurston and Hughes, it is the independence of culture from the social and economic that allows the priority of the racial to emerge. For them, the Negro's cultural activity provides not only (what it did for Locke) "the key to that revaluation of the Negro which must precede or accompany any considerable further betterment of race relations" (Locke, *The New Negro*, 15) but, more powerfully, the key to the very idea of race. Thus the meaning of the genre to which texts like *Not Without Laughter* and *Their Eyes Were Watching God* belong is nothing but the process of racialization, the enactment of the relation between narrator and narrated as a genealogy through which an autonomous racial identity is both authenticated and, through the process of authentication, created.

Aboriginal America

THERE'S A NOTE I'd like to strike. It's about impotence . . . ," says a newspaperman who wants to become a novelist in Sherwood Anderson's *Dark Laughter* (1925), "and if this war isn't a sign of universal impotence . . . then I don't know much."[165] Anderson's journalist is a kind of proleptic parody of Hemingway's Jake Barnes except that Anderson takes him as seriously as Hemingway takes Jake and it was, of course, Hemingway in *The Torrents of Spring* (1926) who produced the parody of Anderson rather than the other way around. In *Dark Laughter*, as in Hemingway and Madison Grant and Lothrop Stoddard, the war is identified with the failure of white reproductive ability and the increased prominence of nonwhites in America: "brown men, brown women, coming more and more into American life . . ." (74). But in the nativist texts, the rising tide of color is understood as the ultimate cause of Nordic sterility; contemplating the economic disruptions produced by immigration, Stoddard says, "When we think of all the American homes broken up or never founded and all the American children who were never born, we begin to get some conception of the 'sterilizing' effects of the vast alien tide" (*Re-Forging*, 151). It's as if Jake Barnes were not only "sterile" in comparison to Robert Cohn but had been sterilized by Cohn. In Anderson, by contrast, the effect of color is to *restore* whites to potency. The dark laughter of the title is produced primarily by "two negro women" (253) who embody the primitive wisdom of a people who, when they want to, just "'takes up' with each other" (291) and who, knowing instinctively that Anderson's main characters Bruce and Aline will have an affair, are amused to watch it develop: "The two negro women in the house watched and waited. Often they looked at each other and giggled. The air on the hilltop was filled with laughter—dark laughter" (253). Where in Stoddard et al. the potency of color is a threat, in Anderson it's an incentive—"Now she would have a child," Aline realizes, "a son perhaps" (257).

In Anderson, then, impotence and sterility have meaning only as the expression of a certain postwar exhaustion. In *The Torrents of Spring*, however, as its subtitle, *A Romantic Novel in Honor of the Passing of a Great Race*, suggests, they begin to assume their properly racial significance. If the Negro is an antidote to impotence in *Dark Laughter*, in *The Torrents of Spring* the Negro virtually disappears and is replaced by the Indian. Thus the inability of the high Nordic Yogi Johnson (his parents are from "Sweden or Norway") to "want a woman" is "cured" by the appearance of an Indian "squaw," "clad only in a pair of worn moccasins."[166] The "vague primordial feeling" she stirs up "inside him" (77) is, Yogi tells the Indians he's been drinking with, the first sexual desire he's experienced since the war, and, peeling off his own clothes, he sets out in pursuit of her: " 'White chief snappy dresser,' the tall Indian remarks, holding up an initialed shirt. 'White chief going get pretty cold,' small Indian remarks" (85). The parody of Anderson is obvious but so is the resemblance to Hemingway's own work, in *The Sun Also Rises* (where a version of impotence makes Jake white) and in the Nick Adams stories (where the "squaw" Prudence Mitchell is Nick's first girlfriend). The point here is that white impotence is defined by opposition to Jewish potency and then cured by absorption into sex with Indians ("the only real Americans" [*Torrents*, 63]), in effect, matching a good potency against a bad one.

But it would be a mistake to think that, for Hemingway, the presence of the Indian restores the procreative powers that Anderson's previously childless Bruce Dudley comes to display in impregnating Aline. *The Torrents of Spring* honors the *passing* of a great race, not its continuation. Its Indians describe themselves as Yogi's "red brother[s]" (75) and one of them is in fact married to the alluring squaw, so Yogi's desire for her has the incestuous tinge that marks the nativist mistrust of marriage and of the miscegenated procreation it makes possible. Indeed, marriage and procreation are persistent objects of horror in Hemingway. Childbirth kills Catherine Barclay in *A Farewell to Arms* and induces the father in "Indian Camp" to kill himself.[167] Of course, the psychology of "Indian Camp" derives the father's suicide from his inability to tolerate his wife's suffering and, in stories like "Mr. and Mrs. Elliot," the inability to have children is presented as a problem. But the nativist commitment to the great race's passing suggests that the Elliots' repeated failures ("Mr. and Mrs. Elliot tried very hard to have a baby" [85]) should be understood instead as a form of success and that the Indian father's death is more a consequence of his inability to tolerate his wife's actually producing a baby than of his inability to tolerate her suffering. To put the point slightly differently, in stories like "Indian Camp," "Mr. and Mrs. Elliot," and "Hills Like White Elephants" (in which "the American" tries to convince "the girl" to have an abortion),[168] the resources of a realist psychology are deployed on behalf of the commitments of a nativist logic. A young man marries an older woman; they are unable to have children and she turns out to be a lesbian. The realist psychology, the psychology, say, of *Dark Laughter*, explains this as a function of the young man's impotence, and psychological critics like Kenneth Lynn describe Hemingway as attacking men whom he envied (in this case, the poets Chard Powers Smith and T. S. Eliot) by impugning their manhood.[169] It's from this standpoint that the failure to have children counts as a failure. But, from the standpoint of nativism and the identification of the disappearing Nordic with the vanishing Indian, the refusal of procreation is the mark of racial purity; lesbianism, like impotence itself, figures as a technology for producing purity.

"A man must not marry" (*Men Without Women*, 37), the Signor Maggiore tells Nick in "In Another Country"; in "Now I Lay Me," where Nick gets exactly the opposite advice—"A man ought to be married" (136)—it is clear he is listening to the major: "so far, I have never married" (137). The problem with marriage, according to the major, is that it places a man "in a position to lose" when what a man wants is to "find things he cannot lose" (37). What the major has lost, of course, is his wife, but it's possible for wives to take things as well as to be taken. Nick remembers in "Now I Lay Me" how his mother "was always cleaning things out and making a good clearance" (131), and how, cleaning out the basement, she burned what Tom Outland would have called his father's Indian "relics." Nick's mother plays, in effect, the role of the Dreyfus-like Roddy Blake, and Dr. Adams, raking "carefully in the ashes" for "stone axes and stone skinning knives and tools for making arrow-heads and pieces of pottery" (133), plays the role of Tom himself, "tidying up the ruins" and taking "possession" of Blue Mesa (251). The job of the father here is to secure the Indian patrimony against the threat posed by the mother. "Were there two sides to Pocahontas?" (127); although Mrs. Adams, unlike the burlesque Pocahontas (and unlike Crane's "well-featured but wanton yong girle") is in no sense sexually promiscuous, the Nick Adams stories, as has often been remarked, repeatedly present her as betraying her husband.

"A man must not marry," then, because he might lose his wife, or he might, through his wife, lose something at least equally valuable. In either case, the criterion of value the major articulates—what is most valuable is what cannot be lost—suggests the power of identitarian ontology: the thing that you cannot lose is the thing that cannot be separated from you; it is not so much *yours* as it is *you*. What marriage puts in question, then, is identity itself. Which is why the incestuous marriage has such appeal but why even incest doesn't work. The fighter in "The Battler" is managed by his sister, and they are always "being written up in the papers all about brothers and sisters and how she loved her brother and how he loved his sister," but when they get married in New York it makes for a lot of "unpleasantness," they start to have "disagreements," "and one day she just went off and never came back" (*In Our Time*, 61). The truth, the narrator of this story says, is that "they wasn't brother and sister no more than a rabbit," but, as he also says (twice), "She was an awful good-looking woman. Looked enough like him to be twins." So the story wants to insist on the incest, and to insist also that although marrying your twin may be as close as you can come to marrying yourself, even a twin may be lost, even the incestuous marriage may jeopardize rather than preserve identity.

In contrast, then, to Anderson's transformation of "the impotence of American life" (45) into the Negro-sponsored fecundity of "a new marriage" (309), the nativist text invents ways to keep the impotence alive and the racial alien out. And this is at least partially true even in texts where the fundamental opposition between the alien and the American has no real place. For example, in D. H. Lawrence's short story, "The Princess" (written in 1924 and published in 1925), the eponymous heroine identifies herself as "British," "not American,"[170] and even though the story is set mainly on a ranch in New Mexico, the question of what it means to be American is never in play. At the same time, however, the characteristic topoi of nativist modernism are. The princess is the "last" of her "race" and she is taught early "the impossibility of intimacy with any other than her father." Furthermore, she doesn't "care for Jews" (167) and, after her father's death, the one man with whom she feels some "kinship" (178) is the "Indian looking" (168) trail guide, Romero (like Hemingway's bullfighter), who is also the "last" of his "family" (167) and whom the Jews avoid: " 'Oh, don't send Romero with us,' the Jews would say. 'One can't get any response from him' " (168). So "The Princess" participates in crucial respects in the discourse of nativist modernism: it presents us with an epitome of purified "blood"; it articulates that blood's purity through its antipathy to Jews; it identifies that purity with what Lawrence himself calls "sterility" (163) and so with the period's twinned vanishing races, Nordics and Indians; finally, making the princess attracted only to her father and then to the Mexican Indian she experiences as "kin," it imagines sexual relations only in the form of incest.

This engagement with the terms of modernist nativism is even more striking, if only because more extended, in Lawrence's major work of 1924, the novella *St. Mawr*, which ends with its heroine, Lou, accompanied by a "dispossessed Indian" (35), retaking possession of "her America" (25) on a ranch in New Mexico. St. Mawr himself is a "high-bred" (29) stallion who seems, like Cather's cliff dwellers, to belong to "another world" (35), "prehistoric"; "Perhaps the old Greek horses had lived in St. Mawr's world." And he is like the cliff dwellers also (or Jake Barnes or the Compson brothers or Zane Grey's and Oliver La Farge's Navajos) in his commitment to being the last of his line. "They raised him for stud purposes—but he didn't answer" (29), his groom tells his new American owner; the proof of "high" breeding is the impossibility of uncontaminated perpetuation.

But the reworking of the vanishing American as a vanishing horse turns out to mark in Lawrence a crucial difference from as well as an extension of the American discourse of modernist nativism. For where, in the nativist text, the refusal of procreation is identified with racial or cultural purity, with "breeding" itself, in Lawrence it is identified with a deeper reality and with masculinity. Thus Lou doesn't care at all about "St. Mawr's breeding" but only about "the horse himself, his real nature" (126), and the brilliant letter that she and her mother imagine sending to the woman who wishes to steal her husband and geld her horse reads: "*Miss Manby, you may have my husband but not my horse. My husband won't need emasculating, and my horse I won't have you meddle with. I'll preserve one last male thing in the museum of this world, if I can*" (97). The refusal to procreate in Lawrence signifies the refusal to belong to "our whole eunuch civilization" (96) (the refusal to perpetuate eunuchry) and marks instead one's allegiance to a world where maleness survives. And although *St. Mawr* finally locates this world in America, that location has nothing to do with American national or cultural identity. Indeed, "America" is as often as not a Dreiserian term in Lawrence, which is to say, a term that describes a set of social and economic ambitions rather than national ones; when Lou arrives at the incredibly remote ranch that will save her from civilization, she finds that the previous owner, a "true

American," has, despite the enormous difficulties, absurdly and pathetically "put in running water, taps, and wash-hand basins inside his house" (141).

What *St. Mawr* values, then, is not America as such but what it calls "wild America" (155), what is called in Lawrence's major American novel, *The Plumed Serpent* (1926), "savage" or "primeval" America.[171] This America is not a culture but an alternative to culture. Insofar as the American Indians are primitives, it may be found among them, but it may be found elsewhere as well: the "aboriginal" (135) Indian who accompanies Lou to New Mexico is doubled by the "aboriginal" (34) Welshman who accompanies her horse. And the maleness of the aborigines is guaranteed by analogy to the stallion. When the Indian asks the Welshman why St. Mawr "doesn't get any foals," the Welshman answers, "Doesn't want to, I should think. Same as me" (46). This proximity of man to the "prehistoric" horse in *St. Mawr* is expressed in *The Plumed Serpent* through the cult of Quetzacoatl, which restores its practitioners to the "old mode of consciousness" of the "ancient barbaric world" (175).[172] The "aboriginal" in "aboriginal America" (261) stands in opposition to "modern"[173] rather than "alien," which is to say that Lawrence's commitment to the "Indian pure and simple" has nothing to do with pluralism. Where, say, La Farge will explicitly value Indian culture, Lawrence values Indians insofar as they don't yet have a culture, insofar as they are different from someone like *The Plumed Serpent*'s heroine, Kate, who, like her friend Mrs. Norris, is a "daughter of culture" (33) and who can be rescued from it only by being brought "into unison" with the "old, antediluvian blood-male" (415).

Perhaps the sharpest contrast here is between Lawrence and Mary Austin. Austin explicitly distinguishes between the "aboriginal" and the "primitive," insisting in particular that "there may arise literary forms which are far from primitive without being any the less aboriginal" (*The American Rhythm*, 45). So where Lawrence represents the modern American (with his "wash-hand basins inside his house") as the antithesis of the aboriginal American, Austin sees a continuity between them and, in fact, describes her own interest in modern American literature as a consequence of her awakening "to the relationships that must necessarily exist between aboriginal and later American forms" (19). The aboriginal for Austin identifies a native and national culture; Stephen Crane, for example, seems to her a great American poet because he employs the "poetic modes" (53) of Southwest Indians like her informant, Washoe Charlie.

Lawrence's nonpluralism is thus the reverse face of his nonnational-ism. The "aboriginal," whether it's English, American, Welsh, Cornish, Indian, Mexican, Celtic, or Iberian (it's all these in either *St. Mawr* or *The Plumed Serpent*), marks for him the importance of a universal prehistory rather than a national history. His anthropology is developmental rather than pluralist, although, of course, the development counts for him not as progress but as decline. And his commitment to "blood" is in this respect significantly different from that of the nativist/pluralist Americans whom (in his American writings) he otherwise so closely resembles. "*Blood is one blood*" (416), *The Plumed Serpent* concludes, but what "one blood" means in Lawrence is not what it means in the American writers of the '20s. We know how central the citation of Acts 17:26—God "hath made of one blood all nations of men"—was to the nineteenth century critique of racism, and Sollors points out that, as late as 1920, W. E. B. Du Bois was proclaiming his belief in a God "who made of one blood all nations that on earth do dwell."[174] But when Sara Smolinski's husband-to-be says to her, "You and I, we are of one blood" (278), he is not reminding her of the universal identity of all human beings, he is reminding her that they come from the same part of Poland. In *Bread Givers*, to be "of one blood" is to be fellow Jews, "*Landsleute*—countrymen," and in nativist pluralism more generally blood is what *constitutes* groups rather than what eliminates them: Jason Compson's "blood is blood" is meant to assert his identity with his niece Quentin and their shared difference from the man in the red tie. But when, at the end of *The Plumed Serpent*, Kate is made to lose any sense of her difference from her Indian servant—"*The blood is one blood. In the blood, you and I are undifferentiated*" (416)—Lawrence's "blood-consciousness" is being invoked on behalf of a primitivist universalism, one that transcends the boundaries of race and nationality.

Lawrence's primitivism, and especially his universalism, will help us to distinguish between American nativist modernism—the central topic of this book—and what might be described as its regional and international variants, a regional modernism being one that deploys the technologies of identitarianism without quite rising to the level of the national, and an international modernism being one that deploys those same technologies at a level meant to transcend the national. Robinson Jeffers's long poem *Tamar* (1924), for example, was inspired (according to Jeffers) not only by the "Biblical story" and by "a reminiscence of Shelley's *Cenci*" but also by "the strange, introverted and storm-twisted beauty of Point Lobos."[175] Tributes to the beauty of the California coast are, of course, conventional in Jeffers, but geography plays a particularly explicit role in *Tamar*: the place Tamar chooses for making contact with the dead aunt who slept with Tamar's father (as she, Tamar, has slept with her own brother) turns out to have been sacred to the Indians, and Tamar must be ritually "used" by the "dead tribe" (26) before she can speak to the spirit of her predecessor. The "sterile and sacred" (16) love of brother and sister is thus articulated as intercourse with Indians, its "sacred" character guaranteed by the fact that the Indians have died out and so are "spirits" or "Gods," its sterility guaranteed by the ultimate death of Tamar and all her family in a fire that leaves nothing but the famous "wind-torn" "old trees" of Point Lobos intact.

It's particularly striking, in this context, that the death of Tamar's brother/lover keeps him from joining the American expeditionary force in France or, as Tamar understands it, from crawling into the "strange beds" (53) of "black-eyed French girls" (63). The war, in Tamar's reading, represents her brother's desire to "go out," and the fire makes sure that no one will go out. It's as if, in *The Professor's House*, Rosamond had taken "possession" of the vanished cliff dwellers' Mesa *with* Tom and then had killed him before he went off to the war for fear that the Germans might not—for fear that he and she might not, like their new ancestors the Indians, vanish. The only thing *Tamar* lacks to make its "introverted" landscape and its Indians truly national is a Louie Marsellus. Or, to put the point differently, the Frenchness of the "French girls" isn't quite enough to make Tamar preeminently American. It is in this respect that *Tamar* should be understood as close to *St. Mawr* or *The Plumed Serpent*, texts which produce the structure of nativist modernism without the nativism; regionalism in Jeffers, like primitivism in Lawrence, displaces nationalism.[176]

But it is the international rather than the regional alternative to the native that matters most here. Although Williams described Pound and Eliot as the dogs who left the United States to run "after the rabbits,"[177] it's not difficult to see what I have described as nativist elements in their work. Most obvious, no doubt, is the anti-Semitism; if it's hard to find equivalents to Louie Marsellus or Robert Cohn in Jeffers, it's easy to find them in Eliot ("But this or such was Bleistein's way:/A saggy bending of the knees/And elbows with the palms turned out,/Chicago Semite Viennese")[178] and impossible to miss them in Pound ("Remarked Ben: better keep out the jews/or yr/grand children will curse you/jews, real jews, chazims, and *neschek*/also super-neschek or the international racket").[179] And at least as important as the anti-Semitism is the accompanying interest in those poets whom Eliot described as his "ancestors" or in those figures from American history—"Jefferson, Quincy Adams, old John Adams, Jackson, Van Buren"—whom Pound described as constituting our "cultural heritage."[180] Pound's "heritage" and Eliot's "tradition" both participate in the genealogical discourse that nativism made central to the work of art and to the idea of culture.

But to begin thinking about Pound and Eliot in this way is immediately to see the nonnativist purposes to which the discourse of genealogy could also be put. For the endpoint of the "heritage" whose origin Pound locates in Jefferson is, as his title suggests, Benito Mussolini: "The heritage of Jefferson . . . is HERE, NOW in *the Italian peninsula* at the beginning of the fascist second decennio, not in Massachusetts or Delaware."[181] This "heritage" is thus in no way distinctively American, any more than it is distinctively Italian. Rather, it is disassociated from any particular nationality and, indeed, from nationality as such, a concept which Pound tended to link disparagingly with "provincialism."[182] And, by the same token, the "ancestors" to whom Eliot appeals in "Tradition and the Individual Talent" (1919) not only extend beyond (insofar as they even include) his American predecessors to "the whole of the literature of Europe" but beyond Europe as well to "all the poetry that has ever been written."[183] Neither Eliot's "tradition" nor Pound's "heritage" is in any sense *national*; in them, as in related figures like Lawrence and E. M. Forster, the deployment of race is more or less explicitly disarticulated from the nation and committed instead to the formation of a distinctively nonnational community.

Along similar lines, Hannah Arendt has identified modern European racism generally with the "decline of the European nation-state" (9) and with the effort, embodied in what she calls the "pan-movements" ("Pan-Germanism," "Pan-Slavism," etc.) to transcend "the narrow bounds of a national community" by asserting the primacy of "a folk community that would remain a political factor even if its members were dispersed all over the earth" (232). There were no plausibly parallel "pan-movements" in Britain or the United States, but the increasing insistence, especially in Britain,[184] on the irreconcilable antinomy in liberalism between the individual and society suggests what the advantage of race in the constitution of a community would be, especially to those who understood themselves as committed above all to the primacy of the individual. Where, for example, a nativist writer like Williams famously derived the "pure products of America" from the "isolate" character of American life, Lawrence, in the same year (1923), insisted even more strongly than Williams on the "isolate" character of the "essential American soul,"[185] but immediately complicated that insistence both with respect to national identity and, indeed, to any collective identity at all, by generalizing it: "The central law of all organic life is that each organism is intrinsically isolate and single in itself" (66). In this formulation, not only is there nothing distinctively American about the "isolate," but also the reference to collective identities implicit in terms like "American" and (the one Lawrence uses most frequently) "white" is compromised by the radical individualism explicit in the claim that "each organism is . . . single in itself" and is, in fact, as Lawrence goes on to say, destroyed when its "isolation breaks down." How, for instance, can Moby Dick be simultaneously "isolate" (165) and "the deepest blood-being of the white race" (160)? How, more fundamentally, can the idea that "men are only free when they are doing what the deepest self likes" be reconciled with the claim that men are only "free when they belong to a living, organic, *believing* community" (6)?

It is, of course, the perceived inability to answer this question that names the crisis of liberalism; at the same time, however, to put the question in this way, to emphasize the problem posed by Lawrence's individualism for the possibility of a "community," is immediately to see the utility to him of the concept of race. For if the danger of what Lawrence calls in *Studies in Classic American Literature* the "social" (47 and passim) is the danger of the "merge," and the consequent failure to "listen in isolation to the isolate Holy Ghost" who "speaks individually inside each individual" and never to "the general world" (79), that danger is met precisely by conceiving the "community" as a "race" rather than as a society. The individual may be enticed from his or her individuality by the social but not by the racial since, while the idea of race refers to others outside the individual, it in no way depends upon any social relation to them. Lawrence likes to quote a remark he attributes to La Bruyère, "*Tous nos malheurs viennent de ne pouvoir être seuls*" (81, 142); if your "community" is your "race," you can belong to it while remaining alone. Thus Cooper's Deerslayer is an "isolate" who is at the same time "pure white" (63); the replacement of the social by the racial makes it possible for "isolate" to be simultaneously and without contradiction an individual and a collective term.[186]

The prominence of race in Lawrence's writing of the early and mid-'20s can thus be understood in structural terms—that is, without necessary reference to his beliefs about the virtues or faults of any particular racial group—since the idea of race embodies for him a collective entity that does not jeopardize the "integrity" (61) of the individual, whose "soul" can be simultaneously "white" and "alone, for ever alone" (61). And it is this possibility of deploying the technology of race *against* the "social" or against what Forster in *A Passage to India* (1924) calls "the herd-instinct" and on behalf instead of a community of "individuals"[187] that makes racism so attractive. I use the term "technology of race" here because *A Passage to India* speaks disdainfully of "racial feeling"; indeed, Fielding is said to have "no racial feeling" because, unlike his fellow Anglo-Indians, "he had matured" in an "atmosphere where the herd-instinct does not flourish" (65). At the same time, however, and despite the disdain for "racial feeling," the fact that, say, the Nawab Bahadur's automobile accident involves an encounter with a ghost immediately assumes the status of what Forster calls a "racial secret": "None of the English people knew of this, nor did the chauffeur [who is "Eurasian"]; it was a racial secret communicable more by blood than by speech" (106). "Blood," insofar as it can be opposed to "speech," seems to designate a link that is more than merely social, more, that is, than the influence of "atmosphere." The "racial secret" that can be communicated only by blood runs deeper than the "racial feeling" that is merely a kind of conformism.

"Blood," then, is deployed by Forster to produce a community that will not be a "herd," and its appeal is complicated but not compromised by the fact that although the "English people" are said not to know of the ghost, at least one English person, Mrs. Moore, *does* know. It is she who, hearing of the accident, shivers and says, "A ghost!" (194). So the "racial secret" can be somehow interracial; the relevant blood needn't be the blood of Indians. And this point is made even more sharply by the return of Mrs. Moore in the religious festival of "Temple" where Professor Godbole not only remembers her but, remembering her memories, *becomes* her. Losing himself in the "universal warmth," Godbole, "though she was not important to him, remembered an old woman he had met in Chandrapore . . . and he impelled her by his spiritual force to that place where completeness can be found. . . . His senses grew thinner, he remembered a wasp seen he forgot where, perhaps on a stone. He loved the wasp equally. . . ." (321). The wasp is, of course, the wasp encountered by Mrs. Moore while hanging up her cloak some three hundred pages and three years earlier; it has never been seen by Godbole and his ability now to remember it requires that his memory of Mrs. Moore be transformed into an identification with Mrs. Moore. Just as Mrs. Moore's knowledge of the ghost linked her to the Nawab Bahadur, Professor Godbole's knowledge of the wasp links him to Mrs. Moore; "spiritual force" repeats the work of "blood."

This is what it means for Forster to be committed to at least the technologies of race. We have already noticed the compatibility between the commitment to race and a certain spiritualism—in Dixon, the Klan consists of the reincarnated souls of Scots clansmen. In Hopkins, the racialization of the reincarnated soul goes one step further; when *Of One Blood*'s hero visits the home of his African ancestors, he is "surprised" to find "that it all seems familiar to me, as if somewhere in the past I had known just such a city as this" (551). This phenomenon is explained in the text by "Plato's doctrine" of "the soul's transmigration" (478); sights that were familiar to Reuel's ancestors can be, at first sight, familiar to him too because he *is* his ancestors. "The Ego preserves its individuality after the dissolution of the body" (562), the Ethiopians say; it is the fact that the "Ego" reincarnated in Reuel's body has already ruled in Ethiopia that allows Reuel to remember things he seems to be experiencing for the first time.[188] And if the naive literalism of Dixon and Hopkins might seem to consign them to the prehistory of cultural identity, we have only to remember that the imagination of the experiences of the dead as one's own, the transformation of history into memory, lies at the heart of Cather's *Death Comes for the Archbishop*. It is the understanding of "European civilization" as the archbishop's "memories" and of Pecos "tradition" as Jacinto's "experience" that turns the things they know into the things they are.[189]

But where, in Cather, the point of such transformations is to establish the irrevocable separateness of identities—"The Mexicans were always Mexicans, the Indians were always Indians"; it's this that counts as Cather's nativism—in Forster, the technologies of racial identity explicitly cross racial lines, a fact that suggests the irrelevance for Forster of those differences that for nativist writers constitute the essence of the commitment to racial identity. While *A Passage to India* is at least as concerned with making men brothers as its nativist counterparts (like *The Professor's House*), the "brotherhood" it idealizes, even in irony—"the brother Aryan"—is explicitly "universal." Thus the misogyny that in the nativist text understands marriage as the miscegenated destruction of the family functions in Forster as a way of acquiring brothers rather than (as in Cather, Faulkner, et al.) as a way of losing sisters. Since only brothers are allowed to see wives in purdah, allowing one's friend to see one's wife is a way of welcoming him to the family: "All men are my brothers, and as soon as one behaves as such he may see my wife" (125), Aziz tells Fielding. He believes "in the purdah" because it is through the purdah that the friend can be acknowledged as and hence transformed into a brother. Thus *A Passage to India* is as replete with intense male friendship as anything in Cather or Hemingway, but where in the nativist text this fraternity is made *necessary* by the propensity of women to "go out," in Forster it is made *possible* by the ability of men to keep them in. Where the promiscuous woman threatens the difference between families, the veiled woman promises to make all families one.

It is this deployment of the categories of race on behalf of what it calls "something universal" (160) that identifies *A Passage to India* as a text decisively influenced by imperialism rather than nativism and concerned therefore with imagining the terms of relation between the British and the Indians rather than with insisting, in the nativist mode, on their differences. Thus, even when those differences are foregrounded (as in the condescension of the ordinary "Turton and Burton" "sahib" and even of Fielding—"They always do something disappointing" [192]), the question of superiority or inferiority is always relevant and hence a common scale of assessment is always assumed. And when, more typically, those differences are diminished, then the promise of brotherhood and friendship becomes explicit—everyone will get to be an "individual." It is as if in Forster the imperial encounter were the vehicle for the universalization of judgment, which must now involve "all men" (125, 321), "everything" (165), "the whole universe" (321), "nothing" (165). These terms are quoted from two affectively very different contexts, Professor Godbole's ecstatic celebration of the birth of the god in the temple and Mrs. Moore's enervating encounter with the echo in the Marabar caves. But the difference in affect serves only to highlight the elimination of "distinction" (163) that is in both cases its object. What is imperialist (and not nativist) about *A Passage to India* is neither its endorsement (there is none) of British rule in India nor its critique of British rule in India but its commitment to judgments that will include both Indians and British. It is imperialist, then, in the sense that it is *antinationalist*, and so it cannot be anti-imperialist because anti-imperialism would involve the kind of commitment to Indian nationalism that Forster explicitly repudiates: "India a nation! What an apotheosis! Last comer to the drab nineteenth-century sisterhood!" (361).[190]

Regarding India's aspirations to nationhood as an anachronism, For-

ster identifies modernity with an imperial universality as explicit as anything in Pound or Eliot. The crimes committed by the British in India are
not, in Forster, committed by Britain against India; because Eliot's "tradition" and Pound's "heritage" are crucially international, the opponents of
tradition and the traducers of heritage are enemies of civilization rather
than of the United States or Britain or Italy. Whether or not Arendt's
dissociation of German anti-Semitism from German nationalism accurately describes the Nazis, the disarticulation of anti-Semitism from anything corresponding to American nationalism is certainly true of Pound
and Eliot. Whereas the emergence of nativist modernism involved, as I
have suggested, the transformation of the opposition between black and
white into an opposition between Indian and Jew, there are in Pound and
Eliot no Indians. The exhortation of Pound's Ben Franklin to "keep out
the Jews/or yr/grand children will curse you" is not, as it would be in
Stoddard, a plea to keep the nation's bloodlines pure (to keep your grandchildren from *becoming* Jewish), it is a plea to save them from the threat
to civilization that the Jews will inevitably pose. Prohibiting Jewish immigration would, in this view, contribute to making America better rather
than, as in the nativist view, to making it more American.

Another way to put this is to say that for Pound and Eliot, as for
Lawrence and Forster, the question of pluralism never arises. Pluralism
is, as we have seen, at the heart of nativism; the point of substituting
"country" for "right or wrong" is to replace the implicit appeal to universal standards with an explicit reliance on one's own position, in respect to
which everything is either "native" or "alien." From the standpoint of
pluralism, the inevitable preference one has for one's own race or culture
must in principle be dissociated from a conviction of that culture's superiority since the very notions of superiority and inferiority imply the
possibility of common criteria of judgment and thus undermine pluralism's foundational commitment to difference. But the European racism
that would emerge triumphant in Nazism was in no sense committed to
the primacy of difference over the axis of superiority and inferiority. The
"Volkish view," Hitler wrote in *Mein Kampf*, "by no means believes in an
equality of the races, but along with their difference it recognizes their
higher or lesser value."[191] For Hitler, the problem with the Jews was not,
as it was for American nativism, that they had a different (un-American
or un-German) culture, but that they had no culture: "The Jewish people,
despite all apparent intellectual qualities, is without any true culture,
especially without any culture of its own."[192] So even though, in the end,

only the Aryan race may properly possess it, culture, for Hitler, is not, as it is for nativism, an irreducibly racial concept. It is, instead, a set of "values" which, embodied in a single race, nevertheless transcends that race to serve as the yardstick against which all races can be measured.

Hence the irrelevance of nationality to international modernism. As early as 1917 (in "Provincialism the Enemy," the essay quoted above) and as late as 1938 (in "National Culture"), Pound condemned the distinction between native and alien, which is to say, the distinction between nations as such, as a form of provincialism.[193] This provincialism shows itself in the "aping of foreign modes" (163) just because they are foreign and in the "fear of accepting foreign work" for the same reason; it shows itself in the "boosting" of inferior work "*because* it is produced at home" or in the "neglect" of superior work for the same reason. Ultimately the very idea of a national culture turns out to constitute a kind of oxymoron. A "developed" national culture "must of necessity include criteria which are, as criteria, capable of comparison with the best alien criteria" (163). But since the relevance of the criteria derives from their being the "best," it isn't at all clear what it means to think of them as "alien" (or native); so "in one sense it can almost be said," Pound concludes, "there are no alien criteria." The difference between better and worse renders the difference between native and alien irrelevant; the international becomes the universal.[194]

This elimination of both the native and the alien as criteria for judgment and the suggestion that the very notion of a criterion undermines the distinction between the native and the alien make Pound's aspirations to "culture" as universalist as Lawrence's contempt for it. Indeed, Pound's commitment to culture is in this respect absolutely interchangeable with Lawrence's primitivism and sometimes emerges as, in fact, a form of primitivism. Thus the *Cantos* begin with a translation of what Pound thought was the oldest part of the *Odyssey*, or rather a translation of a Renaissance Latin translation of the *Odyssey*, rendered in an English that refers to his own translation of Old English in "The Seafarer." The commitment here is to a notion of the aboriginal that, like Lawrence's (but unlike Austin's or Hemingway's, whose Indian "aborigines" are "the only real Americans" [*Torrents*, 63]), is the same everywhere. It doesn't matter, in other words, what place the aborigine is aboriginal to. The *Cantos* are in this respect an anthology of aboriginal moments, juxtaposed to each other not in celebration of their difference but as a way of insisting on their essential similarity. And the translatability of these moments—the conception of culture itself as an effort of translation—only underlines those similarities, producing out of an array of the international the effect of the universal.

Pound's deployment of the Chinese ideogram is exemplary in this regard. Rather than serving as a mark of cultural difference, a sign that must be presented in the original because (like "Cohn") it cannot be translated, the ideogram represents for him a utopian transcendence even of the necessity for translation; this is the meaning of his fantasy about the sculptor Gaudier's ability to understand "the primitive Chinese ideographs" without knowing Chinese and only because "he was so accustomed to observe the dominant line in objects."[195] Art here is identified with universality, as it is in Lawrence where the "music" of the Indians is said to go "straight through to the soul, the most ancient and everlasting soul of all men, where alone can the human family assemble in immediate contact" (*Plumed Serpent*, 126). Thus the *Cantos* (ranging through Europe, China, and America) are meant as a kind of universal history, the tracing *through* culture of Pound's version of those values that Lawrence sought *before* culture.

The Chinese ideogram and the music of the Indian can both stand as universalist counterparts to the untranslatable text of nativist modernism. The nativist text—the text that must not merely mean but *be* American—can only be destroyed by translation. It is, one might say, irreducibly aboriginal since it can exist only in its original language. Pound's Chinese ideogram and Lawrence's Indian music universalize the aboriginal, transforming the text that cannot be translated into the text that need not be translated. Like the Reverend Shegog's sermon in *The Sound and the Fury*, they speak directly to the "heart," "beyond the need for words." But where the Reverend Shegog's sermon is identified with the emergence of racial identity (as his "pronunciation" becomes "negroid") and where the audience for that sermon presents the family ("Breddren en sistuhn") as the model of the race, in Pound and Lawrence the truly "human family" makes racial specificity disappear. Pluralist or nativist racism makes racial difference constitutive of the human; universalist or imperialist racism makes racial difference a failure to be fully human.[196]

Passing

I N HIS 1926 novel of Harlem life, *Nigger Heaven*, Carl Van Vechten's heroine, Mary, puts on a show of African sculpture at the library where she works, a show that is dismissed by some of her older friends as "the work of heathen savages." "They were our ancestors," Mary says in their defense, but this makes no impression. " 'Of course,' Hester replied, 'everybody goes back to savages, but it does no good to unearth that sort of thing.' "[197] This exchange, as Van Vechten understands it, pits those who wish to reclaim what he calls their "primitive birthright" (89) against those whom he describes as "ashamed" of that birthright. But it is only by linking that birthright to Africa and marking it racially that Van Vechten makes it possible for anyone to be either proud or ashamed of it; "everybody goes back to savages," as Hester says, but the fact that the Negro's ancestors can be located not only in the past (in, say, the caves of Lascaux, Altamira, and other sites of modernist primitivism) but in the present—in Africa—transforms what Van Vechten thinks of as the primitiveness of the Negro from a particular relation to the historical past into a particular relation to the racial present. The primitiveness of the Negro race, in other words, consists not in the fact that it has only recently begun to be civilized and is therefore *closer* to the primitive but rather in the fact that it resists civilization and therefore *is* primitive. The "civilized races," Van Vechten says, are "struggling" to "get back to" the primitive. Modernism ("the art of a Picasso or a Stravinsky") is for them an essentially historical effort to recover something they have lost; for Mary, it is the racial effort to be who she is.

The difference in affect between Mary and Hester—one wishing to celebrate the primitive past, the other to repudiate it—is not, in other words, the difference that matters. What matters is that Mary has a properly genealogical relation to her ancestors, seeing them as sources of identity, whereas Hester sees them as points of comparison. Naturally, once you start comparing yourself to savages, it is possible to think of the comparison as cutting both ways. In *The Age of Innocence* (1920), Edith Wharton evokes the discourse of the primitive (the "tribe," the "clan") in ways that repeatedly raise the question of whether the past—the age of innocence—was better or worse than the present. But the answer to this question is less important than the technology that must be put in place in order for it to be asked. The "books on Primitive Man" that Wharton's "people of advanced culture were beginning to read"[198] provide the terms—from primitive to advanced—that will make comparison possible. These are the books Wharton herself had read, concerned with the historical development of civilization out of savagery, and *The Age of Innocence* is offered as a contribution to this history. Its repeated invocation of the "tribal" is thus meant as a reminder of the continuities between the "primitive" and the "advanced," and its anthropology is that of the conjectural history rather than the plural description, the transition from nature to culture, not the difference between cultures.

Simply put, *The Age of Innocence* is a historical novel. This is, of course, literally true since it is set in the (fairly recent) past, but the point here is that its anthropology, unlike *Nigger Heaven's*, is a historical anthropology, committed to the narrative links (more or less primitive, more or less advanced) between societies that the new pluralism will regard as essentially *different* and unlinked by the kind of genetic account that would make comparisons between them (more primitive, more advanced) possible.[199] The importance of this narrative element to *The Age of Innocence* is foregrounded in its title, which identifies innocence with a historical epoch rather than, say, a particular place, and the novel's ironizing of the title—the questions it raises about who really is innocent and about what innocence is—in no way undermines or ironizes this commitment to narrative. Producing increasingly subtle questions about what the narrative really means is a way of *asserting* its power, not reducing it. The twenty-five-year gap between the novel's final two chapters positively insists upon the power of linear narrative: "If things go on at this pace," someone says in chapter 33, "our children" will end up marrying "Beaufort's bastards" (1284); in chapter 34, Newland Archer's son is indeed about to marry the illegitimate daughter of Archer's old enemy, Julius Beaufort. Even Wharton's numerous and somewhat crude technological foreshadowings—"there were people who thought there would someday be a tunnel under the Hudson" (1241)—are mustered to confirm the vision of the present as an organic development out of the past—the vision of a single "culture" (for better or for worse) "advancing." It is this model that the pluralizing of culture will challenge; in the logic of pluralism, no culture can be more or less "advanced" than any other, no culture more or less "primitive" than any other.

If, then, *The Age of Innocence* presents itself as a history of what it calls "the Family," what Wharton means by family is very different from what nativist writers like Cather and Gould would mean by it. The family in Wharton is social, not racial. And if we think of society as the ultimate hero of *The Age of Innocence* (in that its heroic figures, Archer and Ellen Olenska, *are* heroic insofar as they are most deeply committed to society's "discipline" [1271]), then we can see what it means for Wharton's "tribe" to multiply rather than vanish. For in the degree to which the survival of "the Family" is crucial in *The Age of Innocence*, its genealogical purity isn't. That's why the fact that "Beaufort's bastards" will not only be eventually accepted but will—in the person of Fanny Beaufort—actually marry Archer's son counts as a happy ending. That there are losses as well as gains from this process is obvious; the novel is simultaneously committed to the idea that the 1870s were better than its present and to the idea that they were worse. But the survival of something called "society"—the ability of "the Family" by sometimes excluding and sometimes including to continue—is strengthened rather than jeopardized by the threat of illegitimacy. The contrast to texts like *The Professor's House* and *The Sound and the Fury* could hardly be sharper. For in these texts, the survival of the family means the survival not of the society but of the race, and the illegitimate children who represent the continuation of the one have become the miscegenated children who represent the extinction of the other. Society has a history, which is to say that everyone in it descends from someone; race has a genealogy, which is to say that you can't know whether or not you're in it unless you know which ones you descend from.

Thus, where Wharton constructs a primitivism without race, Van Vechten, trading in the universality of savage ancestry ("everybody goes back to savages") for the particularity of racial ancestry ("they were *our* ancestors"), turns the primitive into the racial. And attaching African sculpture to the American Negro instead of to white Europeans, he simultaneously turns the cultural into the racial. African sculpture, Alain Locke wrote in *The New Negro*, has been ignored by American Negroes while serving as "a mine of fresh *motifs*" for modernist Europeans; surely, he argues, "this art can scarcely have less influence upon the blood descendants, bound to it by a sense of direct cultural kinship, than upon those who inherit by tradition only, and through the channels of an exotic curiosity and interest" (256). In Locke, as in Van Vechten, African sculpture is crucially racial. As the idea of the primitive gets connected to the idea of race it gets disconnected, in other words, from the idea of people who have no culture and gets connected instead with the idea of people whose culture is based on their race.

What this means is that the primitive becomes a criterion of racial and cultural authenticity—when you become less primitive you become racially inauthentic. Thus, in nativist modernism, modernization begins to be understood as racial betrayal, and both the primitive and the modern begin to be separated from the history of the development of civilization in which they had their origin. The more closely you identify the primitive with the Negro, for example, the less you identify those qualities deemed primitive with the early stages of civilization as such. Nativist primitivism, in other words, redescribed the primitive not as a stage through which all civilizations eventually passed but as an expression of racial identity. In this respect, the beliefs and practices associated with the uncivilized character of the primitive could be immediately redescribed as the beliefs and practices associated with the civilization of the Negro. Thus the distinctly racial character of modernist primitivism in America (its identification with racial authenticity) begins to transform it into the pluralism that would leave the idea of the primitive behind. Insofar as Negroes who might produce European-looking art could be regarded not as having become (for better or for worse) more civilized but rather as having become less Negro, the differences between African and European art could no longer be measured on the single linear scale—less civilized, more civilized—implied by the term "primitive." In this respect, the racialization of the primitive—its transformation into a criterion of racial authenticity—puts the primitive to use in replacing the idea of a single culture (which some races had more of and some races less of) with the idea of plural cultures, one in equal amounts for each race.

Hence the "primitive birthright" that Mary hopes to reclaim is the birthright of race, the "birthright" that the "Ex-Colored Man" of James Weldon Johnson's *The Autobiography of an Ex-Colored Man* (first published in 1912 and reprinted, with an introduction by Van Vechten, in 1927) laments that he has sold "for a mess of pottage."[200] What the ex-colored man means by his "birthright" is, of course, something more literal than anything meant by Van Vechten's characters; with skin the color of "ivory" (11), he has stopped identifying himself as "Negro" and has lived instead as a white man. But the possibility of passing—the imagination of a racial identity that must be affirmed or denied as well as embodied—is central to *Nigger Heaven*'s minidrama of racial pride and, more importantly, to the constitution of racial identity as a project.

The ex-colored man's response to being told that he's not white is to look "long and earnestly" (11) into a mirror, but it is, of course, of the essence of his situation that no mirror can reveal the truth of his race. The

Supreme Court decision that gave Jim Crow legislation the final stamp of federal approval, *Plessy v. Ferguson* (1896) had grounded the "legal distinction" between "the white and colored races" in "the color of the two races" and had described it as a distinction that would "always exist so long as white men are distinguished from the other race by color."[201] But it is one of the famous ironies of this case in particular and of the American system of racial classification more generally that the color of Homer Plessy's skin was so light that his arrest for riding in a white-only streetcar had to be arranged. The racial difference that the Court "founded in the color of the two races" was not visible in Homer Plessy's skin, and, indeed, the literature of the period is replete with anecdotes of the puzzles made possible by first the identification and then the separation of race and color. Booker T. Washington, for example, describes the dilemma of a conductor confronted in the Jim Crow car with "a man so white that even an expert would have hard work to classify him as a black man"; he "looked him over carefully, examining his hair, eyes, nose, and hands. . . . Finally, to solve the difficulty, he stooped over and peeped at the man's feet."[202] And one of the characters in Frances Harper's *Iola Leroy* (1892) is so white that his friends jokingly urge him to wear a "label" saying "I am a colored man" so that his presence in the "colored car" won't be challenged.[203]

Suggesting, at the very least, as Washington put it, "how difficult it sometimes is to know where the black begins and the white ends,"[204] such stories might plausibly be thought to highlight a certain arbitrariness in the taxonomies of race in America, an arbitrariness made dazzlingly clear in the Supreme Court's insistence that racial identity was a function of "physical differences" and its simultaneous acknowledgment that what exactly those physical differences might be—that is, what "proportion of colored blood" was "necessary to constitute a colored person"—varied from state to state. "Legislation is powerless to eradicate racial instincts or to abolish distinctions based upon physical differences," the Court wrote in *Plessy*.[205] But the question of which racial instincts were ineradicably Homer Plessy's could only be determined according to the laws of the state of Louisiana.

What's most striking about this racial logic, however, is not its incoherence but its utility in making racial identity *more* rather than less important. In *Iola Leroy*, for example, the point about light-skinned Negroes needing labels is not that racial identification is arbitrary and meaningless but that Negroes who could pass for white choose not to. And while in *Iola Leroy* that choice is made for reasons that are not themselves racial—Harper's characters feel they can do more good working among poor Negroes as a Negro, or they scorn to conceal from the white world the "one drop" of Negro blood in their veins—the meaning of passing and of the options it makes available will more characteristically revolve around the emergence of race itself as an object of affect. Thus, even though much of her ancestry is white and although she has been mainly raised by the white members of her family, Clare, in Nella Larsen's *Passing* (1929), is condemned not merely for what amounts to pretending to be white, but more importantly for showing that she "cared nothing for the race. She only belonged to it."[206] Passing is thus understood first as a failure of affection and second as the occasion of its success, since Clare's self-imposed exile from her race produces in her an increasing and over-whelming desire "to see Negroes, to be with them again, to talk with them, to hear them laugh" (200). The estrangement made possible by the identification of and discrepancy between skin color and racial identity is the enabling condition of Clare's emotional rehabilitation here; it is just because she has been able to disguise the fact that she belongs to her race that Clare has learned to care for it.

This point is made even more powerfully in Larsen's first novel, *Quicksand* (1928), where the object of attachment is not merely the particular race to which its heroine, Helga, belongs but the fact of race itself and where the desire produced is not just to be "with" Negroes but to *be* Negro. Helga is the child of a black American and a white Dane, and, although not as light-skinned as Clare, she begins the novel feeling neither black nor white and yearning for the experience of "belonging to herself alone and not to a race" (64). A visit to her mother's family in Denmark and the prospect of marriage to a Dane offer precisely this escape from racial classification but, in Denmark, Helga herself becomes the enforcer of racial identity on the American plan, opposing "mixed marriages, 'between races,' " and disdaining her aunt's arguments that such prohibitions are not to be taken seriously "in connection with individuals" (78). Indeed, the commitment to individuality becomes entirely secondary in Helga's explanation of her refusal to marry the Danish artist Olsen: it's because "she couldn't marry a white man"; "It isn't you, not just personal. . . . It's deeper, broader than that. It's racial" (88).

But this transcendence of the "personal" by the "racial" is not a simple replacement of an individual by a collective identity. Rather, the "irresistible ties of race" (92) now occupy the site of the individuality to which they had seemed to be opposed: "it's just something—something deep down inside of me" (91). In general, it is the possibility of passing that will locate race "deep down inside";[207] here, it is the possibility of losing race altogether. Helga's departure from Denmark is her refusal to be "herself" by being "unique"; "homesick, not for America, but for Negroes," she returns to the United States to claim as her own an irreducibly racialized self. And although it is Negroes, not America, that she misses, the Negroes she misses can exist only in America; only under American laws of racial identity can the thing that's "deep down inside" of Helga be her race; only in America can she be herself by being Negro.[208]

A performance of Dvořák's *New World* Symphony with its "wailing undertones of 'Swing Low, Sweet Chariot' " (92) brings Helga to the "definite decision" to go back to America. A version of that symphony had played a crucial role also in Zangwill's *The Melting-Pot*, where a performance of the Jew David Quixano's *American* Symphony (at a settlement house, on a *shabbos* that is also the 4th of July) marks Quixano's final repudiation of his past, his marriage to the daughter of the Russian nobleman who murdered his family back in Kishineff, and his complete submersion in the "crucible" of America. But where the music helps David "forget" his past and the last sight of his Jewish father, the music helps Helga come to terms with hers and for the first time feel "sympathy" with her black father. The technologies of assimilation are reimagined as technologies of racial identification; it's the prospect of making classical music out of "modern rag-time" and "the old slave songs" (104) that causes the ex-colored man, like Helga, to return from Europe to America. Traveling "back into the very heart of the South" to live among his "people" and "drink in . . . inspiration," he imagines himself claiming his "birthright"; recoiling in "shame" at the sight of a lynching and deciding to pass for white, he imagines himself repudiating it (104, 139). What matters here is not which choice the narrator makes but the fact that he must choose. Because the "ivory"-skinned narrator has the option of denying his race, he also has the option of affirming it. And because denial and affirmation are understood as the repudiation or acceptance of a "birthright," the choice the narrator makes is represented less (as in *Iola Leroy*) as a question of personal honesty and more (as in *Quicksand*) as a question of personal identity. But in taking race beyond the question of personal integrity, Johnson also begins to take it beyond the question of self-discovery. For what the ex-colored man starts to regret about his refusal to identify himself as a Negro is not that he has told a lie about himself or even that he has misunderstood himself but that he has missed his opportunity to be himself.

In *The Autobiography of an Ex-Colored Man*, this opportunity—what I referred to above as the *project* of racial identity—is called, with some irony, "making a Negro out of yourself" (106). The irony depends on what seems to the ex-colored man's white employer the implausibility of the ex-colored man—"by blood, by appearance, by education, and by tastes a white man" (105)—presenting himself or even thinking of himself as black. And, inasmuch as the narrator finds it entirely possible to live his life as a white man, the irony seems justified. The function of his final regret, however, his lament for his lost birthright, is precisely to eliminate the irony, and the point of the narrator's whiteness turns out to be the justification rather than the ironization of the effort to make Negroes.[209] It is precisely because he doesn't seem to be black that the ex-colored man can imagine the need to make himself black. And, in fact, the idea that racial identity is in some sense *made* is characteristically associated with passing for the obvious reason that the possibility of passing foregrounds the role of choice, emphasizing at the very least the element of acceptance that must accompany inheritance in the transmission of a "birthright."

But the idea that racial identity must be created as well as embodied can by no means be limited to those whose physical appearance seems racially ambiguous. Mary, the heroine of *Nigger Heaven*, has skin that's a "rich golden-brown" (25), but it is she, rather than the light-skinned young man she eventually falls in love with, who feels that, like the ex-colored man, she has somehow "lost or forfeited her birthright" (89). What she has lost in particular is the ability to "let herself go" (90), especially with men, and since she identifies this ability with Negro "savagery," she experiences her sexual priggishness as racial failure. In this way, the familiar plight of the novelistic heroine who thinks of herself as immune to sex and then falls head over heels in love is transformed into a drama of racial identity. In other words, insofar as the inability to fall in love is understood as a failure to be black enough, actually falling in love becomes a way of affirming one's blackness. Reclaiming one's racial birthright here goes beyond not pretending to be white when you're really black; it involves more, that is, than the "race pride" displayed by Mary's light-skinned lover when he refuses to pass. For racial pride is supplemented in *Nigger Heaven* by what is understood to be racially appropriate behavior. Mary doesn't need to have the ex-colored man's ivory skin in order to feel something like the necessity of making herself a Negro. If racial identity can involve not just having the right "blood" and not just having the right attitude toward your "blood" but—crucially—having the feelings and exhibiting the behavior that are appropriate to the blood, then you don't have to have ivory skin to try to pass. And you don't have to have ivory skin to refuse to pass. The addition of racially appropriate behavior to the concept of racial identity makes the technology of passing (and the dramas of racial fulfillment and betrayal enabled by that technology) available to everyone.

In Johnson, the ex-colored man's employer maintains that music is "a universal art" that can't be limited to any "race" (105); in Van Vechten, the argument for universality is lost: even Hester, denying the racial specificity of African art and reminding Mary that "everybody goes back to savages," can be made to feel her "birthright" by "the beat of the African rhythm"—listening to the "alien music" of Schubert and Schumann only with "forced or affected attention," she would immediately lose herself "under the sway of Negro music" (89). At the same time, however, *Nigger Heaven* begins to complicate the appeal of racial identity by making its inheritance less secure. Race now becomes something more than an identity that must be inherited and that can at best be proclaimed and at worst denied. It becomes more than something you (automatically) embody: Mary "cherished an almost fanatic faith in her race, a love for her people in themselves, and a fervent belief in their possibilities. She admired all Negro characteristics and desired earnestly to possess them. Somehow, so many of them, through no fault of her own, eluded her" (89). Instead of being embodied in Negroes, "Negro characteristics" may or may not be possessed by them. Identified as in some way belonging to the race (since they are "Negro") but not as determining race (since Negroes might not possess them), these "characteristics" are a new racial entity; it is their existence that gives a nonironic meaning to the project of making yourself into a Negro.

This is why passing, comparatively unimportant as a sociological phenomenon, has nevertheless constituted a significant theoretical advance. The possibility of concealing one's racial identity—of looking and behaving in ways that do not reflect one's race—makes available the desire to reveal it. And the conception of racial identity as the sort of thing that might or might not be revealed by one's behavior extends the regime of race to belief and action. In this respect, passing and the miscegenation that makes it possible are only literalized versions of a racial betrayal that cannot quite be reduced to sleeping with a Jew, to marrying (like the ex-colored man) a white woman, or to selling yourself (like La Farge's Slim Girl) to a white man. Indeed, it is explicit in *Laughing Boy* that simply ceasing to sleep with the American, George, cannot restore Slim Girl to "the People." Because she has been educated in the American school, because she has been made to be like "an American, with an American name, thinking in American" (165), she must now learn to be a Navajo, "to speak familiarly of everything familiar to them, to participate in every phase of their life, to acquire completely the Navajo gesture" (136). Navajo identity in *Laughing Boy* thus requires something more than biological fidelity to the Navajo race; to be a Navajo, in this text, is not only to be born a Navajo but to behave like one. Biology is an essential but not a sufficient condition of an identity that here requires a relatively autonomous set of practices to complete its constitution: *autonomous* because they don't simply follow from the biology (they can be embraced or rejected); *relatively* autonomous because the determination of which practices are the right ones can only be made by reference to biology (that's why Slim Girl's American education couldn't finally make her an American). "I am not a Navajo, nor am I an American, but the Navajos are my people," (47), Slim Girl says. It is because Slim Girl can fail to be a Navajo even though her people are Navajo and because she cannot succeed in being an American because her people aren't American that the project of making a Navajo out of herself can be both imaginable and imaginably successful.

Thus Slim Girl's learning to weave, to ride, and to sleep out under the stars is represented not only as an effort to "acquire completely the Navajo gesture" but also as the exercise of a "right" (62) granted her by birth but stolen from her by the missionaries. "The Americans spoiled me for a Navajo life," she says; the happy ending of *Laughing Boy* requires neither that Slim Girl lead a Navajo life nor (especially) that she give Laughing Boy the Navajo children she longs to bear[210] but that she "die a Navajo" (177). "What is sad about the passing of the Indian," Sapir wrote in "Culture, Genuine and Spurious" (1924), "is not the depletion of his numbers" but "the fading away of genuine cultures" (318). La Farge goes Sapir one better by making the depletion of numbers the occasion for a renewal of the culture, but the key in both texts is that the preservation of the culture has emerged as an issue that must be understood as separable from the preservation of the people. It is not enough for Indians to survive, Indian culture must survive. For without his culture, "the Indian finds himself in a state of bewildered vacuity. Even if he succeeds in making a fairly satisfactory compromise with his new environment . . . he is apt to retain an uneasy sense of the loss of some vague and great good, some state of mind that he would be hard put to define, but which gave him a courage and joy that latter-day prosperity never quite seems to have regained for him" (318). Since the survival of actual Indians cannot guarantee the survival of Indian culture, even "prosperity" is a "compromise'; the pathos of the vanishing race is preserved by being transferred to the vanishing culture.

This commitment to the survival of cultures would, of course, emerge as a professional requirement for anthropologists, and it is worth remembering that La Farge had been trained as an anthropologist and that he had done field work among the Navajos. But the particular ingenuity of *Laughing Boy* consists in its translation of the American anthropologist's affection for Navajo culture into what amounts to a Navajo affection for Navajo culture. That is, by provisionally depriving Slim Girl of her "heritage," La Farge is able not only to depict a heritage as essentially the kind of thing (unlike one's racial biology or one's social practices) that you can get separated from but also to make that thing potentially an object of affect. Thus when Slim Girl camps out, she takes pleasure not in the act of camping out as such and not even in her perception of the night as "beautiful with stars" but in her sense that "camping . . . was a part of her people's heritage. She was doing a Navajo thing" (99). What this involves is the representation of your culture not as the things you love to do but as the things you love to do because they are your culture. The drama of the schoolgirl's separation from Navajo ways thus makes two points: that your cultural practices are yours even if you don't practice them—this is what it means for Slim Girl to have a "right" to weaving even when she can't weave—and that cultural practices are attractive to you insofar as they are yours—this is what it means for her to like "doing a Navajo thing."

The attractions of Navajo things thus consist in the fact of their being Navajo; authenticity becomes a crucial aesthetic concept.[211] Laughing Boy's turquoise and silver jewelry, for example, is admired because it is "strong, pure stuff, real Northern Navajo work, untouched by European influence" (79). And the mark of its purity is that not only tourists but "other Indians" buy it. In *Laughing Boy*, Navajos are represented as a people with a powerful aesthetic sense, concerned above all with doing things "in a beautiful way" (64), and Laughing Boy himself is presented as desiring to make his every action beautiful: "He was thinking hard about what he was doing; he was putting forth every effort to make it good and beautiful" (63). But what the invocation of purity makes clear is that Navajo culture is the criterion as well as the instantiation of beauty; Navajo things are beautiful insofar as they are Navajo. This is, of course, a characteristically anthropological view but, again, it is part of the originality of *Laughing Boy* that it here appears as a Navajo view. The Navajos in *Laughing Boy* understand their behavior not as constituting their culture but as representing it. And this understanding, insofar as it makes possible a discrepancy between behavior and culture, also makes possible both the mistake of straying from your culture and the project of returning to it.

The irreducibility of culture to race is thus doubled by its irreducibility to behavior. For if, on the one hand, your culture cannot be simply determined by your race (which is why you can be induced to or forced to betray your race), on the other hand, your culture is not simply identical to your behavior (which is why you can be induced to or forced to betray your culture). And it is because culture cannot simply be identified with behavior that it must be understood as only relatively autonomous with respect to race. This is why even those writers—like Sapir—who were skeptical of the "current assumption that the so-called 'genius' of a people is ultimately reducible to certain inherent hereditary traits of a biological and psychological nature" (311) were committed nevertheless to the centrality of race.

Insisting that "what is assumed to be an innate racial characteristic" usually turns out to be "the resultant of purely historical causes" and that the transmission of "national" identity must be attributed to "more or less consciously imitative processes" rather than to the persistence of "purely hereditary qualities" (309), Sapir deploys the idea of a culture against the idea of a race. But if culture were nothing more than "imitative processes," then Slim Girl, imitating her American teachers, could never be described as having lost her culture; insofar as the practices she imitated were American, her culture would be American. And the Indian more generally could never have the experience, so powerfully described by Sapir, of having "slipped out of the warm embrace of a culture into the cold air of a fragmentary existence" (318). For if the Indian's culture were simply identical to his behavior and in no way related to his race, then he could never slip out of its warm embrace. In order for a culture to be lost, then, it must be separable from one's actual behavior, and in order for it to be separable from one's actual behavior, it must be anchorable in race.

Sapir's critique of race by culture is actually the continuation of race through culture.

For racial identity to become a project, it must turn to culture; for cultural identity to become a project, it must turn to race. The ex-colored man's ambition to make a Negro out of himself provides a kind of rehearsal for a broader range of identitarian ambitions. Because he can pass for white, he can choose to be black—biology is supplemented by behavior, race is supplemented by culture. But because he cannot choose to be white—he can only pretend to be white—behavior can never replace biology, culture cannot replace race. Slim Girl's ambition to make a Navajo out of herself revises and so generalizes the ex-colored man's project, diagnosing American efforts to assimilate Indians as attempts to make them ex-Indians, revealing the Indian effort to be assimilated as an attempt to pass. The emergence of culture, of behavior that is linked to but neither derived from nor constitutive of race, means that you don't have to be light-skinned to try to pass, and you don't have to be light-skinned to choose not to. Culture, in other words, frees the possibility of passing from its connection to skin color and redeploys it as an essential tool in the construction of racial identity as such, in the construction, that is, of identity as an affective object and in the construction of race as itself constructed, an artifact that must be produced as well as inherited.

Thus the Progressive commitment to Americanization, whether of Indians or of aliens, is, as we have seen, repudiated by nativist pluralism, on the grounds that people cannot become what they aren't. But thus also, the commitment to the technologies of Americanization is preserved, on the grounds that people must become what they are. "No longer do we assume that a man is truly American," according to Boston University Professor of Education John J. Mahoney, "merely because he happens to have been born within our country's confines."[212] Mahoney, no nativist, remains committed to the possibility of Americanizing the alien but begins to focus as well on what he takes to be the more fundamental problem of Americanizing the American: "The conviction has been brought home . . . that it is in large measure the un-American attitude of the native born that has made the Americanization of the immigrant so difficult."[213] Making Americans into Americans takes its place alongside making Negroes into Negroes and Navajos into Navajos. And where, in the Progressive commitment to Americanization, the state had played a central role, both as the agent of assimilation and as the source of that citizenship which was the object of assimilation, in nativism, the state is consigned to a distinctly secondary position.[214] Dixon, modeling his Southern clansmen on Polish freedom-fighters and recruiting Jews for the "White Man's Party," had found in "government" the "organized virtue of the community" (*The Leopard's Spots*, 281). Calvin Coolidge, comparing the "interposition of the government" unfavorably to "the genius of the people themselves" (13), understood Americanism as a matter of "heritage" rather than political affiliation: that's what it meant for him to tell the students and faculty of Wheaton College "We do not need more government, we need more culture" (74–75).

Heritage

W HAT IS Africa to me?" is the initiating question of Countee Cullen's "Heritage," asked in a spirit of skepticism that the poem will seek to eliminate but that has nonetheless prompted Arthur Schlesinger Jr. recently to cite "Heritage" as evidence of a traditional African American indifference to Africa.[215] Schlesinger presumably hasn't read past the poem's first ten lines, but an essay that appears some hundred pages after "Heritage" in Alain Locke's *The New Negro* (1925) does provide some support for Schlesinger's anti-Afrocentrism. The Negro represents "a case of complete acculturation," Melville J. Herskovits wrote in "The Negro's Americanism."[216] Denying the idea of a "cultural genius" (356) that could be identified with any "innate" or racially "African" characteristics, Herskovits denies also that any of the "customs" of "ancestral Africa" have survived in America. Insofar as there is anything in Harlem different from the "white culture" that surrounds it, that difference can best be explained, Herskovits argues, as "a remnant from the peasant days in the South" (359). For "One three centuries removed/ From the scenes his fathers loved," Herskovits's answer to the question "What is Africa to me?" is Nothing: the Negro has become completely "Americanized." "Of the African culture, not a trace."

But in "Heritage," of course, that answer is not allowed to stand. For although the scenes the father loved are initially presented as "unremembered" by the son, the tendency to *forget* (as if Africa were too distant to matter) is immediately reinterpreted as a requirement to *repress* (as if Africa were too near to be forgotten): "One thing only I must do/Quench my pride and cool my blood/Lest I perish in their flood, . . . Lest the grave restore its dead" (250–51), lest an apparently lost ancestral Africa turn out not only to be present but to be a force as strong or stronger than the Negro's Americanization. And this attempt to repress the African past is now presented as a failure, since the metaphor through which Africa is supposed to be kept out—"Though I cram against my ear/Both my thumbs and keep them there"—is in fact the technique through which it is discovered that Africa is already inside—"So I lie, who always hear . . . Great drums beating through the air" (251). Trying not to hear the drums outside involves hearing instead the drums inside, the circulation of one's own "dark blood." Thus Africa is, in the end, triumphantly, not only "remembered" but repeated; in *The New Negro*, "Heritage" appears in a section entitled "The Negro Digs Up His Past."

In *The New Negro*, then, Herskovits's view of the Negro as completely assimilated was anomalous; in the scholarly world more generally, how-ever, as the citations in his own *The Myth of the Negro Past* (1941) make clear, it was widely held.[217] Herskovits quotes Robert Park's claim that it is "very difficult to find in the South today anything that can be traced directly back to Africa" (3), Cleanth Brooks's declaration that for the purposes of linguistic study "the speech of the negro and of the white" should be "considered as one" (5), E. F. Frazier's description of the Negro people as "stripped of its social heritage" (3), and Charles S. Johnson's description of the Negro's "cultural heritage" as "completely broken" (4). But by 1941 (and even, in his private correspondence, as early as 1927), Herskovits himself had come to see things very differently.[218] In 1925, in "The Negro's Americanism," he had argued that "All racial and social elements in our population who live here long enough become acculturated, Americanized in the truest sense of the words, eventually" (360), and that the Negro was no exception; in 1941, in *The Myth of the Negro Past*, he argued that the distinguishing traits of "Italians or Germans or Old Americans or Jews or Irish or Mexicans or Swedes" could not be understood "without a reference to a preceding cultural heritage" (299) and, again, that the Negro was no exception. What he had seen in 1925 as the Negro's likeness to other groups in becoming acculturated, he now saw as the Negro's likeness to other groups in *not* becoming acculturated.

The myth of the Negro past, in other words, was that he had none, that he was either completely a creature of the culture imposed upon him in slavery or that he had no culture at all and, insofar as Negroes were themselves brought to accept this view, Herskovits regarded them as the victims of cultural imperialism. *Native Son's* (1940) Bigger Thomas, for example, is described by Richard Wright as "bereft of a culture." "The

Negro," according to Wright, "possessed a rich and complex culture when he was brought to these alien shores," but it was "taken from" him.[219] Herskovits's argument in *The Myth of the Negro Past* was that it had *not* been taken from him, and that the myth of the Negro's unique cultural "pliancy" was a function of "racial prejudice." His point, then, was to show both that the Negro did have a past and that, like other groups, he had clung to it. The "stereotype of the pliant Negro . . . which contrasts him to the Indian, who is held to have died rather than suffer enslavement" (90), is false, Herskovits claimed. The Indian who died to show his "cultural tenacity" now becomes the model not only for "Old Americans" like Tom Outland and old Jews like Reb Smolinski but for the newly historicized Negro whose "pre-American traditions" make him an ethnic like the others.

Precipitated out of the family "black and white" as the first American race, the Negro—filtered through the Indian—now becomes the last American culture. But here Herskovits is not simply catching up to the '20s, he is advancing the argument. For cultural identity in the '20s required, as we have seen, the anticipation of culture by race: to be a Navajo you have to do Navajo things, but you can't really count as doing Navajo things unless you already are a Navajo. For Herskovits, however (and here *The Myth of the Negro Past* is consistent with "The Negro's Americanism"), racial identity plays no role in the constitution of cultural identity; his "analysis is consistently held to the plane of learned behavior, so that whatever role innate endowment may play, it is not permitted to confuse the issues of the research" (14). Thus where Countee Cullen identified the African heritage genealogically, finding it in the body's "black blood," Herskovits saw the distinctive "Africanisms" of the body as "cultural" rather than "biological": his research assistant, Zora Neale Hurston, he noted, was "more White than Negro in her ancestry," but her "motor behavior" was "typically Negro."[220]

When Herskovits sought to prove that the Negro was not "a man without a past," then, the past he sought to give him was entirely cultural. The idea was to show that many aspects of contemporary Negro behavior could be traced back to African beliefs and practices and the point in doing this was to help the Negro toward a proper "appreciation of his past," for a "people that denies its past cannot escape being a prey to doubt of its value today" (32). When, in *Native Son*, Bigger goes to the double feature the movies he sees are *The Gay Woman* and *Trader Horn*. *The Gay Woman*, as Wright describes it, is about rich white people, "dancing, golfing, swimming and spinning roulette wheels";[221] *Trader Horn* is about "black men and women, dancing free and wild, men and women who were adjusted to their soil and at home in their world . . ." (36). *Trader Horn*, in Herskovits's terms, presents Bigger with the spectacle of an African culture that should be his—a display of those "distinctive" "motor habits" (148) that he is supposed to have brought with him from Africa. But it is a spectacle that Bigger himself cannot see. "He looked at *Trader Horn* unfold . . . and then gradually the African scene changed and was replaced by images in his own mind of white men and women dressed in black and white clothes, laughing, talking, drinking and dancing" (35–36). The white world from which he is shut out is more alluring than the African world with which Herskovits wishes to reconnect him. This, from the standpoint of Herskovits, is what it means to belong to a people that denies its past.[222]

But Bigger's indifference may perhaps be more easily understood as a critique of Herskovits than as a failure to live up to his ideals, and what seems to Herskovits at best the Negro's inability to recognize his past and at worst his commitment to denying his past may be read instead as a question about why the past in question is his. For in his identification of the Negro "people" and, more particularly, in his characterization of African customs as part of that people's past, Herskovits turns out to lean more heavily on the concept of racial identity than his culturalist rhetoric suggests. Indeed, how else can an American Negro of the twentieth century be said to be denying his or her past in denying that his or her practices have their roots in Africa?[223]

In *Laughing Boy*, Slim Girl's *actual* past, the things she has herself done (her American education, her conversion to Christianity, her love affair with an American), are regarded as less crucial to her identity than her people's past, the things her mother and father used to do. "Her past" is "dead," Laughing Boy thinks, and, indeed, he himself represents to her "an axe with which to hew down the past" and "a light with which to see her way back to her people" (45). The way to beliefs she has never held and to customs she has never practiced can seem a way *back* in *Laughing Boy* because race provides the necessary (but, crucially, not sufficient) ground of Slim Girl's identity. Neither what she was born nor what she has done is sufficient to confer cultural identity; she can make herself a Navajo only by doubling Navajo birth with the doing of Navajo things. The discrepancy between Slim Girl's actual past and her people's past is thus the enabling condition for the appearance of cultural identity as a project, the project of lining up her practices with her genealogy. Herskovits, however, cannot afford such a discrepancy between what people do and what their ancestors did. Since his analysis is committed only to a genealogy of "learned behavior," a break in that genealogy (a failure actually to do yourself what your ancestors did) can only count as a complete rupture with the past; there can be no appeal to racial continuity.

Thus Herskovits is required to explain, for example, how the "retention of Africanisms" (*Myth*, 133) was possible for house slaves and others "in close contact with whites." Such people, despite being thoroughly trained in white ways and encouraged in the "adoption of white values" (132), could "reabsorb Africanisms" during the periods when they were released from their duties and could mingle with field hands whose practices had been left relatively untouched or, even better, he suggests, with "newly arrived Africans" whose practices were completely untouched. Whatever the historical plausibility of this explanation, and even though the movement from retention to reabsorption suggests a certain slippage (If you were trained as a house slave, why would absorbing Africanisms count as *re*absorbing them?), its theoretical purpose is clear: to guarantee an unbroken chain of (cultural) Africanisms and so avoid any appeal to "innate endowment."

In fact, however, the appearance of a break in the cultural chain only makes visible what must already be present for the "retention of Africanisms" to count as the acquisition of a "past." For the fact that some people before you did some things that you do does not in itself make what they did part of your past. To make what *they* did part of *your* past, there must be some prior assumption of identity between you and them, and this assumption is as racial in Herskovits as it is in Cullen or La Farge. The things the African Negro used to do count as the American Negro's past only because both the African and the American are "the Negro." Herskovits's antiracist culturalism can only be articulated through a commitment to racial identity.[224]

"What is Africa to me?" The answer, if you are Herskovits's Negro, is "my past." Arthur Schlesinger Jr., as I noted earlier, cites that question as an instance of the rejection by black Americans of the idea that their past is African. But this rejection involves for him only a denial of the Africanness of their past, not a rejection of the idea that black Americans as such have a past or of what he calls the "right" of black Americans "to seek an affirmative definition of their past" (30). He does not, in other words, reject the idea of our past as something more than our personal or actual past. On the contrary, his goal in *The Disuniting of America* (1991) is to reclaim the past from Afrocentrists and others who threaten his vision of who we are and what our past is. And, in this, Schlesinger and his opponents stand on the same ground. For if American historians study what is meant to seem to us, if we are Americans, "our" past ("For history is to the nation rather as memory is to the individual" [20], Schlesinger says),[225] nothing is more common today than the challenge to this description that takes the form of asking who "we" are and demanding that our past be pluralized in response to that question, that the "American" past be understood instead as the Native American past, the African American past, the Jewish American past, and so on.

But why does it matter who we are? The answer can't just be the epistemological truism that our account of the past may be partially determined by our own identity, for, of course, this description of the conditions under which we know the past makes no logical difference to the truth or falsity of what we know. It must be instead the ontological claim that we need to know who we are in order to know which past is ours. The real question, however, is not *which* past should count as ours but why *any* past should count as ours. Virtually all the events and actions that we study did not happen to us and were not done by us. In this sense, the history we study is never our own; it is always the history of people who were in some respects like us and in other respects different. When, however, we claim it as ours, we commit ourselves to the ontology of "the Negro," to the identity of "we" and "they" and the primacy of race.[226]

This is not to say, of course, that all accounts of cultural identity require a racial component, it is only to say that the accounts of cultural identity that do any work require a racial component. For insofar as our culture remains nothing more than what we do and believe, it is impotently descriptive. The fact, in other words, that something belongs to our culture cannot count as a motive for our doing it since, if it *does* belong to our culture, we *already* do it and if we don't do it (if we've stopped or haven't yet started doing it), it doesn't belong to our culture. (It makes no sense, for example, to claim that we shouldn't teach Shakespeare because he isn't part of our culture since to teach him will immediately *make* him part of our culture, but it also makes no sense to claim that we should teach him because he is part of our culture since, if we stop teaching him, he won't be any longer.) It is only if we think that our culture is not whatever beliefs and practices we actually happen to have but is instead the beliefs and practices that should properly go with the sort of people we happen to be that the fact of something belonging to our culture can count as a reason for doing it. But to think this is to appeal to something that must be beyond culture and that cannot be derived from culture precisely because our sense of which culture is properly ours must be derived from it. This has been the function of race. Just as it is only the presumed racial identity between Herskovits's Negroes and their African ancestors that makes what the Africans did part of the Negroes' past, so it is only the idea that the appropriateness of culture can be derived from race that makes it possible to think that a certain culture is the right one for a certain people.

It is this idea also that makes it possible to think of people as losing their culture or, more dramatically, having it stolen from them. Thus, for example, it is often said of white musicians, performing the music and dance characteristically associated with some African Americans, that they stole it from blacks. But why does white men's learning to sing and dance like blacks count as stealing black culture? The assumption that transforms learning into stealing must be that blacks have a *right* to their culture that is violated by whites who take up black cultural practices. Or, to look at it from the other perspective, that whites who sing and dance like blacks are betraying *their* culture. But for either of these descriptions to be true there must be some special relation between race and culture such that racial identity counts as importantly determining cultural identity, that is, as determining the cultural practices that you have a right to if not necessarily the cultural practices you in fact engage in. The idea that whites who learn to sing like blacks are stealing black culture thus depends upon the racialist idea that cultural identity is a function of racial identity.

The modern concept of culture is not, in other words, a critique of racism; it is a form of racism. And, in fact, as skepticism about the biology of race has increased, it has become—at least among intellectuals—the dominant form of racism. Herskovits's commitment to culture was articulated in opposition to the concept of race; more recently, however, arguments like his have sought not to oppose race to culture but to redescribe race *as* culture, to insist, in other words, on what Michael Omi and Howard Winant call "race as a *social* concept."[227] Writers like Omi and Winant reiterate Herskovits's hostility to the explanation of behavior by appeal to a biology of race and criticize more generally efforts to give the concept of race a "scientific meaning" (68), but they decline to abandon the concept of race as such. On the contrary, regarding race as "a pre-eminently *social* phenomenon" (90), they celebrate what they call "the forging of new collective racial identities during the 1950s and 1960s," arguing that "the racial subjectivity and self-awareness which they developed" have taken "permanent hold" in American society (91). And this commitment to racial identity without biology certainly does extend beyond the writings of social scientists like Omi and Winant. In a widely noticed racial identity case in Louisiana, for example, the Fourth Circuit Court of Appeals, remarking that "the very concept of the racial classification of individuals . . . is scientifically insupportable,"[228] ruled that Mrs. Susie Phipps, "who had always thought she was white, had lived as white, and had twice married as white,"[229] was not in fact white because her parents, who had provided the racial information on her birth certificate, had classified her as "colored." "Individual racial designations are purely social and cultural perceptions" (372), the court said; the relevant question, then, was not whether those "subjective perceptions" correctly registered some biological fact about Phipps but whether they had been "correctly recorded" at the time the birth certificate was issued. Since in the court's judgment they had been, Susie Phipps and her fellow appellants remained "colored."

Because Phipps was by credible evidence at least one-thirty-second black, commentators like Omi and Winant cite this case as an example of racial biologism, and F. James Davis in his important book *Who Is Black?* describes the Phipps case as confirming the legality of the one-drop rule.[230] This rule had, of course, a biological meaning. In older racist texts like Robert Lee Durham's *The Call of the South*, the justification for counting as black anyone with a traceable amount of black blood is the conviction that this trace will at some point manifest itself, as when the savagery of his African grandfather emerges in the quadroon Hayward Graham and he rapes his white wife: "With a shriek of terror she wildly tries to push him from her: but the demon of the blood of Guinea Gumbo is pitiless, and against the fury of it, as of the storm, she fights and cries—in vain."[231] The idea, then, is that the black blood makes a difference to the intrinsic identity of the person and even if this difference is ordinarily invisible (even if the person characteristically looks and acts even more white than Hayward Graham, who is "unobtrusively but unmistakeably a negro" [7]), at some point his blackness will show itself.[232] The reasoning, in other words, depends on a commitment to the biology of race. But it turns out that the designation of people who neither look nor act black as nonetheless black does not necessarily depend on the idea that their blackness might actually show itself or might even be the sort of thing that could in principle show itself, which is to say that it's a mistake to see that biological account of race confirmed in the Phipps decision. On the contrary, the court, as I have noted, firmly insists that "racial designations are purely social and cultural perceptions." Mrs. Susie Phipps is "colored" not because of her traceable amount of black blood but because her parents said she was.[233]

What this produces is not a one-drop rule but a no-drop rule, the legal equivalent of the social scientist's "*social* phenomenon." It solves the problem of the scientific establishment of racial identity by denying that racial identity is anything more than a question of "purely cultural" perception. But, of course, this solution is accompanied by a problem. For, if racial identity is no longer understood to have anything to do with "blood," what could Phipps's parents have been thinking of when they thought of themselves and of her as black? If their criteria for racial identity were the same as the state's criteria, they weren't thinking that she had some proportion of black blood; according to the state of Louisiana, "purely social and cultural perceptions," not blood, determine racial identity. But they could not be thinking of her as someone who was *perceived* by them as being black; that is, they could not think that their perception of her as black was what made her black because to think that would be to beg the question of why they perceived her as black in the first place. The perception of blackness, in other words, may be enough to make someone black in the eyes of the state but it isn't enough to explain what blackness is. (And, of course, her behavior can't do this either since, as a newborn, she presumably didn't talk in an imaginably black dialect or exhibit any of the forms of behavior that might conceivably be associated with the cultural behavior of blacks.) What, then, is the perception of blackness a perception of?

The standard interpretation of this case is, as we have seen, that it restored the one-drop rule; since everybody agreed that Susie Phipps did have *some* black ancestry, she counted as black. But, despite this ancestry, if her parents had perceived themselves and her as white, she would— even acknowledging this very small proportion of black blood—have counted as white. Louisiana law, in other words, as articulated by the majority in this decision, insists on "the subjective character of racial perceptions" and takes no account of the ancestry. Perhaps one could argue that Louisiana doesn't go far enough in discounting ancestry; after all, why should Phipps's *parents'* perception of her racial identity matter? As a recent defense of anti-essentialist accounts of racial identity has pointed out, "The Indian Reorganization Act of 1972 appeared to abandon the 'blood quantum' standard of Indian identity in favor of 'self-identification,' only to be evaded by the Reagan Administration's attempt to 'enforce degree-of-blood' requirements. . . ."[234] Maybe the injustice in the Phipps case is that the wrong social perceptions were enforced; Susie Phipps should be white because even though her parents perceived her as black, she perceived herself as white. It is, as Omi and Winant say, her "racial self-awareness" that should be respected. But, of course, this doesn't solve the problem posed by the parental perception of her as black, it just relocates it: What's her perception of whiteness a perception of?[235] When Susie Phipps looks back on the baby that her parents perceived as black, what makes her perceive it as white?

The truth is that Louisiana law, acknowledging that there is no biological basis for the determination of racial identity and therefore refusing to establish a biological standard for the law, has decided instead to establish not biology but people's mistaken accounts of biology as the legal standard. In other words, the fact that Phipps had at least one black ancestor could not make her black under the law, but the fact that her one black ancestor made her parents perceive her as black *did* make her black under the law. The biological determination that the state itself regards as "scientifically insupportable" nonetheless counts as determining as long as the mistake is made by the parents instead of by the state itself. Refusing itself to apply the one-drop rule, the state chose instead to enforce Phipps's parents' application of the one-drop rule. What it means, then, to accept the idea of racial identity as a function of "purely social and cultural perceptions" instead of as biology is to accept the idea of racial identity as the codification of people's mistakes *about* biology. In a way, then, Davis is right to assert that some version of the one-drop rule is being enforced by the Louisiana court, but what is being enforced is not the claim that one drop of black blood makes a person black; what's being enforced is the claim that the *perception* that one drop of black blood makes a person black makes a person black.

According to Louisiana law, Susie Phipps was passing, pretending to be white when she was, in fact, black. Both the law and the very idea of passing require that there be some fact of racial identity, a requirement that was easily met as long as there could be some appeal to science but that the repudiation of scientific racism has made more difficult. The requisite fact must now be cultural rather than biological. Thus, in a recent and powerfully written essay called "Passing for White, Passing for Black," Adrian Piper denies that there is any "set of shared physical characteristics" that "joins" her "to other blacks" because, she says, "there is none that all blacks share" (30). What makes blacks black is rather "the shared experience of being visually or cognitively *identified* as black by a white racist society, and the punitive and damaging effects of that identification" (30–31). This is the Louisiana standard: If you're perceived as black, you are black. But Piper's account of her own experience makes the incoherence of this standard even more obvious than it is in the Phipps case. For Piper describes herself as so light-skinned that she is constantly (both by people whom she identifies as black and by people whom she identifies as white) being treated as if she were white. She is thus made to feel that she is passing for white and, since passing for white seems to her "a really, authentically shameful thing to do" (10), she is led into strenuous efforts to identify herself as black. (The irony that produces her title is that these efforts lead her to be accused—again by both whites and blacks—of passing for black.) But what consequences must these efforts have for her nonbiological definition of racial identity? The point of that definition is that being black means being identified by a white racist society as black. On what grounds, then, can someone who is *not* identified by that society as black be said to be black?

Piper makes this dilemma even clearer by going on to remark that she has "white friends who fit the prevailing stereotype of a black person" (31) and thus have "experiences" "similar" to the ones that make blacks black. If they really do have such experiences, what can she mean by calling these friends "white"? That they can be white even if they are treated as black, that she can be black even if she is treated as white—these facts are tributes to, not critiques of, racial essentialism. The very idea of passing—whether it takes the form of looking like you belong to a different race or of acting like you belong to a different race—requires an understanding of race as something separate from the way you look and the way you act. If race really were nothing but culture, that is, if race really were nothing but a distinctive array of beliefs and practices, then, of course, there could be no passing, since to believe and practice what the members of any race believed and practiced would, by definition, make you a member of that race. If race really were culture, people could change their racial identity, siblings could belong to different races, people who were as genetically unlike each other as it's possible for two humans to be could nonetheless belong to the same race. None of these things is possible in the United States today. And, were they to become possible, we would think not that we had finally succeeded in developing an anti-essentialist account of race but that we had given up the idea of race altogether.

On rehearing, the Louisiana court took the opportunity to remind the appellants that we can't afford to give up the idea of race, that the accumulation of "racial data" is "essential" for "planning and monitoring public health programs, affirmative action and other anti-discrimination measures" (374). Which is only to say that race is "one of the most important principles by which U. S. social relations are organized." My point here is not simply that these claims are wrong, for, at least in one sense, they are obviously right: U. S. social relations have been and continue to be organized in part by race. My point has been to assert that insofar as this organization cannot be scientifically defended, it is the consequence of a mistake, and that anti-essentialist defenses of race amount to nothing more than new ways of making the mistake. As absurd as the one-drop rule of Jim Crow is, the no-drop rule of anti-essentialism is even more absurd. Omi and Winant cite two "temptations" that they believe must be resisted in thinking about race: the first is the temptation "to think of race as an *essence*, as something fixed, concrete and objective"; the second is "to see it as a mere illusion" (68). Their point, of course, is that in seeing race as a social construction we can avoid both the temptations. But if to see race as a social construction is inevitably (even if unwillingly and unknowingly) to essentialize it, then race really is either an essence or an illusion. The two "temptations" are the only choices we have.

From the standpoint of anti-essentialism, then, what's wrong with the idea of race is that it's essentially essentialist or, to put the point a little more precisely, what's wrong with it is that there can be no coherent anti-essentialist account of race. But why should this be a problem? Those who believe that individual racial identity is a biological reality don't need an anti-essentialist account of race; those who don't believe that individual racial identity is a biological reality don't need one either, unless, of course, their commitment to the category of race is so complete that they understand themselves to be required to maintain it at all costs. And this does seem to be the point of the whole debate over racial essentialism, the point, that is, of insisting that the problem with the biology of individual racial identity is that it's *essentialist* rather than *false*. Transforming the question of whether or not there is such a thing as individual racial identity into the question of whether or not race is an "essence" and thus deploying race as the grounds of the question rather than as its object, this debate reinvigorates and relegitimates race as a category of analysis.

Our America

WALDO FRANK'S *Our America* (1919) was essentially an attack on what Frank called "Puritan Industrialism," by which he meant the culture of the "commercial" and "conformist" "American Middle-Class."[236] Articulated from the standpoint of those whom Frank identified as "the younger generation," the critique took as its object not only the middle class but the middle-aged: the "our" in the title refers to the artists and writers who are Frank's own contemporaries and who are identified here as the first outbreak of the "new." What is new about "our America," from Frank's standpoint, is that it is for the first time "ours." There is an important sense, however, in which the claim that America now belongs to Frank's generation is less important than is the fact that what Frank and his generation want to claim is "America." The opposition to the "world of commerce," in other words, is here represented as nationalist; the territory that the younger generation wishes to take from the older is a *nation*.

There is a certain sense, of course, in which this literary nationalism was traditional; the effort to imagine a distinctively American—as opposed to British or European—culture was central to American writing and painting at various moments in the nineteenth century. But the early twentieth century had not really been one of those moments. The writers whom Frank identifies as the admirable but not quite successful forerunners of his own group—above all, Dreiser and London—had interested themselves in American commercial life without interesting themselves in what was distinctively American about it. So Frank's desire to claim "America" is not only traditional but new; and this novelty is emphasized by the fact that the objects of Frank's generational critique are already, albeit insufficiently, American. It's as if, in Frank's view, the problem with American culture was that it had neglected to concern itself with its Americanness.[237] Thus, in *Our America*, the disaffection of a cultural elite from a philistine middle class is represented as the struggle of that cultural elite to become more American.

In Frank, this struggle takes two forms, each crucially but differently (even contradictorily) marked by the Progressive commitment to Americanization. In the dominant form, emblematized by the Russian Jewish composer Leo Ornstein, a truly American culture is to be created out of the transformation of immigrants: "Hebrew the seed: American the fruit" (188). It is, in this model, the experience of the new world, the process of ceasing to be Russian and becoming American, what Frank calls the "lust of a new world's conquest," that creates a music that "will be American." A truly American culture is here the product of Americanization. At the same time, however, there is in Frank an anticipation of what will turn out to be the dominant cultural discourse of the '20s, the rejection of Americanization. The only important theater in New York, he argues, is the immigrant theater, where "gleams of folk-lore, racial confessionals . . . clash with the cheap *patter* of the American assimilation" (213). True culture, in this model, requires the Hebrew seed to become American by bearing Hebrew fruit on American soil.

The potential contradiction between these two models is forestalled in *Our America* by invoking the second in an appreciative but exclusively elegiac mode. The forerunners of the immigrants are the Indians, destroyed by "intermarriage" and by "relentless war" waged upon their "customs" by the "American authorities" (110). Among these, the Pueblo Indian "does not intermarry" and "has preserved his culture admirably" (111), but in the face of Puritan Industrialism he too "is dying and is doomed. There can be no question of this" (115). But if, in *Our America*, it is the Indian and the anti-assimilationist model of American culture that is doomed, in fact, it was the Progressive constitution of American fruit out of alien seed that was in the '20s virtually to disappear. In this respect, *Our America* is an oddly transitional text: the model of the American it proclaims as struggling to be born was dying, the model it describes as dead was being reborn.

For the insistence in *Our America* on national identity as the primary criterion of value would become powerful only in combination with the revision of American national identity as a form of racial identity. Thus assimilation, which to Frank seemed (unfortunately) inevitable, would seem to a writer like Stoddard "absolutely impossible" (*Re-Forging*, 246) since it would involve not merely the social "conformism" that Frank deplored but, more fundamentally, the mixing and thus the betrayal of "blood" (4). The first defining characteristic of nativist modernism is thus its deep hostility to assimilation, its repudiation of the miscegenetic ambitions of Marsellus, Gatsby, and Cohn. And the second defining characteristic is simply the reverse face of the desire not to let aliens become American—it is the desire of aliens to remain alien. "Let all parties realize that the problem is, at bottom, one of *difference*," as Stoddard put it. "We Americans have built up *our* America, and we cherish it so supremely that no one should honestly blame us for our resolve that it shall be kept 'American'" (253–54). We cherish it because it's "ours"; others won't, because it isn't theirs, so "of course," there "is no reason why the alien should like our America, and no moral turpitude should attach to him if he voices his discontent" (254). The American's commitment to remaining American is, in the nativist imagination, immediately doubled by the alien's commitment to remaining alien. Which is why Gekin Yashi will die for sleeping with a German and Slim Girl will die for sleeping with an American, or why Sara Smolinski will marry a *Landsleute* and Clare Kendry will yearn for Negroes.

This valorization of difference above all is pluralism, and the new pluralism of the '20s, I have argued, produced at least a theoretical intensification of the commitment to race. For claims to racial superiority inevitably involved the appeal to standards that were understood as common to all races; it is only as measured against such standards that one race could be judged superior to another. Thus the superiority of the race could be asserted only by appeal to criteria that were themselves independent of any particular race and could be deemed valid for all races, that is, universal. In pluralism, however, the possibility of such an appeal is denied. Asserting that races are different from each other without being either better or worse, the pluralist can prefer his own race only on the grounds that it is his. Hence "our America." The particular contribution of pluralism to racism is to make racial identity into its own justification.

The point now is to be what one is, to speak, believe, and act in accordance with one's identity. And although this ambition originates in (and, in fact, requires the continuing contribution of) race, it may present itself disarticulated from and even in opposition to avowedly racial programs. Thus, in *Theories of Americanization: A Critical Study* (1920), Isaac Berkson distinguishes between his own "Community" theory of ethnic identity and Horace Kallen's "Federation of Nationalities" theory by arguing that for Kallen the "identity of race is pivotal; the argument is made to rest primarily upon the proposition that 'we cannot change our grandfathers.' The 'Community' theory, on the other hand, would make the history of the ethnic group, its aesthetic, cultural and religious inheritance, its national self-consciousness, the basic factor."[238] Where Kallen's

Jewishness is a racial inheritance from his grandfathers, Berkson's Jewishness is made a function of "History . . . as it manifests itself in the life experiences of the Jewish people" and "Culture as it expresses itself in the rich inheritance of the Jewish people" (100).

It's difficult to see, however, how the appeal to history can successfully distinguish Berkson from Kallen: What makes Jewish history your history unless your grandparents were Jews? And, although culture seems a more promising criterion of Jewishness—to be Jewish is simply to do what Berkson called "Jewish things" (57)—it's equally difficult to see how the reduction of Jewish identity to the doing of "Jewish things" can underwrite the desire to avoid assimilation, the "loyalty" to an "ethnic community" (103) that Berkson plausibly presents as the crucial feature of cultural identity. For if your grandchildren do not do the things that you have done, and if your culture is nothing more than what you do, how can they be understood to have lost *their* culture? To what "community" have the assimilated children been disloyal? Berkson tries to justify "loyalty" to the "ethnic community" as loyalty to your "culture" instead of to your "grandfathers," but how can the fact that your grandchildren do not do what you did count as your grandchildren's having lost their culture unless the crucial fact in the determination of which culture is theirs is the fact of who their grandparents are?

Insofar as Berkson succeeds in bypassing the appeal to the grandfathers that would make his position indistinguishable from Kallen's, he does so finally not by relying on culture but by transforming it. "The defense of the right of the ethnic group to preserve its identity," he points out, "is usually based upon a claim to unique cultural possessions" (121). But this "approach" seems to him itself "indefensible." For the "ethnic group is not a system of ideas," a philosophy that might be judged on its merits, compared to others, and, if found wanting, discarded. An "ethnic group" is a "nationality," and "every nation must be conceived" not as "a system of ideas" but "as a personality": "In considering whether a person is worthy of living or not, we do not require that he be indispensable. . . . So, too, every nation must be conceived as a personality. . . . Some nations are greater, some more gifted, some have longer and richer traditions—but they are all nations and each has the same right to live" (121).

By understanding cultural identity as a form of personhood rather than as a particular set of beliefs and practices, this national "right to life" (122) makes assimilation a kind of murder or suicide. Redescribing the disappearance of certain beliefs and practices as the death of a person,

Berkson produces the pathos of personal death out of the fact of cultural change. And at the same time, he forestalls any question about the continuity of heritage—the effort to unite people of the present to people of the past through the appeal to a common history—by imagining the historical community as a single person: we share a history with ancient Jews because, as participants in the ethnic personality, we *are* the ancient Jews. The work we have seen done elsewhere (in Dixon and in Hopkins) by reincarnation is done here by personification. Cultural identity can take the place of racial identity either insofar as it already is a form of racial identity or insofar as it can be transformed into personal identity.[239]

The emergence of racial pluralism is thus simultaneous with the emergence of cultural pluralism, which is to say that, by understanding identity as the privileged object of social contest, pluralism makes race and culture structurally equivalent and formally interchangeable. For many writers, of course, already committed to the idea that culture was an expression of race, racial pluralism and cultural pluralism always seemed entirely compatible. For an increasing number of others, however, they would seem utterly incompatible—the whole point of the appeal to culture would be to supplant the appeal to race. But insofar as the appeal to culture was genuinely pluralist, insofar, that is, as it did not involve preferring any one set of cultural practices to another set on the grounds of its being *superior* to the other, racial identity remained an essential component of cultural identity. For, in pluralism, our preference for our own practices can only be justified by the fact that they are ours; our desire to do the things our "community" does can only be justified by what Berkson calls our "loyalty" to it—we do "Jewish things" instead of "Navajo things" (or vice versa) not because we think Jewish things are better than Navajo things (or vice versa) but because we are Jews (or Navajos). So the assertion of cultural identity depends upon an identity that cannot be cultural—we are not Jews because we do Jewish things, we do Jewish things because we are Jews.[240]

To put the point as bluntly as possible, "cultural pluralism" is an oxymoron; its commitment to culture is contradicted by its commitment to pluralism. For, on the one hand, the pluralist claim that our practices are justified only because they are better for us requires us to be able to say who we are independent of those practices and so requires us to produce our racial identity. But, on the other hand, the cultural claim denies the relevance of race and so leaves us unable to appeal to facts about who we are as justifications for what we do. Cultural pluralists are thus required to choose between culture and pluralism. And insofar as they choose pluralism they commit themselves to the primacy of identity; instead of who we are being constituted by what we do, what we do is justified by who we are. Cultural pluralism is thus committed in principle to identity essentialism, which is to say that in cultural pluralism, culture does not constitute identity, it reflects or, more precisely, expresses it.[241]

It is the production of racial/cultural identity, which is to say, of a cultural identity derived from and irrevocably linked to race, that has been the central topic of this book. The Progressive prehistory of that identity, the installation of whiteness as the essential criterion of American citizenship, made no appeal to culture. In the Dixonian vision of a Progressive America, race was sufficient; the difference between white and black was deployed as the essential organizing principle of the citizenry, against the difference between rich and poor or the difference between Englishman and Jew. Pre-Progressive writers like Page, James, and, to some extent, Hopkins had been either indifferent (Page), insufficiently alert (James), or overtly hostile (Hopkins) to the role racial difference could be made to play in the constitution of American identity. Indeed, they had failed to see the importance and utility of the very idea of American identity, a failure marked by their various Anglophilias and by their selective nostalgias for the forms of race relations imaginable before the Civil War, for slavery and for miscegenation. Dixon, repudiating the nostalgia for prewar gentility and for "the family, black and white," rewrote the death of a civilization as the birth of a nation, and made allegiance to "the new America" (*The Leopard's Spots*, 404) the only test of "the true citizen" (441).

But the differences between black and white that could be used to transform the second-class citizens of, say, the Russian empire into first-class citizens of the United States could, as it turned out, be deployed both against those new citizens and against the very concept of American identity that had encouraged their citizenship. More sophisticated technologies of racial distinction made it possible to draw lines not merely between blacks and whites but between Nordics, Alpines, and Mediterraneans, and more sophisticated accounts of nationality (America is not "a government, it is the cultural and spiritual birth right of all true Americans" [Stoddard, *Re-Forging*, 226]) made it possible to think of American identity as something that could by no means be reduced to a matter of political allegiance. In this transformation of citizenship into cultural identity, the commitment of the Progressive state to making Americans is largely repudiated and the very idea of the American is disconnected from allegiance to a set of political ideals and connected instead to inheritance from a cultural past founded in the explicitly "prenational" history of America. The heroes of the Civil War are replaced by the early explorers and settlers of the continent and increasingly by the Indians—the true native Americans—as the origins and exemplars of American identity. Citizenship may be achieved but culture is inherited, and the claim that "American institutions" are "inherently excellent" and should thus be adopted by "all peoples" (Speranza, 65) gives way to the claim that they are excellent only for those with "historic American conceptions and ideals" and not for the "culturally-alien" (Speranza, 77).

Repudiating a universalist white supremacy and embracing the pluralism intrinsic to its conception of culture, nativist modernism invented a new form of racism and produced a new model not only of American identity but of the other identities that would now be available in America. Promoting a conception of identity as both description and responsibility, it made Americanness into a racial inheritance and culture into a set of beliefs and practices dependent on race—without race, culture could be nothing more than one's actual practices and therefore could never be lost or recovered, defended or betrayed—but not reducible to race—if it were nothing but race, it could also not be lost or recovered, it could only be a fact, never a project. More generally, nativist modernism helped to make identity itself into an object of cathexis, into something that might be lost or found, defended or surrendered.[242] And it may well be the emergence of this notion of identity that will come to seem the crucial feature of modernism, around which future studies of the subject will organize themselves.

My aim in the preceding pages, however, has been neither to examine this conception of identity as such nor to analyze its function in the many discursive areas (sexual, psychological, commercial) to which it might be thought relevant. I have been concerned only to trace its emergence in American nativism and to analyze its contribution to a modernist (i.e., racialized) conception of culture. Because that conception of culture found its fullest expression as a literary phenomenon and (not, in my view, coincidentally) because the decade of the '20s produced a great number of exceptionally interesting literary works, I have focused most of my attention on American literary modernism. Whether or not the privileged position of literature as the carrier of cultural heritage is enviable, it is real and, even though it would certainly be useful to deal with a range of phenomena wider than I have attempted, I believe that any account of nativist modernism would end up making American literary history central.

I have also criticized the idea of cultural identity as it was developed in the '20s and as it is sometimes used today, but it should be clear that my criticism of cultural identity and my history of its nativist origins are separate. What's wrong with the current conception of cultural identity is not that it developed out of racial identity (although the fact that it did may well explain *how* what's wrong with it got to be wrong with it); what's wrong with cultural identity is that, without recourse to the racial identity that (in its current manifestations) it repudiates, it makes no sense.

Notes

1 William Faulkner, *The Sound and the Fury*, ed. David Minter (New York, 1987), 176. Subsequent references are to this edition and are cited in parentheses in the text.

2 John Higham, *Strangers in the Land* (New Brunswick, 1955; reprint 1988), 4.

3 *Congressional Record—House* (1924), 5677. The speaker is Congressman Watkins from Oregon, and the complete sentence reads: "The sooner this Congress lays down the proposition of not admitting the people of those nations who can not assimilate, who can not become a part of our blood, our tongue, our life, and our ways, the sooner will we begin to mirror the sentiments and the wishes of the great body of Americans who want America for Americans. [Applause.]"

4 *Congressional Record—House* (1924), 5693. The speaker here is Congressman Allen who, after observing that the "primary reason for the restriction of the alien stream . . . is the necessity for purifying and keeping pure the blood of America," goes on to remark that the "danger line has been reached, if not passed. The percentage of illiterates here is too large and the percentage of unassimilable aliens is also excessive."

5 Calvin Coolidge, *America's Need for Education* (Boston, 1925), 56. Subsequent references are cited in parentheses in the text.

6 Nathaniel Hawthorne, *The Scarlet Letter*, ed. Sculley Bradley, Richmond Croom Beatty, E. Hudson Long, and Seymour Gross (New York, 1978), 172. Subsequent references are to this edition and are cited in parentheses in the text.

7 Stephen M. Ross accurately remarks that "However despairing or nihilistic a given reader may find *The Sound and the Fury*, the momentary ameliorative affirmation engendered by the Easter sermon is almost universally acknowledged" (*Fiction's Inexhaustible Voice: Speech and Writing in Faulkner* [Athens, 1989], 36). But it's essential to recognize that the opposition between the redemptive aspirations of the sermon and the presumed nihilism of the rest of the book is a false one; in the effort to make blood be blood, incest is as good as Easter. Insofar, then, as the sermon counts as an "affirmation," what it affirms is the preference for identity over representation that every other section of *The Sound and the Fury* also affirms.

8 Arguing against what he characterizes as the "Lost Generation" interpretation of this period, Charles C. Alexander asserts that "renewed inquiry into the history of American thought and culture in the twenties highlights the potent workings of a hopeful,

often buoyantly confident cultural nationalism," and he identifies this nationalism with Frederick Lewis Allen's hope that "the time had come when the most powerful nation in the world might rid itself of its cultural subjection to Europe" (Charles C. Alexander, *Here the Country Lies: Nationalism and the Arts in Twentieth-Century America* [Bloomington, 1980], 110). But while it is certainly true that postwar disillusion has virtually no explanatory value with respect to "the complex history of ideas and art in the American 1920s" (108), Alexander's own failure to connect the critique of "cultural subjection to Europe" with the attack on immigration and "cultural nationalism" with nativist racism leads him to misunderstand both phenomena and to replace the empty profundities of the Lost Generation with the equally empty (albeit more broadly applicable) profundities of the American struggle for cultural independence. For a more useful cultural history of the '20s, one that unfortunately appeared too late for me to take its insights into account, see Ann Douglas, *Terrible Honesty: Mongrel Manhattan in the 1920s* (New York, 1995).

9   Horace M. Kallen, *Culture and Democracy in the United States* (New York, 1924; reprint 1970), 200. Subsequent references are to this edition and are cited in parentheses in the text.

10 Willa Cather, *The Professor's House* (New York, 1973), 132, 78. Subsequent references are to this edition and are cited in parentheses in the text.

11 F. Scott Fitzgerald, *The Great Gatsby* (New York, 1925), 17, 131, 146. Subsequent references are cited in parentheses in the text.

12 Charles W. Gould, *America, A Family Matter* (New York, 1922), 163. Subsequent references are cited in parentheses in the text. It is perhaps worth mentioning that Gould, like the more influential racist writer Lothrop Stoddard, was published by Scribner's, as were Hemingway and Fitzgerald. The point here is not that Scribner's was distinctively preoccupied with race (in 1926, for example, Cather's publisher, Knopf, brought out Frank H. Hankins's *The Racial Basis of Civilization* and Carl Van Vechten's *Nigger Heaven*), but rather that an interest in racial questions was not consigned to the margins of American intellectual life.

13 In fact, European immigration had already begun to be restricted by the immigration law of 1921 and, of course, Asian immigration had long been restricted both by act of Congress and by the gentlemen's agreement between Roosevelt and the government of Japan in 1908.

14 "If any gift of particular fitness, begged, unearned, lies anywhere in an individual or an association, it lies there, in the natural or ethnic group. That imparts to it its first impulse, its characteristic skill, and its spontaneous direction. All else is acquired" (Kallen, 201). Kallen's identification of ethnic identity with nature suggests also the continuity between Faulkner's revision of the Hawthornian "heart's native tongue" and his deployment of that tongue through the increasingly "Negroid" speech of the Reverend Shegog. In neither Hawthorne nor Faulkner does the emergence of a "natural" language embody a true gesture toward universality, but where Dimmesdale speaks to those whose common nature bespeaks a shared political identity, the Reverend Shegog speaks to those who share a common racial or ethnic identity.

15 Theodore Dreiser, *An American Tragedy* (New York, 1964), 19.

16 Sinclair Lewis, *Babbitt* (New York, 1980), 48–49.

17   Lothrop Stoddard, *Re-Forging America* (New York, 1927), 238. Subsequent references are cited in parentheses in the text.

18   Thomas Dixon, *The Traitor* (New York, 1907), 328. *The Traitor* is the *Trilogy's* last volume; it was preceded by *The Leopard's Spots* (1902) and *The Clansman* (1905).

19   Hannah Arendt, *The Origins of Totalitarianism* (New York, 1973), 25.

20   With respect to Jason, the point is only driven home by the fact that his Memphis girlfriend calls him "daddy" (117) (and that he gives her money instead of paying her) and by his inability to take the point of his own understanding of the meaning of money: "After all, like I say money has no value; it's just the way you spend it. It don't belong to anybody, so why try to hoard it" (117). The miser's transformation of the conventional value of money into the natural value of the hoard repeats the transformation of the prostitute into the daughter. And they call Benjy "the natural" (97)!

21   Gino Speranza, *Race or Nation* (Indianapolis, 1925), 103. Subsequent references are cited in parentheses in the text.

22   In analogizing here the position of the African American to that of the Jew or Italian, I do not mean to suggest that their positions were, in fact, analogous. Indeed, in the Americanizing discourse of Progressive racism, their positions are almost diametrically opposed; the "Negro" defines the limits of Americanization. But it is an important feature of the nativist discourse of the '20s that the "New Negro" comes to be regarded as a national group like any other; this is one of the things that makes the "New Negro" new. And it is interesting to note that the recent recourse to the term "African American" explicitly redeploys the analogy between blacks and immigrant groups like the Jews and Italians.

23   Prescott F. Hall, "Immigration Restriction and World Eugenics," quoted in Lothrop Stoddard, *The Rising Tide of Color Against White World-Supremacy* (New York, 1920), 259. Subsequent references to *The Rising Tide* are cited in parentheses in the text.

24   Hart Crane, Letter to Otto H. Kahn, September 12, 1987, *The Letters of Hart Crane*, ed. Brom Weber (Berkeley, 1952), 307. Subsequent references are cited in parentheses in the text.

25   Ernest Hemingway, *The Sun Also Rises* (New York, 1970), 116. Subsequent references are cited in parentheses in the text.

26   From this standpoint, recent criticism of the anthropological idea of culture and of cultural pluralism as "perpetuating" rather than, as was originally claimed, repudiating "hierarchies of differential value" seems to me to miss the point. Discussing what she describes as the Israeli "obsession with ethnicity," Virginia R. Dominguez persuasively argues that many supposedly "traditional" customs of non-European Israeli immigrants, while generally attributed to "their culture," are in fact a response to their "encounter with discrimination in Israel, the Israeli bureaucracy, and the material conditions of their lives in Israel" ("Invoking Culture: The Messy Side of 'Cultural Politics,'" *South Atlantic Quarterly* 91:1, Winter 1992, 34). Her point here is that inherited differences in culture are invoked as an alibi for the perpetuation of social and economic inequalities; the difficulties that non-European Jews experience in Israeli society are attributed not to injustices in that society but to the immigrants' "culture." But she persistently misunderstands the force of her own point; what's wrong with the use of "culture" in Israel, she says, is that "Any positive reference to

culture almost always implies a European and Eurocentric culture which [the users] can claim as their own and in contrast to which they disparage others" (37). But the injustice in attributing the immigrants' difficulty in Israeli society to "their culture" is not that it devalues their culture but rather, as she herself has shown, that it falsely attributes to cultural inheritance differences that are in fact the product of economic inequality. And this false attribution is made possible by the pluralist commitment to regarding all cultures as equally valuable and therefore treating all cultural differences as worthy of respect. First, in other words, you identify a response to social injustice as a traditional cultural practice, then you value it (as opposed to altering both it and the conditions that in fact produced it) because it expresses the identity of the people whose practice it is. The problem with cultural pluralism, in other words, is not that it is insufficiently pluralistic and therefore serves only to mask a commitment to the superiority of European culture; the problem with it is that, insofar as it is *genuinely* pluralistic, it expresses a commitment to the irrevocability of cultural differences and therefore to their basis in race.

27 I characterize *The Leopard's Spots* and the other two novels in *The Trilogy of Reconstruction* (*The Clansman* [1905] and *The Traitor* [1907]) as anti-imperialist despite the fact that *The Leopard's Spots* describes the war in Cuba as a triumphant proclamation of "the advent of a giant democracy" (Dixon, *The Leopard's Spots* [New York, 1902], 407). (Subsequent references are to this edition and are cited in parentheses in the text.) The Congressional resolution under which the United States went to war with Spain had explicitly abjured "sovereignty, jurisdiction, or control" over Cuba and by 1902, the year in which *The Leopard's Spots* was published, the Platt Amendment had granted the Cubans complete independence. (For accounts of this process, see Ernest May, *Imperial Democracy* [New York, 1961], and Walter LaFeber, *The New Empire* [Ithaca, 1963].) Hence it was the invasion and annexation of the Philippines that served as the focus of American anti-imperialism—indeed, some anti-imperialists explicitly distinguished the "war for humanity against the Spanish in Cuba" from "the war for conquest against the Filipinos" (J. Laurence Laughlin speaking at the Chicago Liberty Meeting of April 30, 1899, reprinted in *The Anti-Imperialist Reader*, vol. 1, ed. Philip S. Foner and Richard C. Winchester [New York, 1984], 290–91)—and it is the arguments against annexation of the Philippines that I describe below as playing a central role in Dixon's novels. These arguments tended to take two forms: first, racist assertions that Filipino self-government was the only way to avoid burdening the United States with what Mrs. Jefferson Davis called "fresh millions of foreign negroes," even "more ignorant and more degraded" (in *The Anti-Imperialist Reader*, vol. 1, 236) than those at home, and, second, political appeals to the unconstitutionality and, more generally, antirepublican character of imperial acquisition. These latter arguments were sometimes antiracist, but even when, as was more often the case, they displayed a certain amount of racial contempt for the Filipinos, that contempt was only incidental to the political point. If, then, anti-imperialist critiques were generally *either* racist *or* constitutional, one way of beginning to understand Dixon's contribution is by noting that in the trilogy, the racial and constitutional arguments against imperial conquest are not only understood as equally important but also (for reasons I give below) as inextricably linked.

28   Ernest Howard Crosby's *Captain Jinks, Hero* (1902; reprinted in *The Anti-Imperialist Reader*, vol. 2, ed. Philip S. Foner [New York, 1986], 267–394) is virtually the only anti-imperialist text I know that deals explicitly with the events in the Philippines, and *Captain Jinks* is more plausibly described as antimilitarist than as anti-imperialist since it is concerned primarily with burlesquing as a "peculiar kind of insanity" the "preoccupation with uniforms and soldiers, and the readiness [of Jinks] to do anything a man in regimentals tells him to" (393).

29   "Platform of the Liberty Congress of Anti-Imperialists Adopted in Indianapolis, August 16," in *The Anti-Imperialist Reader*, vol. 1, ed. Philip S. Foner and Richard C. Winchester (New York, 1984), 309.

30   Edwin Burritt Smith, "Liberty or Despotism," in *The Anti-Imperialist Reader*, vol. 1, ed. by Foner and Winchester, 293.

31   The term "war of conquest" was employed so frequently in anti-imperialist descriptions of the invasion of the Philippines (by people like Bishop Spaulding and Carl Schurz as well as by the anonymous authors of the "Platform" quoted above) that it is difficult not to believe that Dixon intended his audience to hear their voices echoed in the voice of his Lincoln.

32   "We have come as a people to the parting of the ways. Which shall it be: Nation or Empire? . . . Let us look this imperialism squarely in the face and realize what it means. It means the surrender of American democracy. It means a menace to free American citizenship" (*Liberty Tract No. 12* [1900], reprinted in Foner and Winchester, vol. 1, 306–7). This analysis of imperialism as a threat above all to *self*-government tends to be overlooked by those (like Lenin, for whom American anti-imperialists were "the last Mohicans of bourgeois democracy") who criticize what Robert L. Beisner has called the "impotence" of American anti-imperialists and who see them as essentially "conservative" (Beisner, *Twelve Against Empire* [Chicago, 1985], 222). If we understand American anti-imperialism as committed above all to the revisionary rescue of the concept of American citizenship described in this section, then we must also understand it to have been largely successful and, in its conceptual alliance with what Joel Williamson has called "radical" racism, hardly conservative.

33   Thomas Nelson Page, *Red Rock* (Ridgewood, New Jersey, 1967), viii. Subsequent references are cited in parentheses in the text.

34   In his psychobiographical reading of *The Leopard's Spots*, Joel Williamson emphasizes "the affinity of Dixon for Dick" and, characterizing *The Leopard's Spots* as Dixon's attempt "to get right with womanhood generally and with his mother specifically," reads Dick's lynching as displaced punishment for Dixon's feelings of sexual guilt (Williamson, *The Crucible of Race: Black-White Relations in the American South Since Emancipation* [New York, 1984], 169). For Williamson, "Racism is essentially a mental condition, a disorder of the mind in which internal problems are projected upon external persons" (151), and *The Leopard's Spots* is thus of interest as evidence of how "the deeply personal and largely secret psychic needs of an individual might impel that person to extreme racism" (151). But, however implausible this reduction of racism to psychological abnormality (not to mention the even more blatant implausibility of the implication that late twentieth-century liberal views on race are evidence of psychological normalcy), Williamson's study of American racism since

the Civil War is an exceptionally insightful and powerful one, and has, particularly in its emphasis on and analysis of the rise of racial "radicalism," been crucial to my own understanding of the topic.

35 On the Klan's nationalism and, especially, on the use made of Dixon by D. W. Griffith in *The Birth of a Nation*, see Michael Rogin, "The Sword Became a Flashing Vision," in *Ronald Reagan, The Movie and Other Episodes in Political Demonology* (Berkeley, 1987), 190–235.

36 In fact, after winning the elections of 1894 and 1896, the fusionists were soundly defeated by the Democrats in 1898 and, after the disfranchisement of blacks in 1900, North Carolina followed Louisiana, Mississippi, and South Carolina into the ranks of the solid Democratic South. Charles L. Flynn Jr. has recently argued that because the Southern Democracy (he is speaking of Georgia in particular but the argument can be generalized) was held together by "a conspiracy theory of national politics," Democrats were "unable to conceive of legitimate dissent outside of their party" ("Procrustean Bedfellows and Populists: An Alternative Hypothesis" in *Race, Class and Politics in Southern History: Essays in Honor of Robert F. Durden*, ed. Jeffrey J. Crow, Paul D. Escott, and Charles L. Flynn Jr. [Baton Rouge, 1989], 102). Emphasizing the similarity of populist and Democratic views in fundamental issues, his point is to revise C. Vann Woodward's account of the destruction of radical populism at the hands of conservative Democrats by suggesting that the ideological differences between the two groups were not as great as the more properly political ones; what the Democrats found most disturbing about the populists, in effect, was that they were not Democrats. And Flynn traces this nonideological loyalty to the Democratic Party back to the Reconstruction identification of Republicans as a "money aristocracy" out to plunder the South. His emphasis on the nonideological character of loyalty to the Democratic Party seems to me powerfully suggestive, but I would also argue that it is crucial not to think of this loyalty as simply the continuation of provincial or sectional paranoia. For Progressives (Southern and national), the one-party state could be understood less as a relic of Reconstruction than as a harbinger of the disappearance of partisan politics altogether and of their replacement by (as in Colonel House's *Philip Dru, Administrator*) the "commission"-run, administered state.

37 Herbert Croly, *The Promise of American Life* (1909; reprinted New York, 1965), 340. Subsequent references are cited in parentheses in the text.

38 Describing a "typical entry" (from December 29, 1853) in the diary of one Duncan McCall of Jefferson County, Mississippi, Eugene D. Genovese writes, "He had, he recorded, killed a hog for his guests—'Mr. Watson's family, black and white'" (*Roll, Jordan, Roll* [New York, 1974], 73). Genovese's point is both that slave culture was shaped by a "special sense of family" that "brought black and white together" and that this same sense required not only slaves but also women and children "to accept subordination and obey the head of the white family" (74). It is noteworthy in this context that Progressive racism's critique of the family—its effort to replace family with race—was compatible with and often (as in the case of Ellen Glasgow) central to Progressive feminism's critique of the family, its effort to free wives and daughters from patriarchy.

39 For a more detailed discussion of the invisibility of racial identity in *The Clansman* and related texts, see Walter Benn Michaels, "The Souls of White Folk," in *Literature and the Body*, ed. Elaine Scarry (Baltimore, 1988), 185–209.

40 Mark Twain, *Pudd'nhead Wilson and Those Extraordinary Twins,* ed. Sidney E. Berger (New York, 1980), 60.

41 It is worth noting that this commitment to the Constitution significantly distinguishes American Negrophobia from the German anti-Semitism that was mobilized for Nazi totalitarianism. Totalitarianism's "defiance," as Arendt puts it, of "all, even its own, positive laws" (462) involved an indifference to constitutionalism so complete that, as Arendt points out, the Nazis never even bothered to revoke the Weimar Constitution. The political meaning of Dixon's Negrophobia, by contrast, is incomprehensible if separated from his identification of the law with the state.

42 This identification of anti-imperialism with a commitment to the racial state finds a powerful if indirect confirmation in another novel of 1905, Abraham Cahan's *The White Terror and the Red* (New York, 1905). *The White Terror and the Red* begins with a Russian prince disgusted by the "similarity in physical appearance" between "born aristocrats" and "untitled people" and wishing that "common people" were "black," like American "darkies," so that in Russia, as "in some countries," there would be "some difference between noble people and common" (10). In Cahan's Russia, there are no "darkies," of course, but the relation between the "question of race" and the "question of class" (386) is nonetheless central to the novel, which takes as its fundamental problem the position of Jews in the revolutionary party, the Will of the People. Thus, on the one hand, the party promises the elimination of racial differences; after the revolution "there won't be any such thing as a Jewish . . . question" (145) and, in the meantime, the Russian prince turns revolutionary and even marries a Jewish girl. But, on the other hand, the party treats the great pogroms of 1881 as hopeful manifestations of revolutionary consciousness; when the prince sees the rioters in the streets, he thinks triumphantly, "So our people are *not* incapable of rising" (367), and when he sees the victims of the pogrom, "the panic-stricken men, women and children with oriental features" running past him, he is "simply" unable to "rouse himself to the sense of their being human creatures like himself" (367). The "oriental features" of the Jews fulfill the wish for a physical "difference" between the classes while at the same time, like Dick's lynching in *The Leopard's Spots*, offering the promise of a class-free society.

Nor is this ambivalence about class and race experienced only by the prince; both the Jews in the novel and the novel itself are absolutely unable to make up their minds about whether the solution to "the Jewish question" consists in the assertion through Jewish nationalism of Jewish racial identity or in the elimination through socialism of Jewish racial identity. Hence the relevance of America, which appears in the novel both as the exemplar of racial distinction and as a "shelter" (416) for Jews. In America, where the significant differences in "physical appearance" are, as the novel has begun by pointing out, between whites and "darkies," Jews can be nationalists and socialists at the same time. Thus, although those whom the novel calls the "Americans" (those who have decided to emigrate) are relatively minor figures in *The White Terror and the Red*, the novel is very much an American novel, written by an

"American" (Cahan emigrated in 1882 as a result of the pogroms) and depicting the Jewish experience in Russia as a rehearsal for American citizenship. Cahan's Jews get involved in anti-imperial politics out of their desire to be Russians: "When I think of the moments of joy the movement affords me," says a Talmud boy turned revolutionary, "of the ties of friendship with so many good people—the cream of the generation, the salt of the earth, the best children Russia ever gave birth to . . . I feel that I get a sort of happiness which no Rothschild could buy" (74). But anti-imperial politics in Russia, as in the United States, turns out to depend upon rather than repudiate racial difference. So Progressive America makes it possible for Jews to be revolutionaries by making it possible, as Dixon himself would suggest in his representation of the Jewish storekeeper in *The Traitor*, for Jews to be white. In America, the prince's desires for class equality and racial difference both can be fulfilled.

43　Stoddard's anti-imperialism went in both directions: he meant to defend whites against the colored races but he also disapproved of at least some of the attempts of whites to "flout legitimate Asiatic aspirations to independence" (223).

44　Quoted in Raymond A. Cook, *Thomas Dixon* (New York, 1974), 63. Dixon, Cook says, "held Jews, Catholics, Indians, and many foreign peoples in high regard."

45　Mary Antin, *The Promised Land* (Princeton, 1985), 227. Subsequent references are cited in parentheses in the text.

46　Gatsby's "enabling act," as Herbert N. Schneidau puts it in *Waking Giants* (New York, 1991), is "the creation of a new identity" that begins with the replacement of his actual family by something a good deal more glamorous: "In unrooted America, especially the West, the Family Romance becomes as valid as any other genealogy" (92). *Waking Giants* is a wonderfully insightful study of what Schneidau calls "the presence of the past in Modernism" but one that, because of its relative indifference to the specifically genealogical nature of that presence, is relatively indifferent also to the nativist commitments embodied by those genealogies.

47　Insofar as the desire for a different future is the desire to belong to a different class, the desire for a different past that replaces it should be understood as the desire to belong to a different race. If, in other words, Progressive racism turned class difference between whites into racial *identity*, the new racism of the '20s turned class difference between whites into racial *difference*.

48　The ambiguity of Gatsby's background—the fact that what appear to be social conditions are presented by Fitzgerald as racial phenomena—is eliminated in *The Sun Also Rises* by making Cohn's class origins unproblematic, which is to say, by making his Jewishness the only relevant fact about him: where Gatsby needs to change his name to begin to count as a Jew, Cohn can be Jewish by leaving his alone. The closest *The Sun Also Rises* gets to the appearance of social class is the reflection—in relation to the Englishman Wilson-Harris—that "You couldn't tell how English would mix with each other" (130), and even this, as I show below, is eventually translated out of class into race.

49　Ernest Hemingway, *A Farewell to Arms* (New York, 1969), 185.

50　The contrast with Nick, "growing up in the Carraway house in a city where dwellings are still called through decades by a family's name" (177), is especially sharp.

51　F. Scott Fitzgerald, *The Beautiful and Damned* (New York, 1950), 408.

52　Madison Grant, introduction to Stoddard, *The Rising Tide of Color*, xxx.

53 The rationale for this claim is provided in *The Rising Tide* in a long quotation from the racist writer Prescott Hall who, appealing to what he describes as a racial Gresham's law, insists that the "poorer" of two races "in the same place tends to supplant the better. Mark you, *supplant*, not drive out . . ." (257); some members of the superior race migrate, Hall says, "*but most are prevented from coming into existence at all.*" Hence, according to Stoddard, "The whole white race is exposed . . . to the possibility of social sterilization and final replacement or absorption by the teeming colored races" (298). Similar observations were commonplace. In *America Comes of Age, A French Analysis* (New York, 1927), for example, Andre Siegfried remarked that in "certain classes of Americans" (he instanced "intellectuals and university graduates"), "reproduction seems almost to have ceased," and he cited "figures" "published and quoted all over the country" showing that "On the basis of the present ratio, 1,000 Harvard graduates . . . will have only fifty descendants at the end of two centuries, whereas 1,000 Rumanians in Boston will have 100,000" (111).

54 Critics of *The Professor's House* tend either to ignore or play down the question of anti-Semitism, attaching it (when they bring it up at all) to Cather's ambivalence about Isabelle McClung's Jewish husband or to her general hostility to the American "preoccupation with material wealth" (David Stouck, *Willa Cather's Imagination* [Lincoln, Nebraska, 1975], 109). This seems to me a mistake but not exactly one I mean to correct here since my own interest is less in anti-Semitism as such than in the role played by anti-Semitism (as by love of the classics and admiration for dead Indians) in the reconstruction of American citizenship.

55 The Johnson-Reed Act was anticipated by the Immigration Act of 1921 which, despite its status as what John Higham calls "a makeshift designed to hold the gate while a permanent plan was worked out," nevertheless "established the underlying principle of national quotas based on the preexisting composition of the American population" (Higham, *Send These to Me* [Baltimore, 1984], 54). The 1921 law created quotas based on the number of foreign-born Americans recorded in the 1910 census. The 1924 law used the 1890 census as a base and cut back the percentage of immigrants to be admitted from 3 to 2 percent of each nationality. It went on to provide that, after appropriate study of the ancestry of the *entire* American population (the native as well as the foreign-born), immigration be limited to a total of 150,000, to be distributed among the various nationalities in proportion to their current representation in the American population. For a detailed discussion of the act of 1924, see John Higham, *Strangers in the Land* (New Brunswick, 1988), 312–24.

56 The following citations are drawn from Francis Paul Prucha's compilation, *Documents of United States Indian Policy* (Lincoln, Neb., 1975).

57 In Zane Grey's *The Rainbow Trail* (New York, 1961) the Indian is called Nas Ta Bega and is based on a Paiute named Nasja Begay who, with John Wetherill, guided Grey to the giant natural arch Nonnezoshe and through Monument Valley in 1913 (41). It was Wetherill's brothers, Richard and Al, who in December 1888 had discovered the Anasazi ruin that they called Cliff Palace and that became Cather's Cliff City.

58 Frederick E. Hoxie, *A Final Promise: The Campaign to Assimilate the Indians* (Cambridge, 1989), 236.

59 Robert F. Berkhofer, *The White Man's Indian* (New York, 1978), 177. The conjunction of the Immigration Act and the Indian Citizenship Act is noted also by Brian Dippie,

who remarks pointedly that "At a time when the embattled Anglo-Saxon could see in other ethnic types only a threat, nativism welcomed the native into the fold" (*The Vanishing American* [Lawrence, Kan., 1991], 257).

60 Perhaps the broadest form which this distinction can take is in the difference between what Peter H. Schuck and Rogers B. Smith call the principle of "consensual membership" ("which holds that political membership can result only from free individual choices") and "birthright citizenship" (which "holds that political membership is entirely and irrevocably determined" by the "natural, immutable circumstances of one's birth") (4). For an extended discussion and critique of each of these principles, see Schuck and Smith, *Citizenship Without Consent: Illegal Aliens in the American Polity* (New Haven, 1985), especially 9–41.

61 For a brief history of Memorial Day, see Michael Kammen's encyclopedic *Mystic Chords of Memory: The Transformation of Tradition in American Culture* (New York, 1991), 103–4.

62 Speaking of "the period from the nineties through the First World War," John Higham asserts that the "great evil native white Americans associated with blacks in this era was essentially identical to what they discerned in immigrants. The evil in both cases was pollution . . ." (*Send These to Me*, 195). Although there is certainly some truth to this claim—Progressives were hostile, for example, to the big-city bossism that they associated with manipulation of the immigrant vote—it is important to note that blacks and immigrants were more easily opposed (as in Dixon) than equated. Hence the massive prewar educational campaigns to Americanize the immigrant could have no parallel among African Americans, with respect to whom the very goal of the Americanization programs—assimilation—was unthinkable. The point of Americanization was to make immigrants more like native Americans; the point of Jim Crow was to erect impassible barriers between African and native or European-born Americans. (It is worth remembering in this context that Woodrow Wilson tolerated his own Cabinet's efforts to segregate the federal government but that he refused to support the Congress's first efforts to restrict European immigration and that he would not sign the immigration bill of 1921; Harding did.)

63 Willa Cather, *24 Stories*, ed. with an introduction by Sharon O'Brien (New York, 1987). Subsequent references are cited in parentheses in the text.

64 The song "America" also played a prominent role in the literature of Americanization. David, the hero of Israel Zangwill's *The Melting-Pot* (1909), is introduced singing it and the final curtain "falls slowly" to the "softened sound of voices and instruments joining in" to perform it. Abraham Cahan's *The Rise of David Levinsky* (1917) features both songs; when, at a Catskills resort, the hotel musicians play "The Star-Spangled Banner," the diners rise "like one man, applauding": "Love for America blazed up in my soul," Levinsky says, "I shouted to the musicians, 'My Country,' . . . and we all sang the anthem from the bottom of our souls" (423).

65 Sharon O'Brien convincingly describes "The Namesake" as an "autobiographical" account of Cather's developing commitment to an "art" with its "source in American soil, American history, and American lives" (*Willa Cather: The Emerging Voice* [New York, 1987], 329). The question, however, is what is meant by "American."

66 Indeed for Griffith, as Michael Rogin points out in a brilliant essay on race, nationality, and aesthetics in *The Birth of a Nation* and Progressivism more generally, the

movie itself could be understood to succeed the Klan and Wilsonian Progressivism in a series of "linked attributions of national paternity" ("The Sword Became a Flashing Vision," in *Ronald Reagan, the Movie and Other Episodes in Political Demonology* [Berkeley, 1987] 192).

67 Although "The Namesake" is one of Cather's earliest stories, she had already used its title once, for a poem in memory of her uncle, William Siebert Boak, who (like the sculptor Lyon Hartwell's uncle in the story) had been killed in the Civil War. But where the poem deploys its genealogical interest on behalf of a personal and vocational ambition—the poet wants to be as heroic in her way (as a writer) as the uncle was in his way (as a soldier)—the story nationalizes that ambition: the inspiration of the dead ancestor makes the sculptor great by making him American. And it is this national ambition that will find its fullest expression in Tom Outland's attachment to the "relics" left behind by his "poor grandmothers" on Blue Mesa, an attachment that distinguishes him not so much from other ambitious artists as from the Dreyfusard Roddy Blake and the Jew Louie Marsellus. One can, in other words, trace the trajectory of Cather's invocation of an idealized ancestry from the uncle she imagines to preside over the proclamation of her personal ambition (in the poem) through the uncle who helps Lyon Hartwell to see that he is an American despite his years in Rome to the cliff-dwelling grandmother who makes Tom a *native* American rather than an American Jew. Indeed, this trajectory should probably be understood to continue on into the 1930s, at least through the long story "Old Mrs. Harris," which connects the dead grandmother to the fallen uncle by modeling her on Rachel Boak, Cather's own grandmother and the mother of her uncle William Boak. In "Old Mrs. Harris," however, the national ambitions of "The Namesake" and *The Professor's House* have been discarded; to be Mrs. Harris's granddaughter Vickie is to be exceptional but not to be exceptionally American. Hence the Jewish couple who play so prominent a role in "Old Mrs. Harris" have no desire to join the family—they wish to appreciate Mrs. Harris without wishing to replace her. And, in fact, their attractively "foreign" presence in the story marks in Cather the separation of genealogy from nativism. The attraction of "blood" ("Mr. Templeton came of a superior family and had what Grandmother called 'blood' [131–32]), the desire to keep one's daughter in one's house ("I want to keep my little daughter as long as I can" [109]), the commitment to learning Latin ("Between the first and second parts . . . there was inserted the *Dies Irae* hymn in full. She stopped and puzzled over it for a long while" [106])—all appear in "Old Mrs. Harris," but they appear emptied of their nativist content. If "Old Mrs. Harris" and the two stories published with it—"Neighbour Rosicky" and "Two Friends"—are all elegies (the title of the volume in which they appeared, *Obscure Destinies* [New York, 1932], comes from Gray's "Elegy Written in a Country Churchyard") and if "Old Mrs. Harris" is, as virtually all critics have agreed, by far the greatest of the three and in some respects, perhaps, the last truly great work Cather produced, that may be because "Old Mrs. Harris" not only mourns Rachel Boak but also reproduces and regrets the passing of those preoccupations that energized the masterpieces of the mid-'20s—*A Lost Lady, The Professor's House,* and *Death Comes for the Archbishop*.

68 Madison Grant, *The Passing of the Great Race* (New York, 1916), 174.

69 The Nordicized Spaniard is central also to *The Sun Also Rises* as the exemplar of

aficion, and the link between Spanish and American racial purity is given a further cogency by the fact that the Jews were expelled from Spain in the year of America's discovery: "On the very day in 1492 that Christopher Columbus set sail from Palos for what turned out to be the New World, he noted in the log the shiploads of Jews and *conversos* leaving under threat of death their Old World home of a millennium" (Marc Shell, *Children of the Earth* [New York, 1993], 30). And even Columbus was not immune to racial criticism: Siegfried quotes the Klan magazine *The American Standard*, complaining in October 1925 about the "efforts of the Roman Catholic hierarchy to foist upon us the belief that Christopher Columbus was the discoverer of America, and through this fraudulent representation to lay claim to inherent rights which belong solely to Nordic Christian peoples, through the discovery of this continent by Leif Eriksson in the year 1000" (*America Comes of Age*, 138). Kammen describes the formation of a "Norwegian-American historical organization" in 1925 and the effort to designate October 9 as Leif Eriksson Day but makes it sound as if the issue were a competition between immigrant groups instead of—as Siegfried and the Klan understood it—a conflict between immigrant aliens and Americans (Kammen, *Mystic Chords of Memory*, 437).

70 Edward Sapir, "Culture, Genuine and Spurious," in *Selected Writings on Language, Culture, and Personality*, ed. David G. Mandelbaum (Berkeley, 1985), 316. Subsequent references are cited in parentheses in the text.

71 Zane Grey, *The Vanishing American* (New York, 1982), 137. Subsequent references are cited in parentheses in the text.

72 Actually the number of Indians had increased from 237,196 in 1900 to 244,437 in 1920, and would rise to 357,499 by 1950 (Prucha, 57).

73 Many other changes were also required, most of them focusing on Grey's depiction of the missionaries. To take a characteristic example, in *The Ladies Home Journal*, Grey describes the missionary as having "little or no conception of the true nature of his task, *of the blindness with which he is afflicted and must eradicate,* of the absurdity of converting Indians in little time, *of the doubtful question as to the real worthiness of his cause,* and, lastly, of the complications fomented by other missionaries, and employees of the government, the cliques, the intrigues, the inside workings of the machine" (157, italics mine). In the Harper's edition, the italicized sections are deleted so that the double question of whether the missionary can succeed in his mission and of whether his mission is in itself a worthy one is reduced to the single question of whether he can succeed.

74 Higham, *Strangers in the Land*, 301.

75 Although Stoddard, as we have already seen, regarded the war as a disaster for the white race, he himself had led the way in driving a wedge between the Germans and the purest of American racial stocks. Rejecting the "Pan-Germanism" of writers like Houston Stewart Chamberlain, Stoddard claimed that Chamberlain was deploying "pseudo-racial arguments as a camouflage for essentially political ends" (*The Rising Tide*, 202). The arguments *seemed* racial because they were based on a commitment to Nordicism but, in representing "modern Germany as almost purely Nordic" when, in fact, it was "mainly Alpine in race" (201–202), Pan-Germanists were defending the political entity of Germany rather than the racial entity of Nordicism. "To let Teuton

propaganda gull us into thinking of Germany as the Nordic fatherland," Stoddard concluded, was "both a danger and an absurdity" (202).

76 As a way of guaranteeing their un-American status, Grey makes the missionaries "Bolshevists" (157) as well as Germans, proleptically (from the standpoint of the time when the story takes place) retrofitting (from the standpoint of the time when the story was written) the wartime enemy as the postwar enemy alien.

77 This particular form of ethnic ingenuity was by no means limited to popular representations of the Indian. Mary Austin, author of *The Land of Little Rain* (1903) and a much more serious student of the Southwest Indians than Zane Grey, effortlessly performs a Grey-style transformation of whites into Germans and Indians into Americans in *The American Rhythm* (a collection of "Amerindian Songs," "Reexpressed from the Originals" and accompanied by an explanatory essay; it was first published in 1923 and reprinted with additional songs in 1930). Explaining the meaning of the "scalp dance" ("not necessarily an expression of ferocious triumph, but a ritual of adoption of the *manes* of the dead into our tribe"), Austin mentions approvingly a dance that recently took place "around four blond scalps" and was "designed to make peace and kinship between our own dark soldiers and the ghosts of the Germans they had slain" (*The American Rhythm* [New York, 1970], 48. Subsequent references are cited in parentheses in the text). As the blonds become Germans, the Indians become "our tribe." One argument in favor of promoting Indian participation in World War I had been that exposing Indians to military procedures would contribute toward the traditional assimilationist goal of Americanizing them but, as Grey and Austin make clear, the participation of the Indian could just as easily be made to serve the nativist goal of Americanizing the American.

Indeed, the literary point of *The American Rhythm* was precisely to help Americanize Americans by turning the attention of American "literary scholarship" away from "the scrap heap of Europe" and back toward "our native epics" (83). In this respect, Austin's efforts parallel those of the more influential William Carlos Williams, who urged American poets to avoid the "clownish turn of trying to join, contrary to every reasonable impulsion, a literature (the English) with which [they] had no actual connection" (*In the American Grain* [New York, 1956], 217. Subsequent references are cited in parentheses in the text). Williams's poetic model was different from Austin's—where she looked to the Indians, he looked to Edgar Allan Poe—but Poe appears in Williams's *In the American Grain* (published, like *The Vanishing American*, *The Professor's House*, et al., in 1925) as a kind of Indian after all. Williams compares him to Daniel Boone—"His greatness," he says, "is that he turned his back and faced inland, to originality, with the identical gesture of a Boone" (226)—and Boone's greatness is that he sought to "understand" the "New World" and "to be part of its mysterious movements—like an Indian" (137). So insofar as Poe is like Boone, he is like an Indian.

But the relation between Boone and Poe and the Indians goes beyond likeness. For Boone, imagined simultaneously as "a lineal descendant of Columbus" (139) and as a kind of father to those Indians whom he chooses as companions "even out of preference to his own sons" (139), produces by inversion the Nophaie effect of genealogical continuity between white and red: where red Nophaie has white children, white

Boone accepts with equanimity the murder of his eldest son by the Indians and, replacing his son with those Indians, makes his children red. "I do believe the average American to be an Indian," Williams writes, "but an Indian robbed of his world" (128). Boone's genius is to see that America can only be "possessed" "as the Indian possessed it" (137), and Poe's genius is, "with the identical gesture of a Boone," to reclaim the possession of America in poetry.

78   Indeed, by the time *The Vanishing American* was published in book form (1925), the German soldier was already being superseded by the alien immigrant as the enemy of the Indian. Thus Congressman Carter of Oklahoma declares his Indian ancestry and his support of the Immigration Act of 1924 by noting that on "this question of restricting immigration my pale-faced brothers are several generations behind the Indian" (*Congressional Record* [1924], 5927). And although Carter acknowledges (to "[Laughter.]") that the efforts of his "progenitors" to "maintain absolute prohibition of immigration into this country" did not meet with "marked success," his exhortation to his "brothers" to renew those efforts, to keep out people with "foreign ideals" and to "keep America American" is met on the House floor with "[Applause.]"

79   Ernest Hemingway, *The Garden of Eden* (London, 1988), 12. According to Kenneth Lynn, *The Garden of Eden* was begun in 1946, put aside in 1947, returned to off and on in the '50s and definitively given up by the end of 1958 (Kenneth Lynn, *Hemingway* [New York, 1987], 540–41). The published novel is a heavily edited and reduced version of a manuscript that, Lynn says, ran to over a thousand handwritten pages.

80   "It is a brother and sister against the world," the hero of William Carlos Williams's *A Voyage to Pagany* (New York, 1928) is told by his sister, describing *Die Walkurie*. The coupling of incest and Indian is managed less explicitly here: Dev Evans (carrying the "perfect" arrowhead he has saved since childhood [28]), reluctantly refuses his sister's offer to marry him and is himself reluctantly refused by the "partly Indian" (183) woman he wishes to marry. But *A Voyage to Pagany* is as explicit as possible in its formulation of the point of that coupling: "It's our baby, a pure American" (242).

81   Ellen Glasgow, *The Voice of the People* (New Haven, 1972), 197. Subsequent references are cited in parentheses in the text.

82   Willa Cather, *A Lost Lady* (New York, 1972), 9. Subsequent references are cited in parentheses in the text.

83   Cather thought there was no duplication and wrote him that, even if there were, any possible debt had been more than repaid by the pleasure she experienced reading *Gatsby*. But many readers have been struck by a certain resemblance between the texts. James Woodress, for example, noting that the first draft of *The Great Gatsby* is narrated by an omniscient author, suggests that, after reading *A Lost Lady*, Fitzgerald "may have invented Nick Carraway, his point-of-view character" (*Willa Cather: A Literary Life* [Lincoln, Neb., 1987], 351–52) on the model of Cather's Niel Marian, and the comparison between Nick and Niel (especially insofar as Nick is to be understood as a tolerant Tom) is an apt one. Both *The Great Gatsby* and *A Lost Lady* produce the threat of miscegenation and both find ways of rescuing themselves from it at the end. Tom and Daisy are restored to each other and Nick is restored to an America that tries to make Gatsby himself almost indigenous. Marian Forrester is finally, almost as an afterthought, saved by "the right man," an "old Englishman" who carries her off to Buenos Aires. But, especially in Cather, the "right man" can never be

right enough, at least for a woman. As long as women are charged with the responsibility of "keeping everyone in his proper place" (153), people are likely to get out of
place because the feminine preference for "life on any terms" can lead to a loss of the
crucial "faculty of discrimination"; hence Daisy's interest in Gatsby and Mrs. Forrester's in Ivy Peters.

84   *Is the Ku Klux Klan Constructive or Destructive? A Debate Between Imperial Wizard
Evans, Israel Zangwill and Others*, reported by Edward Price Bell, ed. E. Haldeman-
Julius (Girard, Kan., 1924), 14. Subsequent references are cited in parentheses in the
text.

85   Eve Kosofsky Sedgwick's description of the relation between Tom and Roddy as a
"gorgeous homosocial romance" seems to me exactly right ("Across Gender, Across
Sexuality: Willa Cather and Others," *South Atlantic Quarterly* 88 [1989], 68). Cather's
depiction of the relations between Tom and Roddy is certainly less homo*sexual* than
comparable depictions in, say, Crane and Hemingway, but the absence of the homosexual in no way compromises the gorgeousness of the romance.

86   Hart Crane, *The Bridge* (New York, 1992), 22. Subsequent references are cited in
parentheses in the text.

87   Gardner argues (in " 'Our Native Clay': Racial and Sexual Identity and the Making of
Americans in *The Bridge*," *American Quarterly*, vol. 44, no.1 [March 1992], 24–50) that
the distinctive identity of both Indians and homosexuals was altered by the debate
over their participation in World War I. With respect to Indian participation in the
war, some, in an extension of the assimilationism that had long dominated Indian
policy and Progressive immigration policy, argued that Indian enlisted men should
fight "side by side with the white man, not as Indians but as Americans . . ."; others, in
the avant-garde of nativism, insisted that the establishment of "purely Indian units"
would more effectively "arouse the patriotism of the entire country." In this view, as
Gardner puts it, "The Indian, brought back to the Old World as the unique mark of
the American, defined patriotism as the defense against a mixed European identity"
(28).

The debate over homosexuality was quite different; indeed, it was hardly a debate
—Franklin Delano Roosevelt's attempt to purge the Navy of homosexuals at the end
of the war has been described by Lawrence Murphy as "the most extensive systematic
persecution of gays in American history" (Gardner, 32). Nevertheless its effect was in
certain respects to strengthen ideas of gay identity; as Gardner puts it (again quoting
Murphy), "The attempt to bracket deviant sexuality from the definition of the American served instead to educate the nation with 'the first detailed documentary evidence in America of a distinctively homosexual community' " (33).

88   In "The Last Good Country," written during the '50s and first published in Philip
Young's collection, *The Nick Adams Stories* (New York, 1972), the couple really are
brother and sister and their desire for each other is doubled by his desire to be an
Indian and by her desire to be a boy (111–19).

89   In effect, it is Gekin Yashi who has borne the half-breed in place of Marian, not so
much half-Indian, half-American as—through the emergence of the missionaries and
their allies as Germans rather than Americans—half-Indian/American, half-German.
Thus the initial opposition of the novel—American versus Indian—is transformed
into the opposition American versus German, which turns the last Indian into the

first American, so that Marian can describe herself as having, through her experiences in the West, become "more American," "more Indian" (278).

90 Nativism would thus be understood to require the acknowledgment of this derivation. "Americans will never find spiritual stability until they learn to recognize the Indians as their *spiritual* ancestors," the anthropologist Jaime de Angulo wrote to his close friend Ruth Benedict as she was beginning the field work that would lead to the landmark *Patterns of Culture*; "The Sun-father of Egypt is a living symbol yet in the collective unconscious psychology of every European through actual contact with the unbroken chain of organic culture. Only the Sun-father of the American Indian (an entirely different sort of person from that of Egypt) can ever be a father to the white American" (quoted in Margaret Mead, *Ruth Benedict* [New York, 1974], 297). In nativism, the difference between Europeans and Americans is entirely a difference in ancestry so, as Europeans become aliens, Americans must become Indians, trading in their white immigrant father for a native red one.

91 The professor's recourse to originality mimics a strategy deployed by those Indians of the period who described themselves as "the original American race" and identified themselves as "the *real* 100 percent *Americans*" (see Hazel W. Hertzberg, *The Search for an American Indian Identity: Modern Pan-Indian Movements* [Syracuse, 1971], 179–236). Sometimes the claim to originality appears to have been invoked merely in an effort to put the Indian on an equal footing with others; sometimes it was invoked to make invidious distinctions between Indians and those whom the *American Indian Tepee* (the official publication of the American Indian Association) called "the IWW or Red Element and others from European stock, or southern Europe, who come to this country and are non-citizens and can hardly read or write English" (quoted in Hertzberg, 222).

92 "The First American," as such, was never published, but a much altered version of it called "Blue Meridian" eventually appeared in *The New Caravan* (New York, 1936), marking, as Cynthia Earl Kerman and Richard Eldridge note, "the end of Toomer's literary career" (*The Lives of Jean Toomer: A Hunger for Wholeness* [Baton Rouge, 1987], 224).

93 Jean Toomer, "On Being an American," in *The Wayward and the Seeking: A Collection of Writings by Jean Toomer*, ed. with an introduction by Darwin T. Turner (Washington, D.C., 1982), 92.

94 Letter to Horace Liveright, September 5, 1923, reproduced in *Cane*, ed. Darwin Turner (New York, 1988), 157. He was also unhappy that Alain Locke had excerpted bits of *Cane* for publication in *The New Negro* since, as he wrote to Countee Cullen in 1923, the "negro movement" has "no special meaning for me." As Kerman and Eldridge put it, "This new American did not want to be a New Negro . . ." (*The Lives of Jean Toomer*, 112).

95 Joel Williamson, *New People: Miscegenation and Mulattoes in the United States* (New York, 1984), xi.

96 Letter to John McClure, July 22, 1922, quoted in Kerman and Eldridge, 96. A letter to Claude McKay from August 9 of the same year (also quoted in Kerman and Eldridge, 96), uses almost the same phrasing: "a spiritual form analogous to the fact of racial intermingling." It is noteworthy also that each letter goes on to express a certain skepticism about the achievement of this fusion and a certain resignation about being pulled "deeper and deeper into the Negro group."

97 Charles Chesnutt, *The House Behind the Cedars* (New York, 1993), 57. Subsequent references are to this edition and are cited in parentheses in the text.

98 Hazel Carby, *Reconstructing Womanhood: The Emergence of the Afro-American Woman Novelist* (New York, 1987), 141. Plausibly because, as Carby notes, a central character in *Contending Forces* insists that "Miscegenation, either lawful or unlawful, we do not want" (264).

99 Pauline Hopkins, *Hagar's Daughter*, in *The Magazine Novels of Pauline Hopkins*, with an introduction by Hazel Carby (New York, 1988), 82. Subsequent references to *Hagar's Daughter* and to the other two *Magazine* novels, *Winona* and *Of One Blood*, are to this edition and are cited in parentheses in the text.

100 In fact, even *The House Behind the Cedars* flirts with the possibility of overcoming race. At the very end, as Rena too is coming down with a fever, George Tryon decides that "love" can "surmount" those "difficulties" that had previously seemed to him "insuperable" (194) and he goes in search of her, asking people if they've "seen on the road a young white woman with dark eyes and hair" (187). The description, of course, is warranted by Rena's appearance but, in an extraordinary stroke, Chesnutt makes it lead Tryon away from Rena and to a woman whom he describes as "white enough" but with "the sallowness of the sandhill poor white" and from whom Tryon recoils "in disgust": "She was not fair and she was not Rena." It's as if, in *The House Behind the Cedars*, there *must* be one objection that liberality can't overlook, and to sacrifice one's fastidiousness about race is to assert one's fastidiousness about class: the dark but aristocratic (her father was a "rich" and "liberal" "gentleman" [105]) Rena is infinitely more attractive than her "white enough" but sandhill poor stand-in. At the same time, however, *The House Behind the Cedars* distinguishes itself from *Hagar's Daughter* and *Winona* by supplementing the white man's doubts about miscegenation with the black woman's repudiation of it. "You are white, and you have given me to understand that I am black," Rena writes Tryon in response to his first efforts of reconciliation; "I accept the classification, however unfair, and the consequences, however unjust . . ." (172). The text suggests the seriousness of its growing hostility to miscegenation by transferring the responsibility of enforcing it to its newly blackened heroine. So if Hopkins's Jewel must die because her white lover was weak and hesitated before deciding to marry her, Rena must die lest *she* become weak and agree to marry Tryon.

101 Henry James, *What Maisie Knew* (New York, 1966), 138. Subsequent references are cited in parentheses in the text. Toni Morrison has noted that it is possible "to read Henry James scholarship exhaustively and never arrive at a nodding mention, much less a satisfactory treatment, of the black woman who lubricates the turn of the plot and becomes the agency of moral choice and meaning in *What Maisie Knew*" (*Playing in the Dark: Whiteness and the Literary Imagination* [Cambridge, 1992], 13). However one assesses the role of the black woman in question, Morrison's main point—that the meaning of blacks to and in James has gone undiscussed—is well taken. But it is also true that Kenneth Warren's brilliant *Black and White Strangers: Race and American Realism* (published in 1993 and so unavailable to Morrison) goes a long way toward meeting the point.

102 Kenneth W. Warren, *Black and White Strangers* (Chicago, 1993), 20, 38. My sense of the function of race in James and especially of its limits is indebted also to an unpublished seminar paper by Alex Love.

103   Henry James, *The American Scene* (Indianapolis, 1968), 375. Subsequent references are to this edition and are cited in parentheses in the text.

104   George W. Cable, "The Freedman's Case in Equity," in *The South Since Reconstruction*, ed. Thomas D. Clark (New York, 1973), 278.

105   Or, alternatively, as the unwillingness to let one's whiteness determine one's identity; this is what it means to turn "white" into "White Eagle."

106   Another way to put this would be to say that Hopkins's England reproduces the structure of Page's old Virginia, where family takes precedence over race and "honor" and "ancient lands and name" confer a position that the law must eventually acknowledge. Even *Winona*'s chief villain, Major Thompson, turns out, like the ambitious clerks and overseers of *Red Rock*, to be a class interloper—he too fled England, where he was a "valet" (think of Twain's Valet de Chambres) and where he actually committed the murder of which White Eagle was unjustly accused. But if in Page the overseers achieve their success by allying themselves with the more discontented Negroes, in Hopkins they achieve success by persecuting them, which is only to say that the enemy in Hopkins is not simply the antifamilial state of Reconstruction but the antifamilial and *racialized* state of Dixonian Progressivism. Thus the slaveholding patriarchal "family black and white" of the plantation is both repeated and revised in *Winona* by "the great family of fugitives" that dwells together "in guileless and trusting brotherhood under the patriarchal care of Captain [John] Brown" (373). Redescribing the mid-nineteenth-century fight against slavery as the turn-of-the-century fight against racism, Hopkins imagines the retrofitted plantation family as the institution through which racial difference will disappear. In John Brown's Kansas, as in aristocratic England, the triumph of social equality makes civil equality unnecessary.

107   In an illuminating survey of some of the uses to which this quotation has been put, Werner Sollors cites Timothy Smith's remark that it was "the favorite text of Black preachers" (*Beyond Ethnicity* [New York, 1986], 60), and himself catalogues its appearance in writers from Samuel Sewell through Harriet Beecher Stowe to W. E. B. DuBois.

108   Pauline E. Hopkins, *Contending Forces: A Romance Illustrative of Negro Life North and South*, with an introduction by Richard Yarborough (New York, 1988), 151.

109   Hopkins, *Contending Forces*, 295.

110   Israel Zangwill, *The Melting-Pot* (1909; reprint New York, 1975), 34. Subsequent references are cited in parentheses in the text. For a history of the melting pot as symbol, see Philip Gleason, *Speaking of Diversity: Language and Ethnicity in Twentieth-Century America* (Baltimore, 1992), 3–31. Gleason makes rather heavy weather of the fact that sometimes the melting pot could be invoked on behalf of the effort to create a new American race and sometimes on behalf of the effort to turn new immigrants into copies of the old ones (if the use of one symbol to mean different things testifies to the "fundamental ambiguity" [15] of the symbol, then all symbols are fundamentally ambiguous), but his account of the term's origins and of its triumph over proposed competitors (from the helpfully bureaucratic "transmuting pot" to the forthrightly skeptical "dumping ground") is a useful one.

111   The italics are mine. And it is perhaps also worth pointing out that at least at one moment in *The Melting-Pot*, Zangwill adds to his usual European list, almost literally as an afterthought, "black and yellow" (184).

112 Jean Toomer, *Cane* (New York, 1988), 29. Subsequent references are cited in parentheses in the text.

113 Letter to Sherwood Anderson, December 29, 1922, in *Cane*, ed. Darwin Turner (New York, 1988), 149.

114 Thus, although readings of *Cane* tend to focus on the question of which race Toomer and his various protagonists understand themselves to belong to, my focus here is on the question of what it means to belong to a race in the first place. For a subtle reading of *Cane* as an exploration of its author's "Afro-American heritage," see Nellie Y. McKay, *Jean Toomer, Artist* (Chapel Hill, 1984); for an energetic critique of Toomer's eagerness to "escape" his racial identity, see Donald B. Gibson, *The Politics of Literary Expression* (Westport, Conn., 1981); for a provocative insistence that *Cane* be read as a "biracial" text, see George Hutchinson, "Jean Toomer and American Racial Discourse," *Texas Studies in Language and Literature*, vol. 35, no. 2 (Summer 1993), 226–50.

115 See especially John Higham, *Send These to Me: Immigrants in Urban America*.

116 Quoted in Werner Sollors, "A Critique of Pure Pluralism," in *Reconstructing American Literary History*, ed. Sacvan Bercovitch (Cambridge, 1986), 270, 271.

117 Ibid., 262.

118 *Is the Ku Klux Klan Constructive or Destructive? A Debate between Imperial Wizard Evans, Israel Zangwill and Others*, 14.

119 The most important recent (literary) critic of pluralism has been Werner Sollors, both in *Beyond Ethnicity* and, especially, in "A Critique of Pure Pluralism," where, citing Horace Kallen's 1924 description of the choice facing Americans as one between "Kultur Klux Klan" and "Cultural Pluralism," Sollors calls attention to the "notion of the eternal power of descent, birth, *natio*, and race" (260) that Kallen shares with his racist opponents. Students of cultural identity (especially the skeptical ones) owe Sollors a great debt. It is essential to see, however, that pluralism can no more be thought of as a simple extension of racism than it can be thought of as a repudiation of racism since, as I argue here, it produces a fundamental change in what racism is. And it's important also to note, as I argue below, that the substitution of culture for race (the idea that ethnic identity is culturally rather than genetically transmitted) can never, as long as cultural identity counts as anything more than a description, be complete.

120 Frank H. Hankins, *The Racial Basis of Civilization* (New York: 1926; rev. ed., 1931), 264.

121 Ibid., 293.

122 Another way to put this is just to say that white supremacy requires a commitment to universal standards that pluralism discards. As P.-A. Taguieff puts it, "*la position d'une inégalité entre les 'races' ou les 'cultures' réintroduit de l'universel dans la pensée raciste: car il faut pouvoir comparer les 'identités' collectives pour les rapporter à une échelle comparative. . . . L'interpretation inégalitaire des différences, du fait qu'elle les réinscrit dans une hiérarchie universelle, corrige l'idéologie différentialiste. Toute hiérarchisation postule une comparabilité des termes hiérarchisés, et suggère qu'ils ont une nature commune*" (*La force du préjugé* [Paris, 1987], 322–23).

123 Thus although Elazar Barkan, in his extremely useful book, *The Retreat of Scientific Racism* (Cambridge, 1992), argues that there was a "shift in the balance of power from the racists to the egalitarians during the twenties" (104), it is important not to mis-

take this shift for a critique of the deployment of race as what Barkan calls "an element of causal cultural explanation." On the contrary, racism in the '20s was increasingly egalitarian without being any the less racist; indeed, inasmuch as racial identity (rather than racial superiority) became the primary term of justification, the commitment to race was *intensified* by the shift to a nonhierarchical racism. Thus the white supremacist Hankins proposed to eliminate race as a criterion of suitability for immigration; *his* idea of a biologically "sound immigration policy" involved admitting "all those of whatever race who can prove themselves free from hereditary taint and pass intelligence tests which show them to be above the average of the present population . . ." (ix). Only once you replaced concern about the superiority or inferiority of the immigrant with concern about his or her difference could racial identity assume its rightful place in the logic of exclusion.

124   Stephen Vincent Benét, *John Brown's Body*, with an introduction by Henry Seidel Canby (Chicago, 1990), ix. Subsequent references are cited in parentheses in the text.

125   In *Reading Race: White American Poets and the Racial Discourse in the Twentieth Century* (Athens, Ga., 1988), Aldon Lynn Nielsen praises Benét for precisely this refusal, saying that he "saw more plainly than many the dangers attendant upon attempting to appropriate the voice of the other" (41). The sanctity of otherness is, of course, fundamental to racial pluralism.

126   Anzia Yezierska, *Bread Givers* (New York, 1975), 210. Subsequent references are cited in parentheses in the text.

127   Thus in Lewis Wirth's classic sociological study, *The Ghetto* (Chicago, 1928; reprint 1982), a chapter about assimilation—"The Vanishing Ghetto"—is followed immediately (and, according to the logic of nativism, necessarily) by a chapter about the repudiation of assimilation—"The Return to the Ghetto." Wirth cites a 1925 editorial in the Jewish paper *The Sentinel* which, acknowledging what Zangwill proclaims—"the number of intermarriages in this country is quite high"—nevertheless asserts that "All of us . . . are agreed in our opposition to intermarriage" (273). The solution to this problem, according to *The Sentinel*, is to train Jewish "youth" in "the ways of Jewish life": "Torah v'avodah, study, and practice" will keep Judaism alive by discouraging "Jewish young men and women" from "marry[ing] out of their race."

128   Oliver La Farge, *Laughing Boy* (New York, 1971), 33. Subsequent references are cited in parentheses in the text.

129   La Farge's Navajos think of both Americans and Hopi Indians sometimes as "aliens" (38) and sometimes as "foreigners" (24).

130   In Samson Raphaelson's play *The Jazz Singer* (New York, 1925), the desire (in this case, of the son) to assert his Americanness against his father's Jewishness is similarly compromised: Jakie Rabinowitz, the cantor's son, becomes Jack Robin, the "black-face comedian," but Jack Robin gives up his Broadway career and blackface to become the image of "his own great grandfather in the Russian ghetto . . . praying to a forbidden God" (132). Jack and his Gentile girlfriend keep saying that Broadway is "in his blood" but, when the play ends, he's singing Kol Nidre and marriage to Mary has been put on indefinite hold. By contrast, the movie that appeared two years later allowed Jack to sing Kol Nidre *and* "My Mammy"; it promised, as Michael Rogin says, "that the son could have it all, Jewish past and American future, Jewish mother and gentile wife" ("Blackface, White Noise: The Jewish Jazz Singer Finds His Voice,"

Critical Inquiry [Spring 1992], 426). But the real meaning of this promise, as Rogin reads it, is assimilation, and blackface—the ability to put on and to take off "the mask of a group that must remain immobile, unassimilable, and fixed at the bottom" (431)—"is the instrument that transfers identities from immigrant Jew to American" (434). There can be no doubt that Rogin is right about the use of blackface; the father of Al Jolson in this regard is Dixon's Sam Nicaroshinski, and even in the play, where blackface has a less prominent role than in the movie, the speech Jack gives as he "blacks up" is about his desire to be "part of America" (107). At the same time, however, Rogin's reading of the cantor's hostility to his son's jazz as an alibi for nativist "prejudices against Jews" (426) underestimates the appeal to Jews of the new pluralism, and his complaint that *The Jazz Singer* attempts to turn "Jewish history in the United States into family melodrama" fails to acknowledge the degree to which the history of American Jews *as Jews* had necessarily to be understood as family melodrama.

131 Hugh Kenner, *A Homemade World* (New York, 1975), 145.

132 The thematic point of these disruptions is characteristically articulated by reference to Cohn: when Cohn decides he doesn't like Paris and wants to go to South America, Jake dismisses both ideas as having come "out of a book." (Indeed, Jake thinks that "all of Paris" [42] is experienced by Cohn through books, and through Mencken in particular.) Paris, Jake tells him, "is a good town" (11) that's "nice at night" (12). "Good" and "nice" don't come out of a book, they come out of an experience of Paris as direct as the experience of the concierge's French.

133 In connection with Cohn's efforts to speak Spanish, it is worth remembering something of the history of the Jews in Spain, not because Hemingway was interested in it but because of the difference that history made to the institution of the bullfight, which is, of course, central both to the Hemingway aesthetic in general and to *The Sun Also Rises* in particular.

The bullfight emerged as the great Spanish national festival in the sixteenth century, which is to say, in the wake of the Christian reconquest, which, "culminating in the expulsion of the Jews in 1492 and of the Muslims in 1502," was, as Marc Shell has put it, "*the* nationalist event in Spanish history" (*Children of the Earth*, 26). At the heart of this reconquest were the Statutes of the Purity of the Blood, which enacted distinctions not merely between Christians on the one hand and Jews and Muslims on the other but between "original Christians and conversos." The statutes changed the difference between Christians and non-Christians from a difference of religious practice into a difference of blood, and not only converts but even those whose ancestors had converted to Christianity emerged, by the standard of blood purity, as insufficiently Spanish. Shell identifies this transformation with what he regards as the underside of Christianity's universalist understanding of all humans as brothers —those who are not my brothers are not human. The bullfight, in his view, "helps to fix ideologically the difference between national and nonnational" (30); it commemorates the emergence of Spain as a nation of "brothers." Whether or not one wishes to follow Shell in his reading of Christian intolerance, the identification of the bullfight as an element in an essentially racial nationalism is obviously suggestive for a reading of *The Sun Also Rises*. In Hemingway, *aficion* plays the role of pure blood, defining the group to which the Jew Robert Cohn cannot belong and structuring his attempts to join it (by sleeping with Brett, by imitating Jake) as inevitably failed efforts of conversion. The attraction of the bullfight, then, is its utility in the construction of a race—not, to be sure, a Spanish race but rather one that is nativist American in structure and international Nordic in personnel.

134   William Carlos Williams, *The Embodiment of Knowledge*, ed. Ron Loewinsohn (New York, 1974), 143, 144. Subsequent references are cited in parentheses in the text. Williams argues here that even "the spaces between the words" count as an element of language, not because they signify something (since signification is what is being superseded) or even because they have a diacritical function—you might count the spaces "for measurement's sake," Williams says, but you don't need to since they should "properly" "be considered themselves words—of a sort" (141). The point, then, is that when signification is eliminated as the criterion of the linguistic, the spaces between words can be seen to be as much a part of the poem as the words; if what it means to be part of "language" is to be part of the "materials" of the poem, then it is obvious that the white spaces on the page are essentially part of those materials. Hence Williams's famous attention to where those white spaces should be put and to how much of them there should be; in what may constitute the ne plus ultra of the materialist aesthetic in poetry, he is even reported to have *weighed* his poems, as if once one recognized that the modernity of the modern poem consisted in its claim to be "itself" rather than to mean something else, all the physical features of the poem (what it looked like, what it sounded like, how heavy it was) became its defining characteristics.

135   William Carlos Williams, *The Autobiography of William Carlos Williams* (New York, 1951), 146.

136   William Carlos Williams, *Spring and All*, in *The Collected Poems of William Carlos Williams*, ed. A. Walton Litz and Christopher MacGowan (New York, 1986), 206. Susequent references are cited in parentheses in the text.

137   William Carlos Williams, *In the American Grain* (New York, 1925), 221. Subsequent references are cited in parentheses in the text.

138   In *A Coherent Splendor: The American Poetic Renaissance, 1910–1950* (Cambridge, 1987), Albert Gelpi points out that "'All' recurs four times in the poem," and that "it rhymes internally with 'fallen, tall, small'" (339), and he convincingly cites various other forms of alliteration and assonance that amount to a "network of verbal echoes and sound play." He is less convincing, however, in his explanation of what these patterns do: the use of "reiterated dental consonants," for example, is said to "suggest the balked stasis of the scene," and repetition in general is said to "integrate the individual details into the picture." The problem here is the effort to instrumentalize the "materials," to put them to the use of representation when it is their resistance to representation that mattered to Williams. The point is not that the poem has no meaning but that these elements are foregrounded and yet are not part of that meaning.

139   *The Letters of Ezra Pound 1907–1941*, ed. D. D. Paige (New York, 1950), 124. In addition to making fun of Williams's claim to be a "REAL American," Pound quotes a few lines deprecating the very idea of literary nationalism, a position worth remembering should it come to comparing Pound's anti-Semitism to the more properly nativist commitments described below. Although such a comparison will be sketched out

later, it is worth noting here that Pound's indifference to the idea of a native poetry and his hostility to pluralism suggest a set of racial commitments different not only in degree but in kind from those discussed in this section.

140   For a discussion of separation as the attempt "to separate words from things," see Joseph Riddel, *The Inverted Bell: Modernism and the CounterPoetics of William Carlos Williams* (Baton Rouge, 1974), 225–26.

141   This is not to say that a materialist poetic as such *need be* a nativist or even a nationalist poetic. Williams might, for example, have conceived of American identity as the sort of thing that could be achieved without in any sense also being inherited and so might have admitted the possibility that someone who wasn't American could easily become American. He might, in other words, have been committed to the account of poetic identity that I describe him as holding without being committed to the account of national identity that I describe him as also holding, in which case he would not have identified poetic independence with national independence. In this sense, of course, the fact that he held both these views is contingent. My point in beginning this paragraph with the claim that the relation between the terms in which Williams describes poetry and the terms in which he describes Americans is *not* contingent is just to emphasize that the connection between poetry and American-ism is anchored in a deeper connection between poetry and national identity. Thus the relation between his terms of description (for poetry and American identity) is neither coincidental nor an expression of enthusiasm for attractively American qualities; the fact that the terms he uses are the same expresses his commitment to the idea that the conditions of identity in poetry are the same as the conditions of identity in nationality.

142   *Culture and Democracy in the United States*, 177. Indeed, according to Kallen, even miscegenation can't destroy racial identity. With respect to race, miscegenation too is an environmental influence, conferring upon people the "traits" of different races but leaving the traits themselves untouched; hence, "intermarriage . . . is not racial assimilation." This scenario preserves the integrity of the race at the expense of the integrity of the body; thus Faulkner's Joe Christmas, running from a lynch mob, incomprehensibly ends up hiding "where he must have known he would be certainly run to earth" and, carrying a loaded gun, fails to fire at the man who catches and then kills him: driven alternately and incoherently by his "black blood" and his "white blood," he is unable to "let his body save itself" (Faulkner, *Light in August* [1932; reprinted New York, 1985], 443, 449). The races compete rather than mix in Joe Christmas; his body doesn't have a racial identity, it is a site occupied by (more than one) racial identity.

143   Willa Cather, *Death Comes for the Archbishop* (New York, 1927), 286. Subsequent references are cited in parentheses in the text.

144   For an earlier formulation of the same point, see Horace Kallen's remark, "An Irishman is always an Irishman, a Jew always a Jew" (*The Structure of Lasting Peace* [Boston, 1918], quoted in John Higham, *Send These to Me*, 206).

145   Woodress, *Willa Cather: A Literary Life*, 396. The remark is quoted from a letter to Fanny Butcher.

146   The passionate Padre Martinez is the exception that proves the rule. A "native" priest who refuses celibacy and who has children and grandchildren throughout the area,

he is rendered by the bishop's arrival "really impotent" (141). And this impotence makes him a bulwark of rather than a threat to nativist identity; he begins "already" to be "picturesque," something "left over from the past," like the Indians who are also, of course, "dying out" (122).

147   Willa Cather, *On Writing* (Lincoln, Neb., 1988), 9. This remark comes from Cather's 1927 letter to *The Commonweal* discussing the composition of *Death Comes for the Archbishop*. Subsequent references are cited in parentheses in the text.

148   I borrow this phrase from Kathy Acker's *In Memoriam to Identity* (New York, 1990), much of which is an elaborate and inventive rewriting of *The Sound and the Fury*.

149   What makes them crazy is what makes them pure, the inbreeding of "old names," a "promiscuity" that produces "deaf-mutes." The "isolate lakes and valleys" of New Jersey make the setting of this poem a topographic equivalent of the "separate" "reality" of "pure writing." Its central figure, a "desolate" girl "with a dash of Indian blood," expresses "the truth about us" by embodying in her desolation the truth of poetry's separation (its purity) and of America's isolation (its purity).

150   The specificity of this claim may be indicated by contrasting it to related discussions (in, for example, Michael Fried, *Realism, Writing, Disfiguration: On Thomas Eakins and Stephen Crane* [Chicago, 1987], and Walter Benn Michaels, *The Gold Standard and the Logic of Naturalism* [Berkeley, 1987]) of the meaning of a certain preoccupation with the materiality of writing in American literature at the turn of the century. I would distinguish here between what might be called a premodern insistence on materiality as a form of metaphysical inquiry into the conditions of identity—what makes writing writing—and the nativist insistence on materiality as a way of making identity primary, and so of distinguishing between different identities—what makes American writing American. In the poetic under discussion here, the point is not the artifactuality of the poem but the Americanness of the artifact.

151   Kenner wittily retraces as criticism Hemingway's own route through the English to the Indian: "To write off the big empty words is to return to the small full words, small because Saxon and rooted, full because intimate with physical sensation, the ground, the knowable. But the small full words have dangers of their own; they tend to contract and grow fewer, and approximate to the grunt" (*A Homemade World*, 156). In La Farge's hands, the devotion to Hemingway's principles produced something called the "test of monosyllables," designed to measure the effectiveness of one's prose style and made literal in a chart by T. M. Pearce comparing the percentage of monosyllabic words in a page of *Laughing Boy* to the percentage in a page of *A Farewell to Arms*. *A Farewell to Arms* wins, 78.2 to 73.8 (T. M. Pearce, *Oliver La Farge* [New York, 1972], 71–72).

152   *In the American Grain* frequently identifies Americans as Indians, as in the famous remark, "I do believe the average American to be an Indian, but an Indian robbed of his world" (128), and even its most explicit denial of this identification—"No, we are not Indians . . ." (39)—immediately turns into a way of reasserting it, replacing the "blood" we don't inherit from the Indians with the "spirit" we do, so that "It is we who ran to the shore naked, we who cried, 'Heavenly Man!' These are the inhabitants of our souls, our murdered souls . . ." (39). Rhetorical strategies like these should no doubt be understood as expressions of what Williams elsewhere calls the desire to "steal" "some authenticity" from the corpses of "dead Indians" (74).

153   Albert C. Barnes, *The Art in Painting* (New York, 1925), 306.

154   Alain Locke, ed., *The New Negro* (1925; reprinted New York, 1968), 267, 261. Subsequent references are cited in parentheses in the text.

155   As Houston A. Baker Jr. puts it, the "inner objective" of *The New Negro* was "to found a nation of Afro-Americans on the basis of RACE" (*Modernism and the Harlem Renaissance* [Chicago, 1987], 79).

156   Zora Neale Hurston, "Characteristics of Negro Expression," in *The Sanctified Church* (Berkeley, 1981), 58. This essay was first published in 1934 in Nancy Cunard's anthology *The Negro*.

157   In *The Souls of Black Folk* (1903), for example, Du Bois contrasts "segregation by color" to the "natural clustering by social grades common to all communities" and complains that "the best of the whites and the best of the Negroes almost never live in anything like close community" (*The Souls of Black Folk* [New York, 1986], 477). At its most extreme, this produces an almost Page-like description of slavery when, "through the close contact of master and house-servant in the patriarchal big house, one found the best of both races in close contact and sympathy" (477). Du Bois is not, of course, nostalgic for slavery; he is, however, eager to deploy the "rule of inequality" (421) *within* the races in the service of insistence on equality *between* the races.

158   I don't, of course, mean to imply here that only the decision *not* to pass involves a commitment to racial essence; on the contrary, the very concept of passing—requiring, as it does, the possibility of a difference between one's apparent racial identity and one's real racial identity—involves such a commitment. For if there could be no difference between one's real racial identity and one's apparent racial identity, no one could ever pass: what you passed for would of necessity be what you were.

159   In this judgment, Braithwaite understands himself to be following William Dean Howells, while at the same time he agrees with Dunbar that Howells's enthusiasm for Dunbar's dialect poems was disastrous for Dunbar himself and for the "versifiers" who were his immediate successors. For a related but more complex sense of Dunbar's practice in the dialect poems, see Shelly Eversley's dissertation-in-progress (Johns Hopkins).

160   Langston Hughes, *Not Without Laughter* (New York, 1969), 240, 244.

161   In *The Signifying Monkey* (New York, 1988), Henry Louis Gates Jr. argues for the particular importance of "a dialect-informed free indirect discourse" in *Their Eyes Were Watching God*, characterizing it "as a mediating third term that aspires to resolve the tension between standard English and black vernacular" (215). To put the point this way is to think of Hurston as feeling pressure to choose between the standard and the dialect (as if between middle class or "white" and lower class or "Nigger") and resorting to free indirect speech as "a third language" that, combining the dialect with the standard, becomes the "ultimate sign of the dignity and strength of the black voice" (215). If, however, the point in Hurston is not to incorporate dialect into the standard but to make dialect the object of (self-)representation, then the production of blackness would depend on maintaining rather than resolving the tension between the two, since it is only this tension that makes the project of representation and hence the articulation of racial autonomy through class difference possible.

162   Antonio Gramsci, *Selections from the Prison Notebooks*, ed. and trans. Quintin Hoare and Geoffrey Nowell Smith (New York, 1971), 5, 10.

163 Hazel Carby, "The Politics of Fiction, Anthropology, and the Folk," in *New Essays on Their Eyes Were Watching God*, ed. with an introduction by Michael Awkward (Cambridge, 1990), 75, 76. The whole point for Hurston, however, is that the idea of race *does* resolve these contradictions. Carby compares Hurston unfavorably to Richard Wright, suggesting that Wright's efforts "to explode the category of the Negro" reveal him to be a "modernist," while Hurston is left "embedded in the politics of Negro identity" (79). Carby is surely right to think of Hurston as committed to the politics of Negro identity but, from the standpoint of the history that I have been tracing, it is precisely this commitment that makes her the real modernist.

164 Robert E. Park, "Understanding a Folk Culture," originally published as the introduction to Charles S. Johnson, *The Shadow of the Plantation* (Chicago, 1934) and reprinted in *On Social Control and Collective Behavior*, ed. with an introduction by Ralph H. Turner (Chicago, 1967), 20, 22.

165 Sherwood Anderson, *Dark Laughter* (New York, 1925), 42. Subsequent references are cited in parentheses in the text.

166 Ernest Hemingway, *The Torrents of Spring*, in *The Hemingway Reader* (New York, 1953), 74, 75, 79, 77. Subsequent references are cited in parentheses in the text.

167 The gesture here is identical to St. Peter's (in *The Professor's House*) when he tries to kill himself upon learning of his daughter's pregnancy. "Indian Camp" is the first story in *In Our Time* (New York, 1925); subsequent references to it and to other stories in that collection will be cited in parentheses in the text.

168 Ernest Hemingway, *Men Without Women* (New York, 1925), 39. Subsequent references are cited in parentheses in the text.

169 Kenneth S. Lynn, *Hemingway*, 244–48.

170 D. H. Lawrence, *St. Mawr and Other Stories*, ed. Brian Finney (Cambridge, 1983), 190. Subsequent references to "The Princess" and to *St. Mawr* are to this edition and are cited in parentheses in the text.

171 D. H. Lawrence, *The Plumed Serpent*, ed. L. D. Clark (Cambridge, 1987), 78, 117. Subsequent references are cited in parentheses in the text. The setting of *The Plumed Serpent* is, of course, Mexico, which, given Lawrence's identification of the American with the "savage," seemed to him more American than anything in the United States.

172 It's striking that the final figure for the Indian in *St. Mawr* should be an animal: "On one of the roof-planks a pack-rat was sitting erect like an old Indian keeping watch on a pueblo roof. He showed his white belly, and folded his hands, and lifted his big ears, for all the world like an old immobile Indian" (152). Since the attraction of the ranch is its wildness, the comparison absorbs the Indian into that wildness, making his attraction a function of his animal-like nature. Along the same lines, the "aboriginal" Welsh groom seems so "to sink himself in the horse when he rides" that his mistress is unsure when she speaks to him whether she's "speaking to a man or to a horse" (38).

173 By the same token (i.e., insofar as "Indian" essentially means "ancient" or "barbaric") "Anglo-Saxon" essentially means "modern": "You think like a modern woman," the "dark" Don Ramon says to the "white" Kate, "because you belong to the Anglo-Saxon or Teutonic world . . ." (204). The difference in Lawrence between the Anglo-Saxon and Indian worlds is just the difference in their distance from barbarism. This is why, despite Kate's expressed distaste for "contact" (188) between brown skin and white,

her marriage to an Indian can turn out to be so unproblematic (or why, from the other side, a white woman can so easily be made into an Indian goddess, Malintzi). Because the marriage between Kate and Cipriano both enables and requires her to give up her modernity, it effaces the "racial" difference between them and cannot count as miscegenation.

174   Sollors, *Beyond Ethnicity*, 64.

175   Robinson Jeffers, *Selected Poetry* (New York, 1937), xvi. Subsequent references are cited in parentheses in the text. My attention was first drawn to *Tamar* by John Irwin's description of it, in *Doubling and Incest/Repetition and Revenge* (Baltimore, 1975), as a text from which *The Sound and the Fury* is descended, that is, as a text centrally concerned with incest and more particularly with what Irwin understands in Faulkner as "an incestuous, suicidal struggle" between the "narrator" and "his dark twin, the story" (20). Although Irwin reads incest in these texts as an essentially psychological phenomenon and I read it as an essentially cultural one, I think he is absolutely right to suggest a connection between the "incestuous struggle" and what he both blandly and wittily describes as a certain "creative ambivalence to the homeland" (21). It is, of course, the modernist reconstitution of the idea of the "homeland" that is my particular concern here.

176   This regionalism achieves a kind of literal apotheosis in Jeffers's poem "Roan Stallion" (1927), which, like *St. Mawr*, is the story of a woman and her horse. But where, in *St. Mawr*, the woman admires the horse and flirts with Indians, in "Roan Stallion," she sleeps with the horse and is an Indian, and her name is California. The roan stallion, unlike St. Mawr, is successfully put to stud but the experience makes him feel cheap and, when California gives herself to him that same night, it not only wipes out "the shame of the day" (151), but also prepares the way for his death; just as Tamar kills her lover, California kills hers. The point in both instances is to keep him from or punish him for going "out"; "Roan Stallion," in its most nativist moment, calls it "wrestling with the stranger," and thereby comes closer than *Tamar* to supplying a Louie Marsellus. Lawrence's St. Mawr "don't seem to fancy the mares" (29), so he needn't die, and although he is last seen following "almost slavishly" "at the heels of . . . [a] long-legged black Texan mare" (132), by this time in the novel he has become irrelevant, an "illusion" (137). It is *St. Mawr*'s heroine, not its hero, who will finally live up to the responsibility of sterility, and she will do so by giving herself to the "wild spirit" that inhabits her New Mexico ranch and that "wants" her "more than men" do (155). "Roan Stallion," identifying the horse with God the "father" and its owner with "Mary" (148) (and naming her daughter Christine) is, like *The Sound and the Fury*, more committed to an explicitly Christian extinction. That's what makes the apotheosis literal.

Hence the poem begins by juxtaposing the question, "Did you buy something, Johnny, for our Christine?" with the reminder that "Christmas comes in two days, Johnny" (141). The point will be to put the Christ back in Christine, which will mean redescribing her birth as a virgin birth, exchanging her human father, Johnny, for the roan stallion and reimagining her mother, California, not as Johnny's wife but as "the stallion's wife," which is to say, as "God's wife" (148). The stallion, then, rescues California and redeems her from promiscuity ("Johnny and other men have had me" [153]) by taking the place of her "outcast" husband and retroactively installing himself as Christine's divine parent, "the Father himself" (150). If, then, the coupling of California and the stallion is from one point of view an "unendurable violation" (154), it must, from another point of view, not even count as sexual penetration: "Not entering not accepting entrance, more equally, more utterly, more incredibly conjugate/With the other extreme and greatness; passionately perceptive of identity . . ." (153). The absence of penetration, the tribute of "the whole to the whole" (153), is what will mark Christine's birth as virgin. Indeed, the very idea of the virgin birth is a kind of tribute to identity, a repudiation not merely of the miscegenetic promiscuity of a Pocahontas but of sexual penetration itself. California can only be "covered by a huge beast" (154) because the beast, turning into a "creature" with "wings," is the Holy Spirit. And intercourse with Him, like intercourse with a sibling, will meet the criteria of nativist purity.

177   William Carlos Williams, *Paterson* (New York, 1963), 3. These lines are from book 1, which first appeared in 1946.

178   T. S. Eliot, *The Complete Poems and Plays* (New York, 1926), 24. The lines are taken from "Burbank With a Baedeker: Bleistein With a Cigar," which was published in *Poems* (1920).

179   Ezra Pound, *The Cantos* (New York, 1972), 257. These lines are from Canto LII, which first appeared in 1940.

180   Ezra Pound, *Jefferson and/or Mussolini* (New York, 1935), 12, 27.

181   Ibid., 12.

182   See, for example, "Provincialism, the Enemy," first published in *The New Age* in 1917 and reprinted in Ezra Pound, *Selected Prose*, ed. with an introduction by William Cookson (New York, 1973), 189–294. Subsequent references to this essay and, unless otherwise specified, to Pound's other essays, are to this edition and are cited in parentheses in the text.

183   T. S. Eliot, "Tradition and the Individual Talent," in *Selected Prose*, ed. with an introduction by Frank Kermode (New York, 1975), 38, 40.

184   For an account of British debates about liberalism in the early twentieth century and especially for a discussion of the relation between these debates and the work of Pound and Eliot, see Mark Schoening's dissertation (Johns Hopkins, 1994), "Modernism and Liberalism."

185   D. H. Lawrence, *Studies in Classic American Literature* (New York, 1964), 62. Subsequent references are cited in parentheses in the text.

186   Wyndham Lewis's attack on Lawrence (in *Paleface: The Philosophy of the 'Melting-Pot'* [London, 1929]) is thus mistaken, albeit in an interesting and revealing way. Lewis understands Lawrence's appeal to the "non-individual" as a kind of "communism," and he compares it to the search for a "higher unity" promoted by "the latest european advocate of Bolshevism, René Fülöp-Miller," who recommends "marching, keeping in step, shouting 'hurrah' in unison" and "festal singing in chorus" as ways of producing a "new and superior type of humanity" (182). But these are activities, properly speaking, of the group rather than the race and (although, of course, the two may be folded in to one another) the point of race for Lawrence is, as we have seen, that it can be deployed against the group. Indeed, it might be argued that Lewis's criticism of Lawrence indicates his own indifference to the possibilities of race. For, although Lewis denies that "all people are the same" and insists that each

race has its own "soul or 'consciousness,' or whatever you like to call it" (155), and although the main point of *Paleface* is to call attention to the dangers confronting the white race whose fate, if it isn't careful, "might be the same as that of the Redskin" (236), the threat he imagines is not the loss of racial identity but the loss of individuality, the possibility of becoming "*Mass men*" (221). Unlike Lawrence or, as I will argue below, E. M. Forster, Lewis was unable to understand racial identity as a weapon to be used against the "herd." Thus the concerns of his major writings of the '20s are significantly identitarian—in *Time and Western Man* (1927), for example, the "self's" "first law of being" is "to maintain its identity" and refuse "the mongrel itch to *mix*" (132)—but not significantly racial—the villain of *The Childermass* (1928) may be a "paleface" who's "black inside" (171) but that novel's real obsessions are with the "child cult" and the "homosexual." At the same time, however, Lewis's parodically nativist account of "Homo's Rights (*My Passion right or wrong!*)" (249), suggests that he understood homosexuality as a racialized phenomenon and, while his rewriting of allegiance to one's country as allegiance to one's sexual desires seems intended as a critique of identitarianism, it seems obvious that such a rewriting could also make a significant contribution to identitarian ambitions.

187   E. M. Forster, *A Passage to India* (New York, 1924), 65, 131. Subsequent references are cited in parentheses in the text.

188   So if, as Thomas J. Otten has perceptively remarked (in "Pauline Hopkins and the Hidden Self of Race" *ELH* 59 [1992]: 227–256), *Of One Blood's* spiritualism allows it "to reassert an area of black cultural history that much previous black writing had displaced" (239) and thus to open up a new space "for thinking about or rethinking racial heritage" (233), it does so only by depicting that cultural history and that racial heritage as the biography of a single immortal soul. The advantage of this scheme is, of course, that it solves the problem of how things you didn't do can nevertheless be understood as part of your past: in a previous incarnation, you did do them! The disadvantage, at least for current defenders of the importance of cultural heritage, is that it requires you to believe in reincarnation.

189   Trying to explain the contribution of "imagination" ("the one thing beside honesty that a good writer must have") to "good writing" led Hemingway, in 1935, to make a similar point. "Good writing is true writing," which is why it needs "honesty" and, necessarily, something to be honest about, "experience." "Then what about imagination?" Imagination "is what we get for nothing"; in other words, imagination is unearned in the sense of going beyond our experience. Hence "Nobody knows a damned thing about it" but hence also, since good writing is true writing and since Hemingway's conception of the true requires some experience to be true to, imagination may involve our experience after all: "It may be racial experience. I think that is quite possible" ("Monologue to the Maestro: A High Seas Letter," in *By-Line: Ernest Hemingway*, ed. William White [New York, 1967], 215).

190   Edward Said is thus right to see Forster's contempt for Indian nationalism as an expression of imperialism but wrong to identify it with the conviction that Indians "are not yet ready for self-rule" and so "the English had better go on doing it" (*Culture and Imperialism* [New York, 1983], 205). It is nationalism as such that Forster's imperialism attacks, not Indian nationalism in the service of English nationalism. And when Said forgives Forster his condescension toward Indian nationalists on the

grounds that *A Passage to India* is "a novel that deals with personal, not official or national, histories" (204), he is again half right; the novel's imperialism consists precisely in its dealing with "personal"—not instead of but *as opposed to* "national"—histories.

191 Adolph Hitler, *Mein Kampf*, trans. Ralph Manheim (Boston, 1943), 383. Volume 1 was published in German in 1925, volume 2 in 1927.

192 Ibid., 302.

193 In his collection of essays, *In the American Province* (Bloomington, 1985), David Hollinger usefully identifies Pound as one of a group of American intellectuals (including figures like Floyd Dell, Van Wyck Brooks, Harold Stearns, and, above all, Randolph Bourne) who were committed both to "antiprovincialism" and to its reverse face, "cosmopolitanism" (60). But, in insisting on the continuity between cosmopolitanism and a "cultural nationalism" that led Americans to "attempt to bring to their own national culture an intensity and scope comparable to that of European civilization" (61), he underestimates the degree to which the racial discourse of the '20s would make it plausible both for nativist and universalist intellectuals to define their ambitions *against* what increasingly seemed to them the destructively Jewish values of cosmopolitanism. Where, as Hollinger points out, Bourne's antiprovincialism led him particularly to value Jews, Pound's race-based antiprovincialism would make him particularly hostile to Jews. Indeed, what we might call the *portability* of race—the fact that its conception of rootedness could be disconnected from any particular place—would transform the whole question of provincialism.

194 Eliot's hostility to pluralism and to the sense that the difference in standards of poetic judgment (between, say, classicism and romanticism) could be explained by reference to national origin and could be tolerated as expressions of national character was even more explicit: "Surely the reference to racial origins, or the mere statement that the French are thus, and the English otherwise, is not expected to settle the question: which, of two antithetical views, is *right?*" ("The Function of Criticism" [1923], in *Selected Prose*, 72). This is, in effect, the opposite of Williams's "My country, right or wrong."

195 Ezra Pound, *Gaudier-Brzeska* (East Yorkshire, 1960), 46. The first edition was published in 1916.

196 Marc Shell's critique of universalism—making all humans kin, it turns those who aren't kin into something less than human—makes a version of this point. But Shell tends to see all racism as universalist, and indeed to see all universalism as racist, and thus to miss the specificity of modern notions of race in general and of nativist or plural racism in particular. For Shell, all assertions of consanguinity are essentially the same; in *Children of the Earth*, even the difference between literal and figural claims to kinship is challenged on the grounds that since we can never know for certain who "our real blood kin" (6) are, all claims to kinship are ultimately figurative: "The literal disappears in the figural" (4). But the collapse of the literal into the figurative doesn't really work since the fact (if it is a fact) that we can't know which people are our kin and which aren't doesn't mean that we may not, in fact, be kin to some people and not be kin to others. And, more important for the purposes of this study, the meanings of the assertion of consanguinity can vary widely: the claim that we belong to the same family may be deployed against racial identity as well as on

behalf of it; the claim that we belong to different families may be deployed on behalf of racial identity as well as against it.

197 Carl Van Vechten, *Nigger Heaven* (New York, 1926), 70–71. Subsequent references are cited in parentheses in the text.

198 Edith Wharton, *The Age of Innocence*, in *Edith Wharton: Novels* (New York, 1985), 1051. Subsequent references are cited in parentheses in the text.

199 Franz Boas would be a crucial transitional figure here. At least since the publication of George Stocking Jr.'s seminal essay, "Franz Boas and the Culture Concept in Historical Perspective" (in *Race, Culture, and Evolution: Essays in the History of Anthropology* [Chicago, 1968]), Boas has been considered instrumental in the emergence of the modern anthropological notion of culture, a notion Stocking identifies with the replacement of a single evolving culture by "the concept of a plurality of historically conditioned cultures" (213) and that he associates with a "cultural relativism" based on the critique of "any singular standard of cultural evaluation" (228). But Stocking also points out that "Boas was not a relativist in a consistent sense" (231) and, in fact, it could be argued more strongly that Boas's opposition to evolutionism in no way committed him to the refusal of evaluation that Stocking identifies with pluralism. In *Anthropology and Modern Life* (1928), for example, what Boas characterizes as the fundamental differences between primitive and modern cultures are consistently represented in terms either of progress or decline: in some ways modern culture is said to be better than primitive culture ("Knowledge has been increasing apace" [217]), in some ways it is said to be worse ("It is a reproach to our civilization that we have not learned to utilize the vastly increased leisure in the way done by primitive man" [219]); in no case is it merely different. Indeed, in the one area where Boas thinks of the modern as neither better nor worse than the primitive—morals— he argues not that the two are essentially different but that they are essentially the same: "It is quite possible to show an advance in ethical *behavior* when we compare primitive society with our own. Westermarck and Hobhouse . . . have given us an elaborate history of the evolution of moral ideas. Their descriptions are quite true, but I do not believe that they represent a growth of moral *ideas*, but rather reflect the same moral ideas as manifested in different types of society . . ." (220). It is striking in this context that, although admirers of Boas's antiracism (*Anthropology and Modern Life* was mainly undertaken as an attack on contemporary racial thinking) often identify that antiracism with his presumed pluralism, it is, in fact, the racists Boas meant to oppose whose conception of culture was more purely pluralist. Boas himself was a universalist, in search of "psychological and social data valid for all mankind" and "basal for all culture" (207).

200 James Weldon Johnson, *The Autobiography of an Ex-Colored Man*, ed. with an introduction by William L. Andrews (New York, 1990), 154. Subsequent references are cited in parentheses in the text.

201 *Plessy v. Ferguson*, 163 U.S. 540–52 (1896), reprinted in *The South Since Reconstruction*, ed. Thomas D. Clark (New York, 1973), 159.

202 Booker T. Washington, *Up from Slavery* (1901; reprinted New York, 1986), 101.

203 Frances E. W. Harper, *Iola Leroy* (Boston, 1987), 245.

204 *Up from Slavery*, 100.

205 *Plessy v. Ferguson*, 167.

206 Nella Larsen, *Quicksand and Passing*, ed. with an introduction by Deborah E. Mc-Dowell (Rutgers, 1986), 182. Subsequent references are to this edition and are cited in parentheses in the text. Recent criticism, powerfully exemplified not only in Mc-Dowell's introduction but also in Claudia Tate's "Nella Larsen's *Passing*: A Problem of Interpretation" (*Black American Literature Forum* 14:4 [1980], 142–46); Hazel Carby's *Reconstructing Womanhood* (New York, 1987), 163–75; Ann Ducille's "Blues Notes on Black Sexuality: Sex and the Texts of Jessie Fauset and Nella Larsen" (*Journal of the History of Sexuality* 3:3 [1993], 418–44); and Judith Butler's *Bodies That Matter* ([New York, 1993], 167–85) has tended to emphasize the psychosexual questions raised by these texts, sometimes in opposition to (although more often in conjunction with) the questions of racial identity. My own focus here is obviously on race, which is to say, on the projects, desires, and ambitions made available by American racial discourse.

207 It is thus a mistake to identify the possibility of passing with what Judith Butler calls the construction of "race" as "performative." Butler argues that Clare's "color becomes legible" only through "association"; "if she associates with blacks, she becomes black" (*Bodies That Matter* [New York, 1993], 275, 171). But to put the point in this way is to elide the difference between the epistemological question of racial legibility and the ontological question of racial identity. And, of course, the very idea of passing requires the enforcement of this difference; if being legible as black counted as becoming black, if the race you appeared to belong to determined the race you in fact belonged to, then there could be no such thing as passing—what you passed for would be what you were.

208 In *Passing*, Helga's "discontentment" and her ambivalence about race and individuality are distributed among the three main characters: Brian, who wants to escape race by going to Brazil; Clare, who having escaped the Negro race by passing wants to restore herself to it by having an affair with Brian; and Irene, whose "racial consciousness" (192) would never allow her to pass and who, identifying herself as "an American," will not allow herself to "be uprooted" by emigration to Brazil. The intermingling of racial and romantic motives is here even more explicit than in *Quicksand*, where Helga's unrealized desire for Robert Anderson is eventually proposed as the real explanation of her repeated removals.

209 The moral is hammered home by those critics, like Robert B. Stepto, who condemn the ex-colored man's failure to make contact with the "artistic traditions and concerns which would have focused and directed his compositions in such a way that he would have indeed become, for himself as well as his race, a Negro composer" (*From Behind the Veil: A Study of Afro-American Narrative* [Urbana, 1991], 126). Just as the one-drop rule makes the ex-colored man's race "Negro," so the understanding of racial identity as a "birthright" makes his refusal to insist on that one drop a betrayal not only of race but of self.

210 As in *St. Mawr*, the responsibility of sterility is shifted here from male to female shoulders, although Laughing Boy does find himself wishing he were—like Jake or Benjy—a "gelding."

211 Thus Houston A. Baker Jr., praising the "genuine cultural authenticity" of certain Afro-American cultural performances, distinguishes between the authenticity that connotes "powers of certification and invoke[s] a world of rarefied connoisseur-

ship—and a desire, as well, for only the genuine and the original" and an authenticity that is the product of the "everyday world occupied by our grand, great-grand, and immediate parents—our traceable ancestry that judged certain select sounds appealing and considered them efficacious in the office of a liberating advancement of The Race" (*Modernism and the Harlem Renaissance*, 100). The authenticity that accompanies connoisseurship is an artifact of an earlier (but, obviously, surviving) sense of culture as the characteristic aesthetic activities of an advanced civilization; the authenticity of the ancestral "everyday world" is an artifact of the more modern, anthropologized sense of culture as the totality of the beliefs and practices of any given people. The original and the genuine are valued in both conceptions, but what is meant by original and genuine changes. The original on the connoisseurship model is opposed to the derivative; on the anthropological model, it is opposed to the debased or impure. Laughing Boy's jewelry is valued not because it is different from (more original than) the work of other real Navajos but because it is different from the work of those Navajos whose taste has been corrupted by exposure to whites—its originality consists in its being *just like* the work of other real Navajos.

212   John J. Mahoney, "Americanization in the United States." *Department of the Interior, Bulletin* (Washington, 1923), 1–2.

213   Ibid., 2.

214   Thus Stoddard denies that "America" is simply an "area" or a "government" and describes it instead as the "cultural and spiritual birthright of all true Americans," a "birthright" that "we living Americans, who are its present guardians, are resolved to bequeath . . . to our children" (*Re-Forging*, 226). The nativist "America" is not only an inheritance but, crucially, a contested inheritance, and it's the contest that gives meaning to the nativist project: "We know only too well that past errors have impaired the national heritage. But this makes us all the more determined to restore its former potency and to hand it on, improved, to the next generation, who will continue the great task" (227).

215   Arthur M. Schlesinger Jr., *The Disuniting of America* (New York, 1991), 46. Subsequent references are cited in parentheses in the text.

216   Alain Locke, ed., *The New Negro*, 360. Subsequent references both to Herskovits's essay and to Countee Cullen's poem "Heritage" (which originally appeared in *The New Negro*) are cited in parentheses in the text.

217   Melville J. Herskovits, *The Myth of the Negro Past* (Boston, 1990). Subsequent references are cited in parentheses in the text.

218   For an account of Herskovits's career, see Walter Jackson, "Melville Herskovits and the Search for Afro-American Culture," in *Malinowski, Rivers, Benedict and Others*, ed. G. W. Stocking Jr., (Madison, 1986), 95–126.

219   Richard Wright, "I Bite the Hand That Feeds Me," *The Atlantic Monthly* (June 1940), 827–28.

220   Quoted in Jackson, 107.

221   Richard Wright, *Native Son* (New York, 1966), 33. Subsequent references are cited in parentheses in the text.

222   This also is a central aspect of James Baldwin's critique of *Native Son* in "Everybody's Protest Novel" and "Many Thousands Gone," with, however, Bigger's repudiation of African culture read as Wright's inability to express the "tradition" of the American

Negro: "the fact is not that the Negro has no tradition but there has as yet arrived no sensibility sufficiently profound and tough to make this tradition articulate. For a tradition expresses, after all, nothing more than the long and painful experience of a people; it comes out of the battle waged to maintain their integrity . . ." (*Notes of a Native Son* [Boston, 1990], 36). Some recent critics have sought to defend Wright against Baldwin, arguing that "a genuine folk heritage shines forth" from *Native Son* (Houston A. Baker Jr., "Racial Wisdom and Richard Wright's *Native Son*," in *Critical Essays on Richard Wright*, ed. Yoshinobu Hakutani [Boston, 1982], 74), but the role of supplying such a heritage has, of course, been much more frequently assigned to Hurston. For an important critique of this use of Hurston, however, see Hazel Carby, "The Politics of Fiction, Anthropology, and the Folk: Zora Neale Hurston," in *New Essays on* Their Eyes Were Watching God, ed. Michael Awkward (Cambridge, 1990). Asking why *Their Eyes Were Watching God* has become such "a privileged text," Carby goes on to wonder why it is "considered necessary that the novel produce cultural meanings of authenticity" and how "cultural authenticity come[s] to be situated so exclusively in the rural folk" (89). It should be pointed out, however, that her answer to these very useful questions—in essence, that the contemporary critical commitment to Hurston is a response to the current crisis in "black urban America"—speaks more clearly to the question of why authenticity gets located in the folk than it does to the question of the novel's relation to cultural authenticity as such.

223   Where Herskovits wished to attack the idea of racial identity by substituting for it the idea of historical identity, other writers have sought to *save* the idea of racial identity by redescribing it as historical identity. For a brilliant critique of this effort, one that has influenced my critique of cultural identity, see Kwame Anthony Appiah, "The Uncompleted Argument: Du Bois and the Illusion of Race" in *"Race," Writing, and Difference*, ed. with an introduction by Henry Louis Gates Jr. (Chicago, 1986), 21–37.

224   Nervous about Herskovits-style claims for continuous cultural descent, anthropologists have recently begun to criticize the idea of culture precisely because of what they take to be, in James Clifford's words, "its bias toward wholeness, continuity, and growth" (*The Predicament of Culture* [Cambridge, 1988], 338). According to Clifford, it "cannot tolerate radical breaks in historical continuity"; thus the only two available narratives about cultures imagine them either dying or surviving, and these narratives cannot account for the discovery of "new ways to be different," for "complex historical processes of appropriation, compromise, subversion, masking, invention, and revival" (338). Hence, with respect to problems like the legal determination of Indian identity (the particular example is a trial to determine whether the Mashpee Indians can be counted as a "tribe"), Clifford finds the "organicist" criterion of culture irrelevant. While it is true, he argues, that participation in "traditional" Indian practices was intermittent so that Indian culture (understood as the continual participation in these practices) could not be said to have "survived," it was also true that "Indianness" had been continually "reinvented." In court, and according to the anthropological understanding of culture, such reinventions could not be accepted: "An identity could not die and come back to life" (341). In fact, however, it is precisely through such reinventions that "collective structures" "reproduce themselves." "Their wholeness is as much a matter of reinvention and encounter as it is of continuity and survival" (341).

But the opposition here between "reinvention" and "continuity" is problematic. Clifford argues that "any part of a tradition" that can be "remembered, even genera-Avery Gordon and Christopher Newfield, "White Philosophy," *Critical Inquiry*, vol. (341–42). It is this kind of reinvention that constitutes Mashpee identity. The appeal to memory makes it clear that the resumption of a discontinued Indian practice cannot in itself count as a marker of Indian identity; going to powwows, taking up drumming, and starting to wear "regalia" wouldn't turn a New York Jew into a Mashpee Indian. The point of "remembered" as opposed to discovered (or of "reinvented" as opposed to invented) is to identify the traditions in question as appropriate to (already in some sense belonging to) the person who (re)involves himself or herself in them. It is a mistake, then, to think that there is no appeal here to either "continuity" or "survival." On the contrary, it is only the (implied) assertion of continuity between the person who originally practiced, say, drumming, then discontinued the practice and has now once again begun to drum that makes sense of the notion that the practice of drumming is being remembered rather than invented.

But this assertion is, of course, false. The reason there is a question about Mashpee identity in the first place is because there is no such person. But, since there is no such person, it is difficult to see why taking up drumming should be understood as remembering part of a lost tradition. If then, the criteria of Mashpee identity are drumming, dressing in "regalia," and so on, it should be the case that anyone who meets these criteria counts as a Mashpee. But if these criteria aren't sufficient, then some other criterion must be invoked. Clifford rejects culture as a mark of identity because culture tolerates no discontinuities. But he himself can tolerate discontinuity only if it is grounded in a continuity that runs much deeper than culture: drumming will make you a Mashpee not because anyone who drums gets to be a Mashpee but because, insofar as your drumming counts as remembering a lost tradition, it shows that you already *are* a Mashpee. The point here is not that Clifford is secretly depending on some notion of racial identity but that his rejection of cultural identity gets him no further away from racial identity than does the more usual insistence on cultural identity. The problem, in other words, is with the claim for identity.

When the object of anthropological attention is "ethnicity" instead of "culture," the effort to avoid race is even more obviously a failure. Like Clifford, Michael M. J. Fischer seeks to emphasize the creative discontinuities in the transmission of ethnicity—it is "reinvented and reinterpreted" rather than "simply passed on from generation to generation, taught and learned" ("Ethnicity and the Post-Modern Arts of Memory," in *Writing Culture: The Poetics and Politics of Ethnography*, ed. James Clifford and George E. Marcus [Berkeley, 1986], 195). The point here is that ethnicity does not consist in simply following the traditional practices of the ethnic group in question. Rather, ethnicity is "something dynamic, often unsuccessfully repressed or avoided," a "recognition of something about one's essential being [that] seems to stem from outside one's immediate consciousness and control, and yet requires an effort of self-definition" (196–97). Ethnicity here is by no means simply biological (indeed, Fischer never mentions biology and it is difficult to see how a biological ethnicity could be "reinvented" or "repressed" as opposed to just embodied), but neither is it simply transmitted through what Fischer contemptuously refers to as "socialization" (if it were it could hardly be described as "a sense of the buried coming to the surface" and analogized to the Freudian id). In fact, in order to convert ethnicity into something other than socialization, Fischer has no choice but to rely on biology as a necessary but not sufficient condition of ethnic identity: necessary because it confers on the ethnic subject a mark of identity that transcends one's actual practices and experiences, insufficient because without eventual recourse to the appropriate practices and experiences, there can be no reinvention or return of the repressed.

225   The description of historical understanding as "remembering" is, in general, tendentious. Why should learning something about the past that we have never known be described as remembering it? The remembering subject (in order to count as remembering) must once have known and then forgotten what it now comes to know *again* (and so remembers). But who is this subject? This is the question Schlesinger answers when he says that "history is to the nation rather as memory is to the individual" (20). He subsequently warns against the "corruption of history by nationalism" (21) (by which he means the tendency of some historians to subordinate the truth to the "nurture of the nation"), but nationalism in his own account plays a more crucial role in the constitution of history than in its corruption. For history to serve as the nation's memory, the nation must become a subject; without nationalism, history could never become memory. Of course, it is more or less a truism to point out the connection between historical study and nationalism. My point here is only to emphasize that the links between history and nationalism do not depend upon the historian's tendency to produce nationally biased accounts of his or her country's past, it is built into the account of his or her activity as an attempt to *remember* that past. And my further point is that this construction of the historical or remembering subject need not be limited to the nation. Rather, it is part of my argument that at certain moments the notion of *cultural* memory has importantly supplemented or replaced the notion of national memory.

226   For criticism of the (nonracist) models of collective identity required to make events in which we did not personally participate part of "our" past, see Steven Knapp, *Literary Interest* (Cambridge, 1993), 106–136. (Whether racial identity, even if admitted, can provide such a model remains an open question; my interest here is only in those who do not wish to—but, I claim, nevertheless must—appeal to race.) The argument in this section relies also on an unpublished draft of an essay on race and culture written in collaboration by Knapp and Michaels.

227   Michael Omi and Howard Winant, *Racial Formation in the United States* (New York, 1986), 60. Subsequent references are cited in parentheses in the text.

228   479 Southern Reporter, 2d Series, 372. Subsequent references are cited in parentheses in the text.

229   F. James Davis, *Who Is Black?* (University Park, Pa., 1991), 10.

230   Noting that both the Louisiana Supreme Court and the United States Supreme Court refused to review the decision of the court of appeals, Davis argues that "the highest court in the United States saw no reason to disturb the application of the one-drop rule . . ." (11). Although, as will become clear below, I do not entirely agree with Davis's interpretation of *Jane Doe v. State of Louisiana* (which is how the Phipps case was filed), I have learned a great deal from his history of the one-drop rule and from his comparison of racial practices in the United States to racial practices elsewhere.

231   Robert Lee Durham, *The Call of the South* (Boston, 1908), 290.

232   Perhaps the most common version of this scenario involves not the atavistic brutality characteristic of Negrophobic texts but a reproductive atavism that appears either in reality or as a feared specter in a wide variety of racial writings. In Nella Larsen's *Passing*, for example, the light-skinned Clare Kendry describes herself as nearly dying "of terror the whole nine months before Margery was born for fear that she might be dark" (168) and thus reveal to her white husband that Clare herself is a Negro. And, much more recently, the artist and philosopher Adrian Piper describes a white man attempting "to demonstrate his understanding" of her decision not to have children "by speculating that I was probably concerned that they would turn out darker than I was" ("Passing for White, Passing for Black," *Transition* 58 [1993], 11. Subsequent references are cited in parentheses in the text).

233   When the Phipps case went to trial, a 1970 statute declaring that anyone with "one thirty-second or less Negro blood" could not be counted as black was still in effect. But by the time the case reached the court of appeal, that statute had been repealed and the court, basing its own decision on "social and cultural perceptions," declared that it was, in any event, "not relevant" to the Phipps case. The statute that replaced it, according to Davis, explicitly gives "parents the right to designate the race of newborns" (10).

234   Avery Gordon and Christopher Newfield, "White Philosophy," *Critical Inquiry*, vol. 20, number 4 (Summer 1994), 746.

235   The problem with self-identification from the standpoint of racial essentialism is that you can't trust people to tell the truth; the problem with self-identification from the standpoint of racial *anti*-essentialism is that you have no idea what criteria might help you to determine the truth and so no reason to believe that there is any truth.

236   Waldo Frank, *Our America* (New York, 1919), 208, 216. Subsequent references are cited in parentheses in the text.

237   Dreiser's generation, as Frank sees it, gave itself over to the necessary but destructive critique of the "myths upon which America was built" (124), necessary because they freed themselves from "falsehood," destructive because they gave themselves nothing new to believe and thus fell victim to "Despair." The task of his own generation, as Frank presents it, is to transform that despair into "hope," "the hope of Our America" (126).

238   Isaac B. Berkson, *Theories of Americanization: A Critical Study* (New York, 1969), 98. Subsequent references are cited in parentheses in the text.

239   The continuing commitment to the analogy between cultures and persons is exemplified in David Theo Goldberg's recent effort (in *Racist Culture* [Cambridge, 1993]) to explicate the relevance of nonbiological racial distinctions. He imagines a case in which one hundred people, only fifty of whom can be saved, are caught inside a burning hotel. Insofar as we are committed to "the universal value of nondiscrimination," he says, we should rescue people "on the basis of random selection" (212). But what if we were to find out that fifty of the hotel's occupants were the last "surviving members of some racial group (interpreted as culture, though phenotype may help to pick them out)?" A "strong case" can be made, he argues, for "first saving the San" (the racial group in question) "as a means to perpetuating or attempting to revive the culture." But why should we be committed to keeping San culture alive?

The answer cannot be that we find San culture valuable because that answer would rest on a universal calculus of values that might just as easily (depending on who the other fifty patrons were) condemn the San to death. What Goldberg imagines, in other words, is that we want to save the San because they are the last San, not because they are especially good at pottery making or at rocket science—we want to save them not because they are good at what they do but because they are who they are. So if we can't want to keep San culture alive because it's good, why do we care about keeping it alive? What's wrong with a certain number of beliefs and practices (whose value is in principle irrelevant to us) disappearing? It is only because, like Berkson, he understands a culture as a kind of person that Goldberg thinks the cessation of certain (in themselves, by hypothesis, no more valuable than other) practices has the pathos of a death. And, of course, this pathos can be made available even when no actual person dies: suppose the fifty remaining San all move to the suburbs and start hanging out at malls. San culture has died even though there's been no loss of San.

240   The theoretical centrality of race continues to be on display in recent professions of pluralism which mean to make no appeal to race. In a recent critique of multiculturalism, for example, Arthur Schlesinger Jr. produces a characteristic pluralist defense of American values: "We don't have to believe that our values are absolutely better than the next fellow's or the next country's, but we have no doubt that they are better *for us*, reared as we are—and are worth living by and worth dying for" (*Disuniting*, 137). The pluralism, of course, is built into the distinction between "better" and "better for us," which makes the question of who we are central because it makes the worth of our values depend on our identity. Who, then, is the "us" for whom our "values" are "better"? The obvious answer to the question of who we are is that we are Americans, and that American values, while not better than other values for everyone, are better for Americans. But why? The answer cannot be that they are better for us because they are the values we hold since, first, the mere fact of our holding them cannot count as a *reason* for our holding them and, second, the whole debate over multiculturalism exists because not every American holds the same values. Hence the multicultural critique of Schlesinger, that the "us" in "better for us" must be further pluralized, from American to African American, Jewish American, Native American, Mexican American, and so on.

But this effort to give a more persuasive answer to the question of who we are does not answer the question we have just raised, which is, Why should it matter who we are? What is the link that makes certain values "better" for certain people than for others? What distinguishes the people for whom these values are better from people for whom some other values are better? For the racial pluralist, the answer to this question is (logically, at least) straightforward: the thing that distinguishes one group of people from another so that one set of values will be better for one and another set of values better for the other is race. For the cultural pluralist, this answer is obviously unavailable. The cultural pluralist cannot rely on race to distinguish between the groups for whom different sets of values are best without giving up the claim that his pluralism is merely cultural. But, as we have already seen, he cannot rely on culture to make this distinction either, since what he's trying to explain is why one culture is better for some people and another culture better for others. He cannot, in other words, explain why some values are better for some people and other values better for others by pointing out that different people have different values. We know they have different values. What we want to know is why their values are good for them. To say that the culture people have is the best one for them because it goes best with their biology is to make an effort (albeit an unconvincing one) to answer this question. To say that the culture people have is the best one for them because it goes best with their culture is not even to make the effort.

241 The reference here to identity essentialism may be a little misleading, for I do not mean to imply that so-called anti-essentialist accounts of identity (accounts that emphasize the complex, conflicted, mobile, multiple, etc., nature of identity) can evade this dilemma. In my view, there are no anti-essentialist accounts of identity. The reason for this is that the essentialism inheres not in the description of the identity but in the attempt to derive the practices from the identity—we *do* this because we *are* this. Hence anti-essentialism with respect to cultural identity should take the form not of producing more sophisticated accounts of identity (that is, more sophisticated essentialisms) but of ceasing to explain what people should do by reference to who they are and/or what culture they belong to. (Needless to say, and for the same reason, making the *culture* more complex, contradictory, discontinuous, etc., is also just another turn of the essentialist screw.)

242 Charles Taylor's recent defense of cultural identity in Quebec and of the more general claim that once "we're concerned with identity," nothing "is more legitimate than one's aspiration that it never be lost," provides a state-of-the-art example (*Multiculturalism and "The Politics of Rerecognition"* [Princeton, 1992], 40). The crux here is the use of the term "lost" as opposed to, say, "different." It is the use of this term "lost" that leads Taylor—speaking of Quebecois in particular but, more generally, of any "distinct" culture—to identify "the desire of these peoples for survival" as lying at the heart of multiculturalism. The idea is that if their distinct culture disappears, if, say, French Canadians stop speaking French, then their identity will have been lost, the people will not have survived.

But in what sense will a people not have survived? Current debates over intermarriage and Jewish survival make clear one way in which the question of survival should not be understood. "For Jews," as a writer in the *New York Times* puts it, "who lost a third of their population to the Nazi Holocaust, the question of survival is obviously painful" ("Debating Intermarriage and Jewish Survival," *The New York Times*, October 18, 1992, 40). But intermarriage with Gentiles does not, of course, threaten Jewish survival in the way that the Nazis did. The Nazis threatened Jewish survival because they tried to kill all the Jews; intermarriage hardly kills anyone. The desire of Jews not to be killed by Nazis needn't in any way depend on their desire to survive as a people in the sense that Taylor means here; the desire of Jews not to disappear through intermarriage may. But it is a mistake to treat these two desires as if they were the same and, as Taylor's use of the Quebecois makes clear, what he has in mind is the second kind of disappearance: what worries Quebecois is that they will stop speaking French, not that they will be gassed.

Nevertheless, the Holocaust analogy cannot be too easily dismissed. As one writer concerned with Jewish assimilation has put it: "What's the difference between dying of starvation in the Warsaw ghetto and completely assimilating into Protestant culture? Either way, the Jewish people cease to exist" ("U.S. Whitewashes Jews," *The*

Daily Californian, May 12, 1988, 7). The difference I've noted above—assimilation doesn't kill anyone—is irrelevant here; people don't disappear but "the Jewish people" do. It is this desire of Jews *as Jews*, of Quebecois *as Quebecois*, to survive as Jews and as Quebecois that constitutes the multiculturalist "aspiration" that one's "identity" "never be lost."

But what exactly would be lost if everybody in Quebec stopped speaking French or if no one ever again thought of himself or herself as a Jew? Why would someone who used to speak French but now speaks English think of himself as having lost his identity? Why would what he used to do (speak French) determine his identity in a way that what he now does (speaks English) does not? My point here is not that nothing would be lost or even that nothing of value would be lost. French-speaking in Quebec would be lost and, insofar as French might be understood as a particularly valuable language, something particularly valuable would be lost. But without some way of explaining how what people used to do but no longer do constitutes their real identity, while what they actually do does not, it cannot be said that what the former French-speakers, current English-speakers have lost is their identity. My point, then, is not that nothing of value is ever lost but that identity is never lost.

Index

Walter Benn Michaels is Professor of English and the
Humanities at The Johns Hopkins University. He is author
of *The Gold Standard and the Logic of Naturalism* and
coeditor of *The American Renaissance Reconsidered*.

Library of Congress Cataloging-in-Publication Data
Michaels, Walter Benn.
Our America : nativism, modernism, and pluralism /
Walter Benn Michaels.
p. cm. — (Post-contemporary interventions)
ISBN 0-8223-1700-1 (cloth : alk. paper)
1. United States—Civilization—1918–1945. 2. Nativism.
3. Modernism (Literature)—United States. 4. Pluralism
(Social sciences)—United States. 5. United States—Race
relations.
I. Title. II. Series.
E169.1.M6   1995
305.8'00973—dc20   95-12117 CIP